1st Workshop on Information Extraction from Scientific Publications (WIESP 2022)

Online
20 November 2022

ISBN: 978-1-7138-6756-2

Printed from e-media with permission by:

Curran Associates, Inc.
57 Morehouse Lane
Red Hook, NY 12571

Some format issues inherent in the e-media version may also appear in this print version.

Printed with permission by Curran Associates, Inc. (2023)

For permission requests, please contact the Association for Computational Linguistics at the address below.

Association for Computational Linguistics
209 N. Eighth Street
Stroudsburg, Pennsylvania 18360

Phone: 1-570-476-8006
Fax: 1-570-476-0860

acl@aclweb.org

Additional copies of this publication are available from:

Curran Associates, Inc.
57 Morehouse Lane
Red Hook, NY 12571 USA
Phone: 845-758-0400
Fax: 845-758-2633
Email: curran@proceedings.com
Web: www.proceedings.com

AACL-IJCNLP 2022

The 1st Workshop on Information Extraction from Scientific Publications

Proceedings of the Workshop

November 20, 2022

Preface

The number of scientific papers published per year has exploded in recent years, strengthening its value as one of the main drivers for scientific progress. In astronomy alone, more than 41,000 new articles are published every year and the vast majority are available either via an open-access model or via pre-print services. Indexing the article's full-text in search engines helps discover and retrieve vital scientific information to continue building on the shoulders of giants, informing policy, and making evidence-based decisions. Nevertheless, it is difficult to navigate in this ocean of data; finding articles rely heavily on string matching searches and following citations/references. Still, new approaches are necessary to differentiate the signal from the noise more easily (e.g., finding the key articles about the medical condition we are interested in).

Simple string matching has substantial limitations, human language is ambiguous in nature, context matters, and we frequently use the same word and acronyms to represent a multitude of different meanings. Extracting structured and semantically relevant information from scientific publications (e.g., named-entity recognition, summarization, citation intention, linkage to knowledge graphs) allows better selection and filter articles.

The Workshop on Information Extraction from Scientific Publications (WIESP) is a forum to foster discussion and research using Natural Language Processing and Machine Learning. In this space, leading professionals, organizations, early career researchers and students can cooperate towards building the algorithms, models, and tools that will pave the way for machine comprehension of science in the future.

WIESP received 25 submissions, of which 16 were accepted (8 long papers, 4 short papers, and 4 shared task system papers).

WIESP was held on November 20th 2022.

Organizing Committee

Tirthankar Ghosal, Charles University, CZ
Sergi Blanco-Cuaresma, Center for Astrophysics | Harvard & Smithsonian, USA
Alberto Accomazzi, Center for Astrophysics | Harvard & Smithsonian, USA
Robert M. Patton, Oak Ridge National Laboratory, USA
Felix Grezes, Center for Astrophysics | Harvard & Smithsonian, USA
Thomas Allen, Center for Astrophysics | Harvard & Smithsonian, USA

Program Committee

Min-Yuh Day
Hen-Hsen Huang
Jheng-Long Wu
Daniel Acuna
Akiko Aizawa
Hamed Alhoori
Atilla Kaan Alkan
Thomas Allen
Hardik Arora
Premjith B
Partha Basuchowdhuri
Saprativa Bhattacharjee
Yimeng Dai
Xiang Dai
Vignesh Edithal
Sergey Feldman
Edward Fox
Zheng Gao
Daisuke Ikeda
Sarvnaz Karimi
Valia Kordoni
Sarvnaz Karimi
Valia Kordoni
Asheesh Kumar
Rishu Kumar
Sandeep Kumar
Xiangci Li
Shigeki Matsubara
Yoshitomo Matsubara
Sujit Pal
Rajesh Piryani
Trinita Roy
Neil Smalheiser
Wojtek Sylwestrzak
Rohan Tondulkar
George Tsatsaronis

Jan Philip Wahle
Ronin Wu
Wuhe Zou

Table of Contents

Overview of the First Shared Task on Detecting Entities in the Astrophysics Literature (DEAL)
Felix Grezes, Sergi Blanco-Cuaresma, Thomas Allen and Tirthankar Ghosal 1

Classification of URL Citations in Scholarly Papers for Promoting Utilization of Research Artifacts
Masaya Tsunokake and Shigeki Matsubara 8

TELIN: Table Entity LINker for Extracting Leaderboards from Machine Learning Publications
Sean Yang, Chris Tensmeyer and Curtis Wigington 20

PICO Corpus: A Publicly Available Corpus to Support Automatic Data Extraction from Biomedical Literature
Faith Mutinda, Kongmeng Liew, Shuntaro Yada, Shoko Wakamiya and Eiji ARAMAKI 26

Linking a Hypothesis Network From the Domain of Invasion Biology to a Corpus of Scientific Abstracts: The INAS Dataset
Marc Brinner, Tina Heger and Sina Zarriess 32

Leveraging knowledge graphs to update scientific word embeddings using latent semantic imputation
Jason Hoelscher-Obermaier, Edward Stevinson, Valentin Stauber, Ivaylo Zhelev, Viktor Botev, Ronin Wu and Jeremy Minton 43

Full-Text Argumentation Mining on Scientific Publications
Arne Binder, Leonhard Hennig and Bhuvanesh Verma 54

On the portability of extractive Question-Answering systems on scientific papers to real-life application scenarios
Chyrine Tahri, Xavier Tannier and Patrick Haouat 67

Detecting Entities in the Astrophysics Literature: A Comparison of Word-based and Span-based Entity Recognition Methods
Xiang Dai and Sarvnaz Karimi 78

Domain Specific Augmentations as Low Cost Teachers for Large Students
Po-Wei Huang 84

Moving beyond word lists: towards abstractive topic labels for human-like topics of scientific documents
Domenic Rosati 91

Astro-mT5: Entity Extraction from Astrophysics Literature using mT5 Language Model
Madhusudan Ghosh, Payel Santra, Sk Asif Iqbal and Partha Basuchowdhuri 100

NLPSharedTasks: A Corpus of Shared Task Overview Papers in Natural Language Processing Domains
Anna Martin, Ted Pedersen and Jennifer D'Souza 105

Parsing Electronic Theses and Dissertations Using Object Detection
Aman Ahuja, Alan Devera and Edward Alan Fox 121

TDAC, The First Corpus in Time-Domain Astrophysics: Analysis and First Experiments on Named Entity Recognition
Atilla Kaan Alkan, Cyril Grouin, Fabian Schussler and Pierre Zweigenbaum 131

Reproducibility Signals in Science: A preliminary analysis
Akhil Pandey Akella, Hamed Alhoori and David Koop 140

A Majority Voting Strategy of a SciBERT-based Ensemble Models for Detecting Entities in the Astrophysics Literature (Shared Task)
Atilla Kaan Alkan, Cyril Grouin, Fabian Schussler and Pierre Zweigenbaum 145

Conference Program

Overview of the First Shared Task on Detecting Entities in the Astrophysics Literature (DEAL)
Felix Grezes, Sergi Blanco-Cuaresma, Thomas Allen and Tirthankar Ghosal

Classification of URL Citations in Scholarly Papers for Promoting Utilization of Research Artifacts
Masaya Tsunokake and Shigeki Matsubara

TELIN: Table Entity LINker for Extracting Leaderboards from Machine Learning Publications
Sean Yang, Chris Tensmeyer and Curtis Wigington

PICO Corpus: A Publicly Available Corpus to Support Automatic Data Extraction from Biomedical Literature
Faith Mutinda, Kongmeng Liew, Shuntaro Yada, Shoko Wakamiya and Eiji ARAMAKI

Linking a Hypothesis Network From the Domain of Invasion Biology to a Corpus of Scientific Abstracts: The INAS Dataset
Marc Brinner, Tina Heger and Sina Zarriess

Leveraging knowledge graphs to update scientific word embeddings using latent semantic imputation
Jason Hoelscher-Obermaier, Edward Stevinson, Valentin Stauber, Ivaylo Zhelev, Viktor Botev, Ronin Wu and Jeremy Minton

Full-Text Argumentation Mining on Scientific Publications
Arne Binder, Leonhard Hennig and Bhuvanesh Verma

On the portability of extractive Question-Answering systems on scientific papers to real-life application scenarios
Chyrine Tahri, Xavier Tannier and Patrick Haouat

Detecting Entities in the Astrophysics Literature: A Comparison of Word-based and Span-based Entity Recognition Methods
Xiang Dai and Sarvnaz Karimi

Domain Specific Augmentations as Low Cost Teachers for Large Students
Po-Wei Huang

Moving beyond word lists: towards abstractive topic labels for human-like topics of scientific documents
Domenic Rosati

Astro-mT5: Entity Extraction from Astrophysics Literature using mT5 Language Model
Madhusudan Ghosh, Payel Santra, Sk Asif Iqbal and Partha Basuchowdhuri

No Day Set (continued)

NLPSharedTasks: A Corpus of Shared Task Overview Papers in Natural Language Processing Domains
Anna Martin, Ted Pedersen and Jennifer D'Souza

Parsing Electronic Theses and Dissertations Using Object Detection
Aman Ahuja, Alan Devera and Edward Alan Fox

TDAC, The First Corpus in Time-Domain Astrophysics: Analysis and First Experiments on Named Entity Recognition
Atilla Kaan Alkan, Cyril Grouin, Fabian Schussler and Pierre Zweigenbaum

Reproducibility Signals in Science: A preliminary analysis
Akhil Pandey Akella, Hamed Alhoori and David Koop

A Majority Voting Strategy of a SciBERT-based Ensemble Models for Detecting Entities in the Astrophysics Literature (Shared Task)
Atilla Kaan Alkan, Cyril Grouin, Fabian Schussler and Pierre Zweigenbaum

Overview of the First Shared Task on *Detecting Entities in the Astrophysics Literature (DEAL)*

Felix Grezes[1], **Thomas Allen**[1], **Tirthankar Ghosal**[2], **Sergi Blanco-Cuaresma**[1]
[1]Center for Astrophysics, Harvard & Smithsonian, USA
[2]Charles University, Faculty of Mathematics and Physics,
Institute of Formal and Applied Linguistics, Czech Republic
[1](felix.grezes,thomas.allen,sblancocuaresma)@cfa.harvard.edu
[2]ghosal@ufal.mff.cuni.cz

Abstract

In this article, we describe the overview of our shared task: Detecting Entities in the Astrophysics Literature (DEAL). The DEAL shared task was part of the Workshop on Information Extraction from Scientific Publications (WIESP) in AACL-IJCNLP 2022[1]. Information extraction from scientific publications is critical in several downstream tasks such as identification of critical entities, article summarization, citation classification, etc. The motivation of this shared task was to develop a community-wide effort for entity extraction from astrophysics literature. Automated entity extraction would help to build knowledge bases, high-quality meta-data for indexing and search, and several other use-cases of interests. Thirty-three teams registered for DEAL, twelve of them participated in the system runs, and finally four teams submitted their system descriptions. We analyze their system and performance and finally discuss the findings of DEAL.

1 Introduction

A good amount of astrophysics research makes use of data coming from missions and facilities such as ground observatories in remote locations or space telescopes, as well as digital archives that hold large amounts of observed and simulated data. These missions and facilities are frequently named after historical figures or use some ingenious acronym which, unfortunately, can be easily confused when searching for them in the literature via simple string matching. For instance, "Planck" can refer to the person, the mission, the constant, or several institutions. Automatically recognizing entities such as missions or facilities would help tackle this word sense disambiguation problem. In our DEAL shared task, we instigate a community initiative to extract "entities of interest" from astrophysics publications.

[1]https://ui.adsabs.harvard.edu/WIESP/

2 Task

2.1 Definition

The shared task *Detecting Entities in the Astrophysics Literature (DEAL)* (Grezes et al., 2022) consists of Named Entity recognition (NER) on samples of text extracted from astrophysics publications indexed by NASA ADS (Kurtz et al., 2000). The labels were created by domain experts and designed to identify entities of interest to the astrophysics community. They range from simple to detect (ex: URLs) to highly unstructured (ex: Formula), and from useful to researchers (ex: Telescope) to more useful to archivists and administrators (ex: Grant).

2.2 Evaluation

Submissions were scored using both the CoNLL-2000 shared task seqeval F1-Score at the entity level and scikit-learn's Matthews correlation coefficient method at the token level. We also encouraged authors to propose their own evaluation metrics. The task baseline was computed using the astroBERT model (Grezes et al., 2021).

3 Dataset Description

3.1 Data Collection and Creation

The dataset [2] consists of text fragments obtained from the astrophysical literature. The journals that the text fragments were obtained from are the Astrophysical Journal, Astronomy & Astrophysics, and the Monthly Notices of the Royal Astronomical Society. All text fragments are from recent publications, between the years of 2015 and 2021. Each text fragment originates from one of two parts of an article. The first are fragments from the full-text, consisting of all sections of the body of the article, excluding the abstract and acknowledgment

[2]The data is openly available under the CC-BY-4.0 licence huggingface.co/datasets/adsabs/WIESP2022-NER

Proceedings of the 1st Workshop on Information Extraction from Scientific Publications, pages 1–7
Nov 20, 2022. ©2022 Association for Computational Linguistics

sections. The second are fragments from the acknowledgment section of the article.

Thirty-three different entities, comprised of general and astrophysical entities, were manually labeled in each text fragment by a domain expert. The entities that were labeled cover a number of broad categories. One category contains common NER entities, such as Person, Organization, and Location. A second category contains entities related to astrophysical facilities, such as Observatory and Telescope. A third category contains entities related to research funding and proposals, such as Grant or Proposal. A fourth category contains entities relating to astronomical objects and regions. Finally there is a category that contains various entities that are found in the literature, such as URL's and citations.

3.2 Data Segmentation for Shared Task

The overall dataset was separated into four components: the development dataset, the training dataset, the testing dataset, and the validation dataset. The development dataset is a small dataset of only twenty text fragments used to aid in the development of modeling systems. The training dataset consists of 1741 text fragments, 887 of which are from the full-text and 854 of which are from the acknowledgments. Table 3 shows the the number of labeled entities and origin of the text fragment for these entities. The testing dataset consists of 2495 text fragments, 1201 of which are from the full-text and 1294 of which are from the acknowledgments. Table 3 shows the the number of labeled entities and origin of the text fragment for these entities. Finally, the validation dataset consists of 2505 text fragments for the purpose of scoring the submitted models.

4 Participant Systems

Ghosh et al. (2022) proposed an Astro-mT5 model for entity recognition from Astrophysics publications. Primarily, they fine-tune a multilingual Text-To-Text Transfer Transformer (T5) model on the downstream task followed by sequence-labelling using Conditional Random Field (CRF) to get the probability sequence over the possible sequence labels.

Huang (2022) propose a system that uses data augmentation as a low-cost method of teacher-student training to transfer domain-specific knowledge to a larger adapter-based model. The author introduce a framework that uses data augmentation from domain-specific pre-trained models to transfer domain-specific knowledge to larger general pre-trained models for the underlying DEAL task. Specifically, they use the adapter architecture of the DeBERTaV3-large model as the backbone model, and CosmicRoBERTa (a further pretrained version of SpaceRoBERTa, a domain-specific model), as the augmentation teacher model.

Dai and Karimi (2022) investigate two different NER methods, word-based tagging and span-based classification for the DEAL task. They show that their span-based method using RoBERTa-large pre-trained models outperform the widely used word-based sequence tagging method (which uses BIO annotation schema).

Kaan Alkan et al. (2022) proposed a majority voting strategy of a SciBERT-based ensemble models for the DEAL task. Specifically, they used outputs from 32 different SciBERT-based classifiers for the majority voting strategy.

5 astroBERT Baseline

The shared task submissions were evaluated using F-1 score and the Matthews correlation coefficient (MCC) metrics. The F-1 score is a standard measure of model quality and was computed using seqeval (Nakayama, 2018), which uses micro-averaging and ignores the 'O' label. The MCC takes into account every value in the confusion matrix and is generally regarded as a balanced measure; it was computed using scikit-learn (Pedregosa et al., 2011). The F-1 score was computed at the entity level and the MCC score was computed at the token level. Using two metrics help prevent with a submission overfitting by optimizing for a single score.

As a baseline, we finetuned three BERT variants on the shared task. The original BERT from Google (Devlin et al., 2018), SciBERT from AllenAI (Beltagy et al., 2019), and astroBERT from NASA/ADS (Grezes et al., 2021). Each variant was finetuned on the training dataset for 1000 epochs (~5 hours each on dual V100 NVIDIA GPUs).

Table 2 provides the scores of the baselines on the WIESP datasets. Additionally, a model making random predictions based on label frequency was

model	astroBERT		Augmentation (Huang, 2022)		Word vs Span (Dai and Karimi, 2022)		Ensemble (Kaan Alkan et al., 2022)		**Astro-mT5** (Ghosh et al., 2022)	
Metric \ Split	val	test	val	test	val	test	val	test	val	test
MCC	0.8104	0.7939	0.9063	0.8928	0.9138	0.8946	0.9139	**0.8978**	0.9129	0.8954
F-1	0.5779	0.5561	0.7988	0.7799	0.8307	0.7990	0.8262	0.7993	0.8364	**0.8057**
Precision	0.5508	0.5387	0.7854	0.7854	0.8249	0.8076	0.8145	0.8013	0.8296	**0.8137**
Recall	0.6077	0.5746	0.8126	0.7744	0.8366	0.7906	0.8382	0.7972	0.8434	**0.7979**
Accuracy	0.9389	0.9308	0.9692	0.9633	0.9718	0.9640	0.9718	**0.9651**	0.9714	0.9642

Table 1: Main DEAL@WIESP 2022 Shared Task Results. F-1, Precision and Recall are computed using micro-averaging.

included for comparison. Additional standard metric scores (overall precision, recall and accuracy) are included as well. These additional metrics were also computed for the shared task submissions and provided to the participants but were not used to rank them. For each metric, astroBERT outscored BERT and SciBERT. A finer comparison between astroBERT and SciBERT is provided in the appendix figure 1, as well as the confusion matrix between labels for astroBERT on the testing dataset in appendix figure 2.

6 Results and Analysis

We report the results of the four teams that submitted their system papers in table 1 which were also the best performers of the twelve shared task participants on both F-1 score and MCC metrics. All three systems significantly outperform the astroBERT baseline, and are built on top of pre-existing publicly available language models.

7 Findings of DEAL

Each participants system significantly outperformed the baseline using different techniques. Below are the findings each system that we believe to be of importance to the community. From the top participant system astro-mT5 by Ghosh et al. (2022), we highlight the use of Conditional Random Fields (CRF), which validate other studies showing that CRFs help on NER tasks. Kaan Alkan et al. (2022) found that using ensemble methods to combine multiple models made for more robust predictions. Dai and Karimi (2022) concluded that span-based methods outperform word-based. They also showed that non-astrophysics tokenizer may suffer from over-segmentation when applied to astronomy papers. Finally, Huang (2022) highlighted the usefulness of data augmentation when applied to a dataset the size of WIESP.

8 Conclusion and Future Directions

All the participant systems were built on top of existing language models (i.e. general English, not tailored to a domain), and significantly beat the baseline scores. This begs the question: how would these systems performs when built on top of a language model and tokenizer tailored to astronomy? Based on the competition results, the use of CRFs seems especially promising. Furthermore, the wide variety in the methods used by the successful participant systems indicate that the task is far from solved, and that many improvements can be made to the astroBERT baseline.

References

Iz Beltagy, Kyle Lo, and Arman Cohan. 2019. SciBERT: A Pretrained Language Model for Scientific Text. *arXiv e-prints*, page arXiv:1903.10676.

Xiang Dai and Sarvnaz Karimi. 2022. Detecting entities in the astrophysics literature: A comparison of word-based and span-based entity recognition methods. In *Proceedings of the 1st Workshop on Information Extraction from Scientific Publications*, Taipei, Taiwan. Association for Computational Linguistics.

Jacob Devlin, Ming-Wei Chang, Kenton Lee, and Kristina Toutanova. 2018. BERT: Pre-training of Deep Bidirectional Transformers for Language Understanding. *arXiv e-prints*, page arXiv:1810.04805.

Madhusudan Ghosh, Payel Santra, Sk Asif Iqbal, and Partha Basuchowdhuri. 2022. Astro-mt5: Entity extraction from astrophysics literature using mt5 language model. In *Proceedings of the 1st Workshop on Information Extraction from Scientific Publications*, Taipei, Taiwan. Association for Computational Linguistics.

Felix Grezes, Thomas Allen, Tirthankar Ghosal, and Sergi Blanco-Cuaresma. 2022. Overview of the first shared task on detecting entities in the astrophysics literature (deal). In *Proceedings of the 1st Workshop on Information Extraction from Scientific Publications*, Taipei, Taiwan. Association for Computational Linguistics.

model	Random			BERT			SciBERT			astroBERT		
Metric \ Split	train	val	test	train	val	test	train	val	test	train	val	test
MCC	0.1037	0.1083	0.1057	0.7542	0.7405	0.7229	0.8159	0.8019	0.7844	0.8296	0.8104	**0.7939**
F-1	0.0170	0.0166	0.0162	0.4920	0.4739	0.4513	0.5867	0.5601	0.5355	0.6138	0.5779	**0.5561**
Precision	0.0122	0.0119	0.0116	0.4995	0.4780	0.4622	0.5753	0.5463	0.5313	0.5889	0.5508	**0.5387**
Recall	0.0278	0.0273	0.0269	0.4848	0.4698	0.4409	0.5986	0.5745	0.5398	0.6409	0.6077	**0.5746**
Accuracy	0.7146	0.7059	0.6876	0.9256	0.9188	0.9094	0.9430	0.9366	0.9280	0.9468	0.9389	**0.9308**

Table 2: Evaluation of the three BERT baselines. F-1, Precision and Recall are computed using micro-averaging.

Felix Grezes, Sergi Blanco-Cuaresma, Alberto Accomazzi, Michael J. Kurtz, Golnaz Shapurian, Edwin Henneken, Carolyn S. Grant, Donna M. Thompson, Roman Chyla, Stephen McDonald, Timothy W. Hostetler, Matthew R. Templeton, Kelly E. Lockhart, Nemanja Martinovic, Shinyi Chen, Chris Tanner, and Pavlos Protopapas. 2021. Building astroBERT, a language model for Astronomy & Astrophysics. *arXiv e-prints*, page arXiv:2112.00590.

Po-Wei Huang. 2022. Domain specific augmentations as low cost teachers for large students. In *Proceedings of the 1st Workshop on Information Extraction from Scientific Publications*, Taipei, Taiwan. Association for Computational Linguistics.

Atilla Kaan Alkan, Cyril Grouin, Fabian Schussler, and Pierre Zweigenbaum. 2022. A majority voting strategy of a scibert-based ensemble models for detecting entities in the astrophysics literature (shared task). In *Proceedings of the 1st Workshop on Information Extraction from Scientific Publications*, Taipei, Taiwan. Association for Computational Linguistics.

Michael J. Kurtz, Guenther Eichhorn, Alberto Accomazzi, Carolyn S. Grant, Stephen S. Murray, and Joyce M. Watson. 2000. The NASA Astrophysics Data System: Overview. , 143:41–59.

Hiroki Nakayama. 2018. seqeval: A python framework for sequence labeling evaluation. Software available from https://github.com/chakki-works/seqeval.

F. Pedregosa, G. Varoquaux, A. Gramfort, V. Michel, B. Thirion, O. Grisel, M. Blondel, P. Prettenhofer, R. Weiss, V. Dubourg, J. Vanderplas, A. Passos, D. Cournapeau, M. Brucher, M. Perrot, and E. Duchesnay. 2011. Scikit-learn: Machine learning in Python. *Journal of Machine Learning Research*, 12:2825–2830.

A Appendix

Label \ Section	Training		Testing		Total
	Ack	Full Text	Ack	Full Text	
Archive	628	30	1119	50	1827
CelestialObject	110	4521	113	5615	10359
CelestialObjectRegion	0	488	7	1344	1839
CelestialRegion	8	390	27	581	1006
Citation	1097	23665	1650	31923	58335
Collaboration	855	49	1214	45	2163
ComputingFacility	1188	20	1644	9	2861
Database	461	54	649	152	1316
Dataset	102	594	182	1005	1883
EntityOfFutureInterest	0	77	52	724	853
Event	213	8	340	7	568
Fellowship	1426	0	2096	0	3522
Formula	0	10521	4	17856	28381
Grant	7532	26	14610	24	22192
Identifier	68	75	156	145	444
Instrument	224	630	367	1064	2285
Location	1843	28	2932	55	4858
Mission	56	81	143	161	441
Model	64	2980	174	6110	9328
O	59549	412758	86353	553386	1112046
ObservationalTechniques	4	194	1	141	340
Observatory	1713	195	2469	378	4755
Organization	21562	97	31954	87	53700
Person	6081	41	9539	97	15758
Proposal	176	24	312	40	552
Software	679	810	1050	883	3422
Survey	707	751	969	1003	3430
Tag	0	120	0	148	268
Telescope	1044	1136	1699	1627	5506
TextGarbage	14	92	3	483	592
URL	262	44	342	110	758
Wavelength	61	4906	106	7210	12283
Total	107727	465405	162276	632463	1367871

Table 3: Counts of labels in training and test datasets according source origination. Note, that "O" refers to unlabeled words. (note: 'Ack' stands for Acknowledgment)

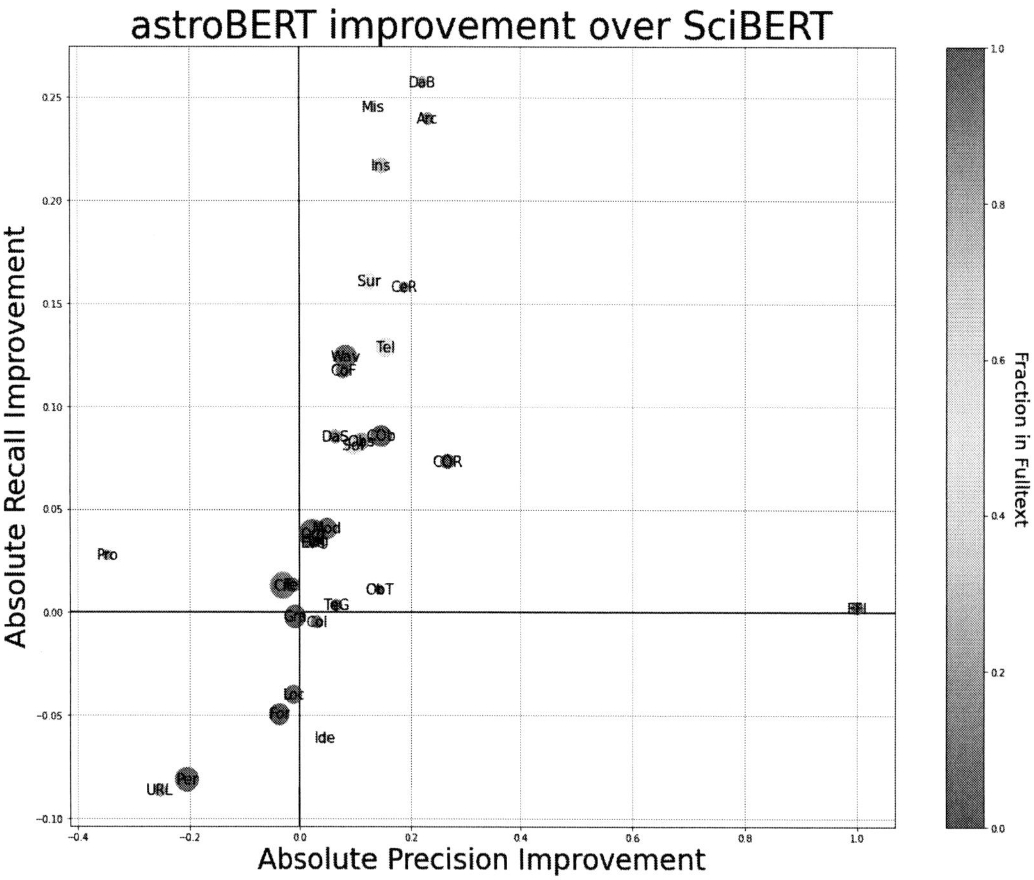

Figure 1: Absolute improvement from astroBERT over SciBERT in precision and recall for each class over the WIESP-TESTING data set, colored by predominance of that class body or acknowledgment sections.

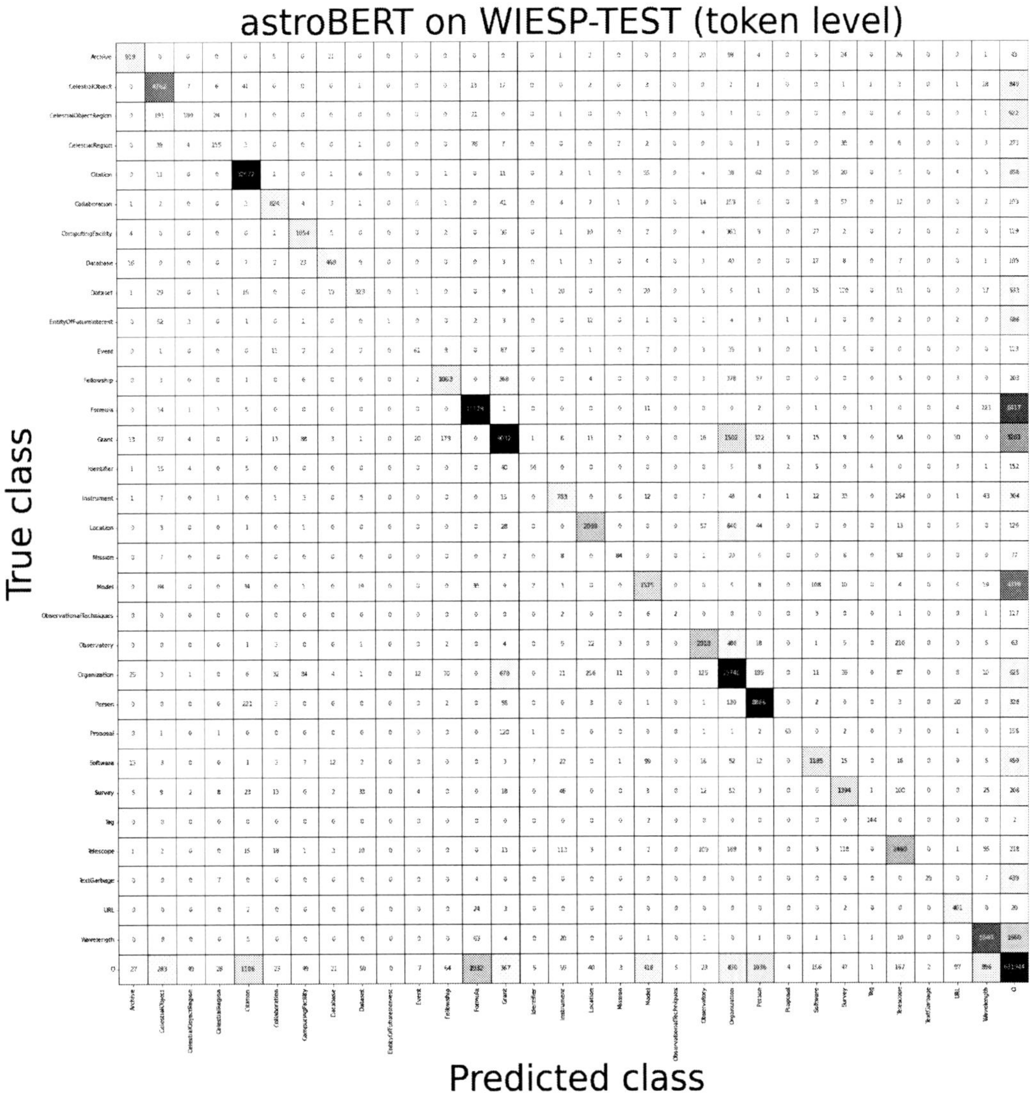

Figure 2: Confusion Matrix between actual labels and predicted labels from astroBERT on the WIESP-TEST tokens.

Classification of URL Citations in Scholarly Papers for Promoting Utilization of Research Artifacts

Masaya Tsunokake*
Research and Development Group,
Hitachi, Ltd.
Tokyo, Japan
masaya.tsunokake@gmail.com

Shigeki Matsubara
Information and Communications,
Nagoya University
Nagoya, Japan
matubara@nagoya-u.jp

Abstract

Utilizing citations for research artifacts (e.g., dataset, software) in scholarly papers contributes to efficient expansion of research artifact repositories and various applications e.g., the search, recommendation, and evaluation of such artifacts. This study focuses on citations using URLs (URL citations) and aims to identify and analyze research artifact citations automatically. This paper addresses the classification task for each URL citation to identify (1) the role that the referenced resources play in research activities, (2) the type of referenced resources, and (3) the reason why the author cited the resources. This paper proposes the classification method using section titles and footnote texts as new input features. We extracted URL citations from international conference papers as experimental data. We performed 5-fold cross-validation using the data and computed the classification performance of our method. The results demonstrate that our method is effective in all tasks. An additional experiment demonstrates that using cited URLs as input features is also effective.

1 Introduction

Open science is an activity for promoting sharing and utilizing research artifacts[1]. One strategy to promote these activities is to provide repositories for research artifacts, and such repositories have been developed recently, e.g., Zenodo[2] and Mendeley Data[3]. In addition, national infrastructures for sharing research artifacts have been developed[4].

To develop a research artifact repository, it is required to register research artifacts and create their metadata[5]. Automating these processes can improve the efficiency of developing repositories and increase the number of research artifacts registered in the repositories. To this end, research artifact citations in scholarly papers can be utilized because scholarly papers citing research artifacts generally describe the name or usage of the artifacts. In addition, information about research artifacts not in existing metadata may be described in the scholarly papers (Kozawa et al., 2010; Singhal et al., 2014). Unlike citations for literature (**paper citations**), there are various ways to cite research artifacts. Therefore, automating the identification of the research artifact citations is not trivial task.

This study focuses on citations using URLs in scholarly papers (**URL citations**) and aims to identify and analyze research artifact citations. Figure 1 shows examples of URL citations. URL citations can refer to not only scholarly papers but also various resources, e.g., datasets, software, homepages, and articles. Therefore, an analysis of URL citations leads to the identification of research artifact citations. In addition, it can clarify the reality of URL citations performed informally.

This paper proposes a method to classify URL citations in scholarly papers according to the following viewpoints:

- The role of resources referenced by the URL in research activities
- The type of resources referenced by the URL

*This work was conducted while the first author was a master's student at the Nagoya University in Japan.

[1]This paper denotes research artifacts as digital objects collected, created, generated, or used in the course of research activities such as tools (e.g., software, program) and data (e.g., measurement data, test data). This definition is similar to that provided by the Association for Computing Machinery (Association for Computing Machinery, 2020).

[2]https://zenodo.org/

[3]https://data.mendeley.com/

[4]e.g., Australian Research Data Commons (https://ardc.edu.au/), European Open Science Cloud (https://ec.europa.eu/), National Data Service (Towns et al., 2016) (http://www.nationaldataservice.org), NII Research Data Cloud (https://rcos.nii.ac.jp/en/service/)

[5]Information about research artifacts (e.g., name, creator, type, and usage)

Proceedings of the 1st Workshop on Information Extraction from Scientific Publications, pages 8–19
Nov 20, 2022.

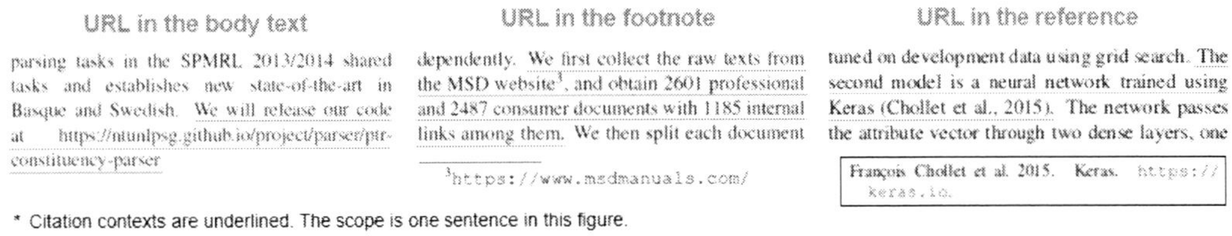

Figure 1: Examples of URL citations

- The reason why the authors cited the resources

Zhao et al. (2019) proposed a classification method using multi-task learning for a similar task. That method inputs a word sequence surrounding the citation (**citation context**) into BERT (Devlin et al., 2019), and the representations obtained from the BERT are fed to a classification layer for each task. This paper proposes utilizing the section title and the footnote text used by the URL citation as new input features. Unlike the study by Zhao et al. (2019), this study newly addresses URL citations using reference sections.

2 Related Work

2.1 Citation Classification

Citations in scholarly papers have long been analyzed (Garfield, 1964; Moravcsik and Murugesan, 1975; Spiegel-Rösing, 1977; Cullars, 1990). Garfield (1964) discussed the reasons for citations and listed 15 motivations such as "Paying homage to pioneers" and "Providing background reading". Moravcsik and Murugesan (1975) investigated paper citations in the physics field to consider the appropriateness of using citations as measures of scientific accomplishments. The discussions in these studies were based on manual classification or the authors' insights. With the development of the computer science, some automatic classification methods have been proposed (Teufel et al., 2006; Abu-Jbara et al., 2013; Jurgens et al., 2018; Cohan et al., 2019). Teufel et al. (2006) proposed a method to classify paper citations based on the authors' reason for the citing (**citation function**) such as statement of weakness and comparison with other work. Jurgens et al. (2018) proposed a method to classify paper citations into six categories, e.g., "BACKGROUND," which means a cited paper provides relevant information, "USES," which means a citing paper uses data or methods in the cited paper.

Ding et al. (2014) summarized such approaches for analyzing citations based on their content as Content-based Citation Analysis (CCA). The CCA has been applied to various tasks, e.g., summarizing papers, recommending citations, and improving metrics for papers (Ding et al., 2014). In addition, some studies have demonstrated that considering the citation functions contributes to the analysis of academic trends (Abu-Jbara et al., 2013; Jurgens et al., 2018), automatic generation of citation sentence (Ge et al., 2021), and prediction of the number of citations (Jurgens et al., 2018).

2.2 Research Artifact Citations

Recently, research artifacts, e.g., datasets and software, have been cited increasingly in scholarly papers. Then, there is a growing movement to establish formal rules for data and software citations, as FORCE11 has declared "Data Citation Principles" (Data Citation Synthesis Group, 2014) and "Software Citation Principles" (Smith et al., 2016). However, widespread adoption of this practice among researcher is a long way off. Howison and Bullard (2016) have demonstrated that there were many informal citations in biology papers. One strategy for automatic identification of the informal citations is to identify research artifact mentions in the body text (Krüger and Schindler, 2020). Some studies address the identification of dataset names (Singhal and Srivastava, 2013; Prasad et al., 2019; Ikeda et al., 2020) or software names (Li and Yan, 2018; Schindler et al., 2020; Du et al., 2021). Another approach finds research artifact citations from explicit citations. Ikoma and Matsubara (2020) attempted to identify bibliographic information referring to linguistic resources (e.g., corpus, lexicon) from reference sections. Since some research artifact citations uses URL, identification of URLs referring to research artifacts in scholarly papers has also been studied (Tsunokake and Matsubara, 2021).

Table 1: List of resource roles and resource types

Resource role	Resource type	description
Material	Dataset	corpus, image sets, etc.
	Knowledge	lexicon, knowledge graph, etc.
	DataSource	source data for the Dataset/Knowledge
Method	Tool	toolkit, software, system, etc.
	Code	codebase, library, API, etc.
Supplement	Document	documents on the Web (e.g., specifications, guidelines)
	Paper	scholarly papers
	Media	games, music, videos, etc.
	Website	other resources on the Web (e.g., services, homepages)
Mixed	Mixed	citations referring to multiple resources

2.3 Classification of URL Citations

With the increase in URL citations in scholarly papers, some studies have attempted to utilize resources referenced by URLs. For example, Yamamoto and Takagi (2007) extracted URLs from papers in the life science domain to develop a system for searching online resources. Parmar et al. (2020) extracted URLs from papers and constructed a portal of academic information (e.g., metadata about papers and authors) in the natural language processing field. Nanba (2018) proposed a method to extract a URL in scholarly papers and the tag representing the URL based on their distributed representations obtained from scholarly papers. There is a study addressing the classification of URL citations. Zhao et al. (2019) applied the CCA (Section 2.1) to URL citations in order to construct search/recommendation systems and knowledge graphs for scientific resources. They proposed a classification method to determine the roles of resources referenced by URLs in scholarly papers and the authors' purposes of URL citations based on the citation contexts.

In this study, our goal is to generate metadata for research data automatically. The resource roles defined by Zhao et al. (2019) contain the "Material" and "Method" roles, and we consider that citations corresponding to these labels are equivalent to research artifact citations. Thus, research artifact citations can be identified by solving this classification task. In addition, information on how referenced resources can be used in research activities can be obtained. URL citations are less identifiable and more ambiguous than paper citations whose bibliographic information are regularly listed in the reference sections. Thus, it would be meaningful for the academic community to realize automatic analysis for URL citations.

3 Task Definition

This study addresses three classification tasks determining the followings for each URL citation.

1. The role that resources play in the context of research activities (**resource role**)
2. The type of resources (**resource type**)
3. The reason why resources were cited (**citation function**)

Zhao et al. (2019) defined two levels of resource roles consisting of general resource roles and fine-grained resource roles. The fine-grained resource roles can be regarded as the type of referenced resources; thus, this study redefines them as resource types. Even if the same URL is cited in distinct papers, the resources that one author refers to may differ from those referenced by other authors. Therefore, in any of the classification tasks, it is necessary to infer from the citation contexts. Our target URL citations are as follows:

1. The URL is described in the body text
2. The URL is described in a footnote
3. The URL is described in the bibliographic references, and the corresponding citation anchor is described in the body text

Figure 1 shows an example of each case. If the URL is described in the footnote (case 2) or the reference (case 3), the corresponding surrounding sentences in the body text are the citation contexts. Note that Zhao et al. (2019) only targeted the case 1 and 2. However, when citing online resources, the resources can be cited as a reference, and the corresponding URL is described in

Table 2: List of citation functions

Citation function	Description
Use	Used in the citing paper's research.
Produce	First produced or released by the citing paper's research.
Compare	Compared with other resources.
Extend	Used in the citing paper's research but are improved, upgraded, or changed to work for other problems in the course of the research.
Introduce	The resources or the related information (e.g., background, applications) are introduced.
Other	The URL citation does not belong to the above 5 categories.

the bibliographic information. It is sometimes recommended that online resources are cited as references; thus, classifying URL citations via reference sections is required.

Table 1 presents the labels for the resource role/type. Since each resource type determines the role it can play, there is a correspondence between the resource roles and resource types. While the labels are based on the setting of Zhao et al. (2019), this study applies some alterations with a view to generating metadata for research artifacts. If the extracted information is used for metadata, the resource types are required to be somewhat fine-grained. However, the only resource type corresponding to "Material" (one of the resource roles) is "Data" in the study by Zhao et al. (2019). Therefore, this paper defines "Dataset," "Knowledge," and "DataSource" as more detailed types. In addition, since this paper considers resource types as types of cited digital objects, labels referring to something conceptual rather than actual digital objects (e.g., "algorithm") were dropped from the resource types. In some URL citations, multiple resources may be referenced simultaneously. Since the URL citation cannot be classified into a specific label in this case, "Mixed" is defined as one of the resource roles/types. The "Mixed" label was defined in some studies addressing citation classifications to consider cases where multiple labels are mixed (Cullars, 1990; Ge et al., 2021). Table 2 presents the labels for citation functions. This is the same setting as in Zhao et al. (2019).

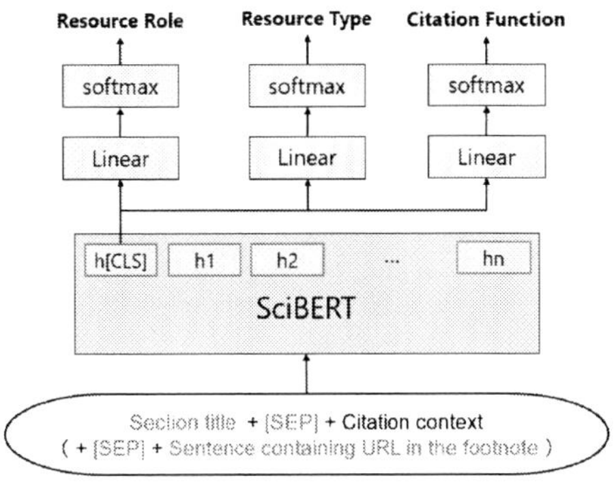

Figure 2: Architecture of our method

4 Method

Zhao et al. (2019) proposed a framework called SciResCLF for a similar classification task. Since there is a certain correlation between labels for each task, they employed multi-task learning in SciResCLF. The SciResCLF employs BERT (Devlin et al., 2019) as the encoder for citation contexts. In the SciResCLF, the citation contexts are taken into the BERT, and the obtained embeddings for the "[CLS]" token are taken into a classification layer for each task. In fine-tuning, the model parameters are optimized based on the weighted sum of the cross-entropy of each task. The SciResCLF only uses citation contexts as the input features. Based on SciResCLF, this paper proposes a classification method using section titles as global context information, and footnote texts used for URL citations.

Jurgens et al. (2018) demonstrated that there was a certain relationship between where paper citations appear in the narrative structure of a citing paper and their citation functions. In our task as well, information about the narrative structure may be useful. For example, scholarly papers may tend to cite used software, code, or datasets by providing the corresponding URL in the sections describing experiments. On the other hand, URLs described in introductory sections may tend to refer to supplements related to the background (e.g., news, web-service). Thus, our method uses the section titles where URL citations appear as input features. In addition, some URL citations do not explain the referenced resources in the body text but explain the resources in the footnotes which the corresponding URL are described in. Therefore, the footnote texts used for URL citations are

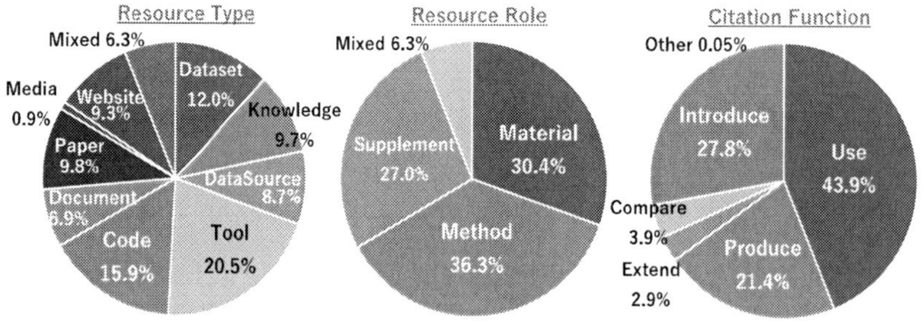

Figure 3: Ratio of each label in the created dataset

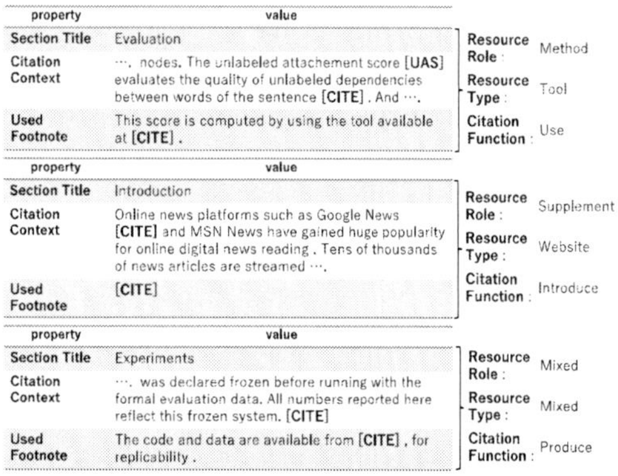

Figure 4: Examples of the created datset

expected to be an effective feature in this classification task.

Figure 2 shows the architecture of our method. In our method, the input for each URL citation is created by concatenating the section title where the citation appears, the citation context, and the footnote sentence containing the cited URL with "[SEP]" [6]. This model is trained in a multi-task learning framework. Thus, the model is optimized based on cross-entropy losses about predicting the resource roles, resource types, and citation functions.

5 Experiment

5.1 Dataset

There was no dataset for the classification of URL citations with the corresponding section titles, footnotes, and this paper's classification labels. Therefore, we created an experimental dataset. We collected the scholarly papers as the source of URL citations from the ACL Anthology[7]. The papers were collected from the proceedings of ACL/EMNLP/NAACL 2000–2021. We collected a total of 15,761 papers. The PDF of each paper was converted to text by PDFNLT-1.0[8](Abekawa and Aizawa, 2016). The URLs[9], footnote numbers in the body text that refer to the footnotes, and the citation anchors referring to bibliographic information in the reference section were detected for each paper. The citation anchors were detected by regular expressions[10] based on those described by Gosangi et al. (2021). They are compatible with both the Harvard and Vancouver referencing style. Using the detected results, paragraphs where the URL citations appeared were extracted as the citation contexts of the citations. We evaluated the performance of identifying the location of URL citations using 65 randomly selected papers. As a result, precision was 0.995 (199/200), and recall was 0.948 (199/210).

The extracted URL citations were annotated by an expert in the natural language processing field. Before the annotation, a part of URL removed mechanically, such as URL citations whose citation context had only a few words and the URLs attached as an auxiliary to the bibliographic information in the paper citation. The annotator was instructed to refer to the label definitions and examples of annotated URL citations before the work and could refer to them anytime during the work.

The created dataset contained 2,037 URL citations from 652 papers. Figure 3 shows the distribution of labels. Although the distribution of labels is skewed, there is a certain balance in the ratio

[6]If a URL citation does not use a footnote, or a footnote used by the URL citation only contains the URL, the second "[SEP]" and the footnote sentence are not concatenated.

[7]https://aclanthology.org/

[8]https://github.com/KMCS-NII/PDFNLT-1.0

[9]Strings beginning with either "http://," "https://," or "ftp://" were identified as URLs.

[10]Details are described in the appendix.

Table 3: Evaluation results for each task

Method	Resource role				Resource type				Citation function			
	ACC.	P.	R.	F1	ACC.	P.	R.	F1	ACC.	P.	R.	F1
Baseline	0.653	0.682	0.598	0.621	0.430	0.450	0.348	0.357	0.663	0.563	0.429	0.437
Our method	†0.694	0.711	0.653	†0.670	0.459	0.452	†0.385	0.391	†0.703	0.571	0.438	0.448

Table 4: Cases where baseline failed to predict but our method correctly predicts

Inputs of our method	True	Prediction	
		Baseline	Our method
Introduction [SEP] Recently, a new benchmark MRC dataset called Natural Questions [CITE] (NQ) has presented a substantially greater challenge for the existing MRC models. [SEP] **NQ provides some visual examples of the data [CITE] .**	Supplement	Material	Supplement
Data [SEP] WikiSum consist of Wikipedia articles each of which are associated with a set of reference documents. [CITE] [SEP] **We take the processed Wikipedia articles from [CITE] released on April 25th 2018.**	DataSource	Knowledge	DataSource
Conclusion [SEP] We have described a dependency-based system [CITE] for semantic role labeling of English in the PropBank framework. [SEP] **Our system is freely available for download at [CITE] .**	Produce	Use	Produce

of corresponding resource types for each resource role. For example, "Dataset," "Knowledge," and "DataSource" defined by this paper correspond to "Material," and there is not much difference in their ratios. In the dataset, the rate of URL citations using footnotes is 0.725, the rate of URL citations using the reference sections is 0.170, and the rate of URL citations in the body texts is 0.105. Figure 4 shows the examples of dataset[11]. Another researcher in the natural language processing field annotated 100 citations in the dataset as with the original annotator. As a result, the Cohen's kappa of the resource roles, resource types and citation functions were 0.644, 0.456, and 0.615, respectively.

5.2 Experimental Setup

A 5-fold cross-validation was performed using the created dataset. Randomly 20% of the dataset was used as the development set, and the rest was used as the training or test set by dividing it into 5 parts. Thus, the training set contained 1,304 samples, the development set contained 407 samples, and the test set contained 326 samples for each split.

The SciResCLF proposed by Zhao et al. (2019) was employed as the baseline, and both the baseline and our method were evaluated by the 5-fold cross-validation. Both methods used SciBERT (Beltagy et al., 2019) as the encoder for the input features. In our method, the section title used as the input was the top-level heading, and the footnote text was the 1 sentence containing the URL in the footnote used by the URL citation. The loss function was the sum of the cross-entropy losses for each task. The optimization function was Adam (Kingma and Ba, 2014)[12].

To assess the classification performance, both methods were evaluated by accuracy and the macro-averaged F1. Accuracy tends to be more dominated by the results of frequent classes than the F1 averaging the result of each class.

5.3 Experimental Results

Table 3 presents the average of evaluation result for each split[13]. Our method outperformed the baseline in all metrics on all tasks. Table 4 presents cases where the baseline failed to predict but our method predicted correctly. Note that the section titles before the first [SEP]s and the footnotes after the second [SEP]s were not taken into the baseline. In the first row, the footnote indicates that the referenced resource is not a dataset but an example visualization as a supplemental resource. In the second row, the footnote indicates that the referenced resource is not a created dataset but the source used for creation of the dataset. These footnotes contributed to the prediction of our method. In the third row, using section titles and footnotes, our model may catch a tendency that authors are

[11] In the same way as Zhao et al. (2019), we replaced the citation locations and cited URLs with "[CITE]."

[12] Details are described in the appendix.

[13] Daggers (†) mean that there was a significant difference between the baseline and our method by the paired t-test. The significance level was 0.05. ACC., P., and R. are accuracy, macro-averaged precision, and macro-averaged recall, respectively.

Table 5: Results of ablation study and additional experiment

Method	Resource role ACC.	Resource role F1	Resource type ACC.	Resource type F1	Citation function ACC.	Citation function F1
Baseline	0.653	0.621	0.430	0.357	0.663	0.437
Our method	0.694	0.670	0.459	0.391	0.703	0.448
- w/o section title	(−) 0.674	(−) 0.653	(+) 0.481	(+) 0.409	(−) 0.701	(+) 0.451
- w/o footnote	† (−) 0.663	(−) 0.626	(−) 0.423	† (−) 0.348	(−) 0.688	(+) 0.457
- w/ URL	(−) 0.679	(−) 0.631	(+) 0.501	† (+) 0.437	(+) 0.715	(+) 0.454

Table 6: F1-score for each label

Resource role	F1-score Baseline	F1-score Our method	Resource type	F1-score Baseline	F1-score Our method	Citation function	F1-score Baseline	F1-score Our method
Material	0.659	0.680	Dataset	0.466	0.448	Use	0.715	0.751
Method	0.688	0.728	Knowledge	0.217	0.243	Produce	0.615	0.729
Supplement	0.605	0.686	DataSource	0.513	0.514	Compare	0.230	0.172
Mixed	0.532	0.585	Tool	0.494	0.533	Extend	0.029	0.000
			Code	0.410	0.476	Introduce	0.671	0.667
			Document	0.179	0.204	Other	0.000	0.000
			Paper	0.493	0.606			
			Media	0.000	0.000			
			Website	0.343	0.348			
			Mixed	0.459	0.536			

likely to add a URL referring to their own created resources at the end of the paper.

5.4 Disscussion

Table 5 presents the result of an ablation study when one of the proposed input features was excluded[14]. As to resource roles, excluding section titles or footnotes from our method degraded the classification performance, which indicates that both features are effective. Similarly, excluding footnotes from our method degraded the performance in resource types, and thus using footnotes is effective. In contrast, excluding section titles from our method improved the performance in the classification of resource types. In addition, "w/o footnote", which added only the section title to the input features of baseline, was inferior to the baseline. These results demonstrate that using the section titles has a negative effect on the classification of resource types. As to citation functions, excluding one feature from our method improved the performance of the F1. However, the both F1s of "w/o section title" and " w/o footnote" were higher than the baseline. Independently, each of these features was effective in the classification of citation functions; however, combining them or the ways by which they were combined resulted in a negative effect.

Table 6 presents the F1 for each label[15] for the baseline and our method. In the classification of resource roles and types, our method outperformed the baseline for all labels except for "Dataset." There were some cases where our method misclassified citations whose resource type was "Dataset" as "DataSource" because the footnote included the text "from [CITE]" (e.g., "The corpus can be downloaded from [CITE]"). While the ratio of "DataSource" in all predicted labels by our method was 0.089, that for cases where the input text included "from [CITE]" is 0.276. However, it was effective in the second row of Table 4. In this case, the resource type is "DataSource" because the URL refers to not the WikiSum dataset but its source articles. Ideally, the ability to identify the target of the citation and infer the relationship between it and the surrounding words indicating research artifacts is required.

[14]The results of the ablation study that were lower and higher than that of our method are marked with "(−)" and "(+)," respectively. Daggers (†) mean that there was a significant difference compared to our method by the paired t-test. The significance level was 0.05.

[15]It is the average for splits in the cross-validation.

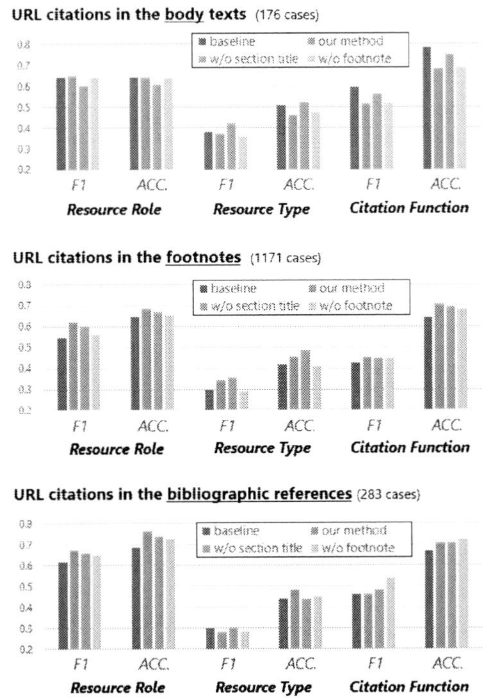

Figure 5: Evaluation results for each URL citation's type based on how the URL are described

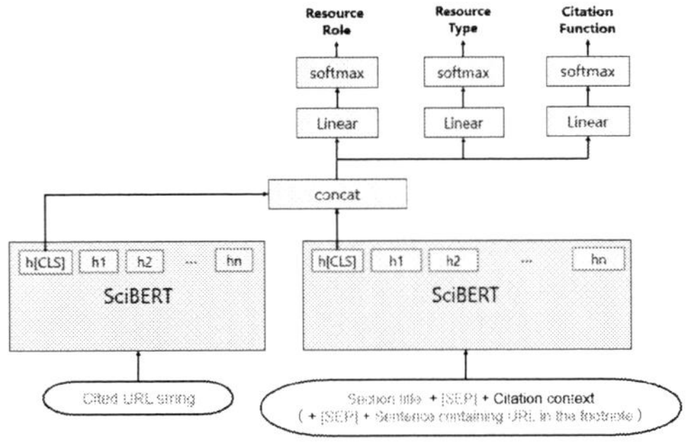

Figure 6: Architecture of classification model using the cited URL strings

As described in Section 3, the URL citations are divided into three types based on how the URLs are described. Figure 5 shows the evaluation results for each type of URL citation. The block of each bin shows the results of baseline, our method, our method without section titles, and our method without footnotes, from left to right. An overview of Figure 5 shows that the valid features depend on the combination of task and how to cite (i.e., the type of the URL citation). Our method basically outperformed the baseline when classifying URL citations in the footnotes and the bibliographic references; however, it tended to exhibit inferior performance compared to the baseline when classifying URL citations in the body. As to the classification of citation functions for URL citations in the body texts, our method was inferior to "w/o section title." In addition, "w/o footnote," which adds section titles to the baseline, was also inferior to the baseline. These results indicate that section titles have a negative effect on the classification of citation functions for URL citations in the body texts. However, there is a different trend for URL citations in footnotes and bibliographic references, which indicates that section titles are effective in the classification of citation functions for both types of URL citations. Different approaches depending on tasks or types of URL citations are required.

URL citations whose URLs are described in the references do not use footnotes. However, in the classification of such URL citations, "w/o section title" feeding cited footnotes into inputs tends to outperform the baseline using only citation contexts. Interestingly, training footnote texts is also useful for some citations that do not use footnotes.

5.5 Improving Classification Performance for Resource Types

While our method was effective for the classification of resource types, the F1-score was lower than that of other tasks. Thus, we extended our method by utilizing the substrings of URLs as input feature for classification. For some cases, the type of resources can be inferred from the domain or directory name constituting the URL. For example, it can be inferred from "data" and "tweets," that the URL "`http://trec.nist.gov/data/tweets/`" points to data related to tweets. Each substring constituting the URLs can contain information about resources on the website. In this approach, for each URL citation, the string of the cited URL is tokenized and encoded by SciBERT. The hidden layer corresponding to the "[CLS]" token is employed as the embedding for the entire substring sequence. Figure 6 shows the classification model used in this approach. The model concatenates the embedding of the cited URL string and the embedding of context information in the citing paper, and the obtained vector is used as the input feature for the linear layer of each task.

Table 5 presents the experimental results[16] The method utilizing the cited URLs (the row of "w/ URL") improved the classification performance of resource types. In addition, the classification of citation functions was also improved.

6 Limitation

In this paper, experimental data was constructed from one domain. Since paper styles, including structure of sections, how to use footnotes, and which type of URL citation the authors prefer may differ according to the domain, constructing experimental data from other domains and verifying our method on the data remain as the future works.

This paper defined the "Mixed" label for multiple resource citations. If citations are classified to the "Mixed" label, the resource roles and types can not be identified. Therefore, in practice, additional classification is required. Otherwise, it can be considered to employ the multi-label classification as with Zhang et al. (2022)'s study which applied the multi-label formulation to the classification of citation function. In that case, it is necessary to discuss how citations using ambiguous terms as referenced resources should be regarded (e.g., "All code and resources are available at [CITE].").

This paper addressed the automatic classification of URL citation to generate metadata of research artifacts. It contributes to the efficient expansion of research artifact repository, enrichment of the existing repositories, and automatic analysis of research artifact citations. However, resources cited by URLs tend to become unreachable within some years (Zeng et al., 2019). To promote utilization of research artifacts cited by URLs, establishing systems and platforms to preserve the artifacts and maintaining them are also required. As for the maintaining, the automatic predicting the longevity of research artifacts cited by URLs (Acuna et al., 2022) might be useful.

7 Conclusion

This paper addressed the classification task of identifying the resource role, resource type, and citation function, for each URL citation in scholarly papers. This paper proposed the classification method using not only citation contexts but also section titles and footnote texts as input features. Our method was evaluated experimentally and the results demonstrated the effectiveness of our method on all tasks. However, the effective features differ depending on the task and how the URL is cited. When classifying resource types, an approach that obtains and uses an embedding for the URL string used for the citation was effective.

[16]If there was a significant difference compared to our method by the paired t-test, daggers (†) are assigned. The significance level was 0.05.

Acknowledgements

This research was partially supported by the Grant-in-Aid for Scientific Research (B) (No. 21H03773) of JSPS.

References

Takeshi Abekawa and Akiko Aizawa. 2016. SideNoter: Scholarly paper browsing system based on PDF restructuring and text annotation. In *Proceedings of the 26th International Conference on Computational Linguistics: System Demonstrations (COLING 2016)*, pages 136-140, Osaka, Japan. The COLING 2016 Organizing Committee.

Amjad Abu-Jbara, Jefferson Ezra, and Dragomir Radev. 2013. Purpose and polarity of citation: Towards NLP-based bibliometrics. In *Proceedings of the 2013 Conference of the North American Chapter of the Association for Computational Linguistics: Human Language Technologies (NAACL-HLT2013)*, pages 596-606, Atlanta, Georgia. Association for Computational Linguistics.

Daniel E. Acuna, Jian Jian, Tong Zeng, Lizhen Liang, and Han Zhuang. 2022. Predicting the longevity of resources shared in scientific publications. *ArXiv preprint*, arXiv:2203.12800.

Association for Computing Machinery. 2020. Artifact review and badging version 1.1. (accessed 26 October 2022)

Iz Beltagy, Kyle Lo, and Arman Cohan. 2019. SciBERT: A pretrained language model for scientific text. In *Proceedings of The 2019 Conference on Empirical Methods in Natural Language Processing and the 9th International Joint Conference on Natural Language Processing (EMNLP-IJCNLP2019)*, pages 3615-3620, Hong Kong, China. Association for Computational Linguistics.

Arman Cohan, Waleed Ammar, Madeleine van Zuylen, and Field Cady. 2019. Structural scaffolds for citation intent classification in scientific publications. In *Proceedings of The 2019 Conference of the North American Chapter of the Association for Computational Linguistics: Human Language Technologies (NAACL-HLT2019) Volume 1 (Long and Short Papers)*, pages 3586–3596, Minneapolis, Minnesota. Association for Computational Linguistics.

John Cullars. 1990. Citation characteristics of Italian and Spanish literary monographs. *The Library Quarterly*, 60(4):337-356.

Data Citation Synthesis Group. 2014. Joint declaration of data citation principles. FORCE11, San Diego, CA, USA.

Jacob Devlin, Ming-Wei Chang, Kenton Lee, and Kristina Toutanova. 2019. BERT: Pre-training of deep bidirectional transformers for language understanding. In *Proceedings of The 2019 Conference of the North American Chapter of the Association for Computational Linguistics: Human Language Technologies (NAACL-HLT2019) Volume 1 (Long and Short Papers)*, pages 4171-4186, Minneapolis, Minnesota. Association for Computational Linguistics.

Ying Ding, Guo Zhang, Tamy Chambers, Min Song, Xiaolong Wang, and Chengxiang Zhai. 2014. Content-based citation analysis: The next generation of citation analysis. *Journal of the association for information science and technology*, 65(9):1820-1833.

Caifan Du, Johanna Cohoon, Patrice Lopez, and James Howison. 2021. Softcite dataset: A dataset of software mentions in biomedical and economic research publications. *Journal of the Association for Information Science and Technology*, 72(7):870-884.

Eugene Garfield. 1964. Can citation indexing be automated?. In *Proceedings of Statistical Association Methods for Mechanized Documentation, Symposium Proceedings*, pages 189–192, Washington, USA.

Yubin Ge, Ly Dinh, Xiaofeng Liu, Jinsong Su, Ziyao Lu, Ante Wang, and Jana Diesner. 2021. BACO: A background knowledge- and content-based framework for citing sentence generation. In *Proceedings of The 59th Annual Meeting of the Association for Computational Linguistics and the 11th International Joint Conference on Natural Language Processing (ACL2021) (Volume 1: Long Papers)*, pages 1466-1478, Online. Association for Computational Linguistics.

Rakesh Gosangi, Ravneet Arora, Mohsen Gheisarieha, Debanjan Mahata, and Haimin Zhang. 2021. On the use of context for predicting citation worthiness of sentences in scholarly articles. In *Proceedings of The 2021 Conference of the North American Chapter of the Association for Computational Linguistics: Human Language Technologies (NAACL-HLT2021)"*, pages 4539–4545, Online. Association for Computational Linguistics.

James Howison and Julia Bullard. 2016. Software in the scientific literature: Problems with seeing, finding, and using software mentioned in the biology literature. *Journal of the Association for Information Science and Technology*, 67(9):2137-2155.

Daisuke Ikeda, Kota Nagamizo, and Yuta Taniguchi. 2020. Automatic identification of dataset names in scholarly articles of various disciplines. *International Journal of Institutional Research and Management*, 4(1):17-30.

Tomoki Ikoma and Shigeki Matsubara. 2020. Identification of research data references based on citation contexts In *Proceedings of The 22nd International Conference on Asia-Pacific Digital Libraries (ICADL 2020)*, pages 149-156, Kyoto, Japan. Springer.

David Jurgens, Srijan Kumar, Raine Hoover, Dan McFarland, and Dan Jurafsky. 2018. Measuring the evolution of a scientific field through citation frames. *Transactions of the Association for Computational Linguistics*, 6:391–406.

Diederik P. Kingma and Jimmy Ba. 2014. Adam: A method for stochastic optimization. *ArXiv preprint*, arXiv.1412.6980

Shunsuke Kozawa, Hitomi Tohyama, Kiyotaka Uchimoto, and Shigeki Matsubara. 2010. Collection of usage information for language resources from academic articles. In *Proceedings of The 7th International Conference on Language Resources and Evaluation (LREC 2010)*, pages 1227-1232, Valletta, Malta. European Language Resources Association (ELRA).

Frank Krüger and David Schindler. 2020. A literature review on methods for the extraction of usage statements of software and data. *Computing in Science Engineering*, 22(1):26-38.

Kai Li and Erjia Yan. 2018. Co-mention network of R packages: Scientific impact and clustering structure. *Journal of Informetrics*, 12(1):87-100.

Michael J. Moravcsik and Poovanalingam Murugesan. 1975. Some results on the function and quality of citations. *Social Studies of Science*, 5(1):86-92.

Hiroki Nakayama, Takahiro Kubo, Junya Kamura, Yasufumi Taniguchi, and Xu Liang. 2018. Doccano: Text annotation tool for human. Software available from `https://github.com/doccano/doccano`.

Hidetsugu Nanba. 2018. Construction of an academic resource repository. In *Proceedings of the Toward Effective Support for Academic Information Search Workshop*, pages 8-14, Hamilton, New Zealand. Kyushu University.

Mark Neumann, Daniel King, Iz Beltagy, and Waleed Ammar. 2019. ScispaCy: Fast and robust models for biomedical natural language processing. In *Proceedings of the 18th BioNLP Workshop and Shared Task*, pages 319-327, Florence, Italy. Association for Computational Linguistics.

Monarch Parmar, Naman Jain, Pranjali Jain, P. Jayakrishna Sahit, Soham Pachpande, Shruti Singh, and Mayank Singh. 2020. NLPExplorer: Exploring the universe of NLP papers. *Advances in Information Retrieval*, 12036:476-480.

Adam Paszke, Sam Gross, Francisco Massa, Adam Lerer, James Bradbury, Gregory Chanan, Trevor Killeen, Zeming Lin, Natalia Gimelshein, Luca Antiga, Alban Desmaison, Andreas Kopf, Edward Yang, Zachary DeVito, Martin Raison, Alykhan Tejani, Sasank Chilamkurthy, Benoit Steiner, Lu Fang, Junjie Bai, and Soumith Chintala. 2019. PyTorch: An imperative style, high-performance deep learning library. In *Proceedings of Advances in Neural Information Processing Systems 32 (NIPS19)*, pages 8024-8035, Vancouver, Canada. Curran Associates Inc.

Fabian Pedregosa, Gaël Varoquaux, Alexandre Gramfort, Vincent Michel, Bertrand Thirion, Olivier Grisel, Mathieu Blondel, Peter Prettenhofer, Ron Weiss, Vincent Dubourg, Jake Vanderplas, Alexandre Passos, David Cournapeau, Matthieu Brucher, Matthieu Perrot, and Édouard Duchesnay. 2011. Scikit-learn: Machine learning in Python. *Journal of Machine Learning Research*, 12(85):2825-2830.

Animesh Prasad, Chenglei Si, and Min-Yen Kan. 2019. Dataset mention extraction and classification. In *Proceedings of the Workshop on Extracting Structured Knowledge from Scientific Publications (ESSP)*, pages 31-36, Minnesota, USA. Association for Computational Linguistics.

David Schindler, Benjamin Zapilko, and Frank Krüger. 2020. Investigating software usage in the social sciences: A knowledge graph approach In *Proceedings of the 17th European Semantic Web Conference Semantic Web (The Semantic Web)*, pages 271-286, Crete, Greece. Springer.

Ayush Singhal, Ravindra Kasturi, and Jaideep Srivastava. 2014. DataGopher: Context-based search for research datasets. In *Proceedings of the 2014 IEEE 15th International Conference on Information Reuse and Integration (IEEE IRI 2014)*, pages 749–756, California, USA. Institute of Electrical and Electronics Engineers

Ayush Singhal and Jaideep Srivastava. 2013. Data extract: Mining context from the web for dataset extraction. *International Journal of Machine Learning and Computing*, 3(2):219-223.

Arfon M. Smith, Daniel S. Katz, and Kyle E. Niemeyer. 2016. Software citation principles. *PeerJ Computer Science*, 2:e86.

Ina Spiegel-Rösing. 1977. Science studies: Bibliometric and content analysis. *Social Studies of Science*, 7(1):97-113.

Simone Teufel, Advaith Siddharthan, and Dan Tidhar. 2006. Automatic classification of citation function. In *Proceedings of the 2006 conference on empirical methods in natural language processing (EMNLP2006)*, pages 103-110, Sydney, Australia. Association for Computational Linguistics.

John Towns, Christine Kirkpatrick, Kenton McHenry, and Kandace Turner. 2016. Towards a U.S. national data service - inaugural report. The National Date Service, Illinois, USA. (accessed 26 October 2022)

Masaya Tsunokake, Shigeki Matsubara. 2021. Classification of URLs citing research artifacts in scholarly documents based on distributed representations. In *Proceedings of the 2nd Workshop on Extraction and Evaluation of Knowledge Entities from Scientific Documents (EEKE2021) co-located with JCDL2021*, pages 20–25, Online. CEUR-WS Team.

Thomas Wolf, Lysandre Debut, Victor Sanh, Julien Chaumond, Clement Delangue, Anthony Moi, Pierric Cistac, Tim Rault, Remi Louf, Morgan Funtowicz, Joe Davison, Sam Shleifer, Patrick von Platen, Clara Ma, Yacine Jernite, Julien Plu, Canwen Xu, Teven Le Scao, Sylvain Gugger, Mariama Drame, Quentin Lhoest, and Alexander Rush. 2020. Transformers: State-of-the-art natural language processing. In *Proceedings of the 2020 Conference on Empirical Methods in Natural Language Processing (EMNLP2020): System Demonstrations*, pages 38-45, Online. Association for Computational Linguistics.

Yasunori Yamamoto and Toshihisa Takagi. 2007. OReFiL: An online resource finder for life sciences. BMC bioinformatics, 8(1):1-8.

Tong Zeng, Alain Shema, and Daniel E. Acuna. 2019. Dead science: Most resources linked in biomedical articles disappear in eight years. In *Proceedings of the 14th International Conference on Information - iConference 2019*, pages 170-176, Washington, USA. Springer.

Yang Zhang, Yufei Wang, Quan Z. Sheng, Adnan Mahmood, Wei Emma Zhang, and Rongying Zhao. 2022. TDM-CFC: Towards document-level multi-label citation function classification. In *Proceedings of the 22nd International Conference on Web Information Systems Engineering - WISE 2021*, pages 363-376, VIC, Australia. Springer.

He Zhao, Zhunchen Luo, Chong Feng, Anqing Zheng, and Xiaopeng Liu. 2019. A context-based framework for modeling the role and function of on-line resource citations in scientific literature. In *Proceedings of the 2019 Conference on Empirical Methods in Natural Language Processing and the 9th International Joint Conference on Natural Language Processing (EMNLP-IJCNLP2019)*, pages 5206-5215, Hong Kong, China. Association for Computational Linguistics.

A Supplement for Creating Dataset

Citation anchors in scholarly papers were detected by regular expressions based on those used by Gosangi et al. (2021). The following code shows the regular expressions for the Harvard referencing style, which was implemented by Python.

```
AUTHOR_NAME = r"([A-Z][\w\-']*?)"
ETAL = "(et ?als?\.?)"
AUTHOR_SECTION = AUTHOR_NAME +
                 r"(?: (?:(?:and|&) (?:de )?" +
                 AUTHOR_NAME + '|' + ETAL + '))?'
YEAR = r"((?:18|19|20)[0-9]{2}[a-z]?)"
PAGE = r"(?:, (?:pages|pp?\.?) \d+(?:-\d+)?)"
YP = f"{YEAR}{PAGE}?"

LEFT_BRACKET = r"[\(\[]"
RIGHT_BRACKET = r"[\)\]]"

CITET = f"{AUTHOR_SECTION} {LEFT_BRACKET}{YP}
        {RIGHT_BRACKET}"
CITEP_SINGLE = f"{LEFT_BRACKET}{AUTHOR_SECTION}
               , {YP}{RIGHT_BRACKET}"
CITEP_MULTI_BEGIN = f"{LEFT_BRACKET}{AUTHOR_SECTION}
                    , {YP};"
CITEP_MULTI_INSIDE = f"(?<=; ){AUTHOR_SECTION}
                    , {YP};"
CITEP_MULTI_END = f"(?<=; ){AUTHOR_SECTION}
                 , {YP}{RIGHT_BRACKET}"

CITATION_ANCHOR = f"(?:{CITET}|{CITEP_SINGLE}|
                  {CITEP_MULTI_BEGIN}|
                  {CITEP_MULTI_INSIDE}|
                  {CITEP_MULTI_END})"
```

In addition, the following code is for the Vancouver referencing style.

```
NUMBER = r"(?:([1-9]\d*)(?:(-[1-9]\d*))?)"
CITATION = f"\\[{NUMBER}(?:, ?{NUMBER})*?\\]"
```

The annotation environment was implemented by Doccano (Nakayama et al., 2018).

B Experimental Setup

In the experiment, the following procedure was performed in each split of the 5-fold cross-validation. For each candidate of hyperparameters, the classification model was trained for up to 50 epochs. Note that training was terminated if the minimum loss for the development set could not be updated within 10 epochs. Then, for each classification task, the trained model with the best classification performance[17] for the development set was applied to the test set to evaluate the method. In this evaluation, accuracy (i.e, micro-averaged F1) and macro-averaged F1 were computed from the classification results obtained on the test set in each split.

The following hyperparameters were verified in the experiment.

- Batch size: 16, 32, 64
- Learning rate: 1.0e-4, 5.0e-5, 1.0e-5, 5.0e-6
- Scope of citation contexts[18]: 1 sentence, 3 sentences (citing sentence and 1 sentence before and after the citing sentence), 5 sentences (citing sentence and 2 sentences before and after the citing sentence)
- Dropout rates: 0.0, 0.3, 0.6
- Maximum sequence length of inputs: 256

The weight of each task in the loss was set equally at 1.0.

In addition, scikit-learn[19] (Pedregosa et al., 2011), PyTorch[20] (Paszke et al., 2019), and Hugging Face's transformers library[21] (Wolf et al., 2020) were used to implement the experiment. Sentence segmentation was performed by ScispaCy[22] (Neumann et al., 2019).

[17] macro-averaged F1-score

[18] A paragraph is one of the semantic units. Therefore, in this study, the scope of the citation context was limited to the paragraph containing the URL citation even when the employed scope included sentences before and after the citing sentence.

[19] https://scikit-learn.org/stable/

[20] https://pytorch.org/docs/1.8.1/

[21] https://github.com/huggingface/transformer

[22] https://github.com/allenai/scispacy

TELIN: Table Entity LINker for Extracting Leaderboards from Machine Learning Publications

Sean T. Yang*
University of Washington
Seattle, WA
tyyang38@uw.edu

Curtis Wigington
Adobe Research
College Park, MD
wigingto@adobe.com

Christopher Tensmeyer
Adobe Research
College Park, MD
tensmeye@adobe.com

Abstract

Tracking state-of-the-art (SOTA) results in machine learning studies is challenging due to high publication volume. Existing methods for creating leaderboards in scientific documents require significant human supervision or rely on scarcely available LaTeX source files. We propose Table Entity LINker (TELIN), a framework which extracts (task, model, dataset, metric) quadruples from collections of scientific publications in PDF format. TELIN identifies scientific named entities, constructs a knowledge base, and leverages human feedback to iteratively refine automatic extractions. TELIN identifies and prioritizes uncertain and impactful entities for human review to create a cascade effect for leaderboard completion. We show that TELIN is competitive with the SOTA but requires much less human annotation.

1 Introduction

Advances in the field of Machine Learning (ML) are typically evidenced by producing better empirical results on benchmark datasets. With over 334k AI papers published in 2021 (Zhang et al., 2022), automated approaches to extract and categorize empirical results would help practitioners track progress in the field.

Leaderboard extraction is challenging because there is no universal lexicon, taxonomy, or structure for reporting empirical results in ML publications. New benchmark datasets and tasks are frequently introduced, and established datasets are updated or repurposed for new tasks or metrics. For example, a publication with a table containing numerical results on "ImageNet" could refer to any particular LSVRC challenge year (2010-2017), task (e.g., classification, object detection, localization), number of classes, dataset version, evaluation metric, etc. These necessary details could be specified in table header cells, table captions, paragraphs referencing the table, or elsewhere in the paper. Additionally, ML publications are often only available in PDF format which infrequently explicitly encodes the underlying document paragraph and table structures.

Prior work on scientific leaderboard construction suffer from the following weaknesses:

(1) Unimodal E.g., tables (Singh et al., 2019), citations (Viswanathan et al., 2021), and knowledge bases (Chen et al., 2020). Leaderboard construction can benefit from processing publications holistically rather than as a single data mode.

(2) Requires LaTeX source files (Singh et al., 2019; Kardas et al., 2020). While extracting document structure is easier from LaTeX files than PDF, many publications are only publicly available in PDF.

(3) Closed Taxonomy (Kardas et al., 2020; Hou et al., 2019). Assuming that the names of all datasets, tasks and metrics are known apriori is unrealistic given the rapid pace of the field.

(4) High Manual Effort. State-of-the-art methods (Kardas et al., 2020; Hou et al., 2019) use supervised models that require large and manually-curated training datasets.

(5) Crowd Sourced. E.g., `paperswithcode.com` generally has precise leaderboard entries, but lack systematic examination of the literature to ensure leaderboard recall.

This work proposes Table Entity LINker (TELIN) as a multi-modal framework that extracts leaderboards from PDF collections of ML publications. TELIN produces (Task, Dataset, Metric, Score) quadruples associated with each paper, which can be grouped and sorted to produce a leaderboard for each (Task, Dataset, Metric) triplet. First, TELIN extracts textual content and tables from all input PDFs and utilizes an off-the-shelf scientific Named Entity Recognition (NER) model, SpERT (Eberts and Ulges, 2020), to identify scientific Named Entities (NE) in the text. Then,

*The work was done while the author interned at Adobe Research.

Proceedings of the 1st Workshop on Information Extraction from Scientific Publications, pages 20–25
Nov 20, 2022. ©2022 Association for Computational Linguistics

TELIN matches NEs to table heading cell text to infer the meaning of table cell values and extract quadruples.As additional publications are parsed and more NEs are recognized, TELIN iteratively propagates these labels to previously seen tables and text. TELIN also allows human feedback to label new NEs in table header text. To facilitate this, TELIN intelligently selects tables for human labeling based on their potential for label propagation.

Our evaluation on the PWCLeaderboards dataset (Kardas et al., 2020) shows that TELIN uses significantly less human supervision on PDF inputs to achieve comparable accuracy with the state-of-the-art leaderboard extraction system, Axcell (Kardas et al., 2020), which requires LaTeX source file inputs. While their accuracy is similar, we conclude that TELIN is likely a more practical tool for leaderboard extraction since it requires less human annotation and can be applied to any publication avaiable in PDF.

2 Methodology

Figure 1 illustrates the pipeline of TELIN, whose objective is to extract empirical result quadruples (Task, Dataset, Metric, Score) from a PDF collection of ML publications. We designed TELIN based on the following observations: **(1)** Many scores are presented in tables, but not all tables display scores. **(2)** In most tables, column header text (and separately row text) contain NEs of only a single NE type - e.g., row headers only have model names while col headers contain only metrics. **(3)** NER on individual table cell texts is difficult since the cell text is often only a few words and the NER model is trained on full sentences. However, table cell NEs are lexically the same as or similar to NEs in the main document text, so NEs recognized by a pretrained model in the main text can help identify NEs within cell text. We now explain each step of the pipeline in detail.

(a) Document Decomposition TELIN first converts an unstructured PDF into a structured document using a YOLO-based object detection model (Redmon and Farhadi, 2018) to identify paragraphs, section headings, captions, and table regions. The rows, columns, heading blocks, and cells are then extracted from each table region using the SPLERGE model (**?**) The PDF text can then be associated with the identified regions to form a structured document. While there are errors in this extraction process, we found that the majority of leaderboard errors are not a result of the extraction process.

(b) Scientific NER on Text NER models typically require heavy supervision, so TELIN applies a pre-trained SpERT (Span-based Entity and Relation Transformer) model (Eberts and Ulges, 2020) to the entire main text of each PDF to identify NEs. SpERT is a BERT-based model for NER that is pre-trained on the SCiERC dataset (Luan et al., 2018) of 500 abstracts from 12 AI conference and workshop proceedings. SpERT classifies scientific entities into 5 categories: Task, Method, Evaluation Metric, Material (dataset), and General, which align well with our quadruple schema of (Task, Metric, Dataset, Score).

Since SpERT is trained on full sentences, it performs poorly on short non-sentence text such as table header cell text. Therefore, TELIN takes the NEs from the main text and compares them with table cell text and propagates NE labels for closely matching text.

(c) Strings Matching After identifying NEs from the main text, we perform string matching between these NEs and the text of each non-numeric table cell. One challenge is that acronyms are often used to shorten method, dataset, and metric names. Another challenge is that exact string matches are not guaranteed. To overcome these challenges, TELIN uses a combination of fuzzy search and short text representations to measure string similarity:

$$char\_s(a,b) = \max(t\_dist(a,b), dist(a,b)) \tag{1}$$

$$score = \frac{char\_s + sim(\mathbf{A},\mathbf{B})}{2} \tag{2}$$

where a, b are the two compared strings, $\mathbf{A}, \mathbf{B}$ are their respective Sentence-Bert (Reimers and Gurevych, 2019) feature vectors, $sim()$ is cosine similarity, $dist()$ is the length-normalized Levenshtein string distance, and $t\_dist()$ computes the difference between the tokenized strings. [1] The implementation of computing character level similarity ratio is able to draw comparison between acronyms. The cosine similarity between

[1] We use the WuzzyFuzzy `https://github.com/seatgeek/thefuzz` library. Specifically, we use `fuzz.ratio()` for *dist*() and `fuzz.token_set_ratio` for *t_dist*(). Higher number means more similar between strings.

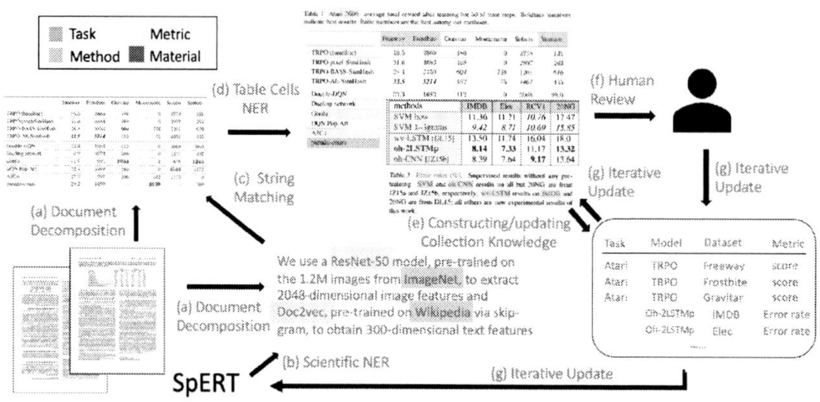

Figure 1: The TELIN framework consumes a collection of Machine Learning publications in PDF and extracts reported results as (Task, Dataset, Metric, Value) quadruples.

the sentence representations indicates how close the strings are semantically.

(d) Table Cells NER SpERT predictions can be inaccurate, and the same or similar strings can be predicted as different entity types. To disambiguate the entity type of a string, we soft-label the string based on majority vote of all predictions for that string across the entire collection text. These labels are then assigned to matching table cell strings. Next, we assign labels to rows and columns of table header cells based on our observation that the type of all cells within a header row/column is often the same. We do this based on cell majority vote and propagate this label to all unlabeled cells. For example, a header row/col with five cells would be labeled when three cells have the same entity type. Then, the 2 remaining unlabled cells would be labeled with this majority type. Finally, the leaderboards are identified when at least three out of the four entities (Task, Dataset, Metric, Model) appear in a table and caption.

(e) Constructing Collection Knowledge We construct a knowledge base from the identified leaderboards and use this as shared knowledge to discover more entities in the documents. The whole collection goes through a few iterations of updates before the human review.

(f) Human Review TELIN integrates a guided human review mechanism to significantly improve the overall entity prediction and quadruple extraction. We compute an influence score E_v for each entity and populate the table with the highest influence score for human annotations. The design philosophy is to prioritize uncertain entities and impactful entities: (1) Uncertain entities have high entropy distributions for predicted entity type distributions from SpERT. (2) Impactful entities are those that can cause a cascade effect for leaderboard completion. A cascade occurs if labeling a string with an entity type and propagating that label to all occurrences of that string throughout the collection would cause a majority labeling of a table header row/col and therefore trigger the propagation of the label to other strings in that table header row/col. Such label propagation may then continue to trigger further cascading of the label.

Note that common entities, such as accuracy (as metric) and COCO (as dataset), do not automatically belong to this category. The proposed design of this task is inspired by identifying influential nodes in a network (Guo et al., 2020; Zhang et al., 2013; Molaei et al., 2020).

First, we compute the uncertainty of a cell by calculate the entropy of the predicted entity type distribution:

$$H_v = \sum_l -p_l \log p_l \tag{3}$$

where p_l is the probability of entity type l for string v. Higher values of H_v indicates higher uncertainty of the entity type.

Then, we compute the uncertainty of the headers.

$$H_h = \sum_{cl \in \Gamma_h} -p_{cl} \log p_{cl} \tag{4}$$

where p_{cl} is the probability of the label l for header h. This step aims to find headers that almost meet the threshold for header labeling.

Next, we construct a heterogeneous network for the purpose of computing the potential of a cell to cause a cascade. Each confirmed entity is a node and edges are formed when two entities appear in the same table header row/col. The "spreading ability" (Guo et al., 2020) of a cell is computed as:

$$H_{uv} = -p_{uv} \log p_{uv} \tag{5}$$

where $p_{uv} = \frac{d_u}{\sum_{l \in \Gamma_v} d_l}$, Γ_v are the immediate neighbors of node v, and d_u is the degree of node u. H_{uv} indicates the spreading ability from node u to node v.

Finally, the influence score of an entity E_v can be acquired by:

$$E_v = H_v + n_{uv} \sum_{u \in \Gamma_v} H_{uv} + \sum_{u \in \Gamma_h} H_h \tag{6}$$

TELIN selects tables including the entities with the highest influence scores for human review. The users are able to confirm or correct the types of the entities on a row/column basis. The user can also label any useful entities in the caption of the table.

(g) Iterative Update The entity type labels from human feedback are treated as ground truth and are used to finetune the SpERT model. The finetuned SpERT model is then used to provide updated NE predictions. This process continues for several iterations until convergence.

3 Experiments and Results

We evaluate TELIN's end-to-end performance on Task, Dataset, Metric, Score (TDMS) quadruple extraction on the PWCLeaderboards (Kardas et al., 2020) task and compare it to the state-of-the-art AxCell model (Kardas et al., 2020). We select AxCell as our main competitor due to its superiority against other existing work (Hou et al., 2019). PWCLeaderboards include 731 papers and 3,445 leaderboards, which include the unique TDMS quadruples in every paper. We follow Kardas et al. for evaluation metrics. We also investigate the performance improvement from the human feedback phase.

End-to-end Performance Table 1 reports the extraction results on PWCLeaderboards dataset. TELIN's performance is comparable to the state-of-the-art results from AxCell with fewer annotations. AxCell includes significant supervision in their pipeline: a table type classification model and a table segmentation model. Both models are trained with 1400 carefully labeled tables. The labeling of these tables require expertise and is time-consuming. The guided human mechanism in TELIN substantially reduces the requirements of human supervision to achieve similar performance as the state-of-the-art.

Table 1: Extraction results on PWCLeaderboards dataset for entire quadruple (TDMS), triple with no score (TDM), and individual entities. The performance of our model is comparable to the state-of-the-art from AxCell with less annotations.

Entity	Micro			Macro		
	P	R	F1	P	R	F1
Axcell (1400 tables)						
TDMS	37.3	23.2	28.7	24.0	21.8	21.1
TDM	67.8	47.8	56.1	47.9	46.4	43.5
Task	70.6	57.3	63.3	60.7	62.6	59.7
Dataset	70.2	48.4	57.3	53.5	52.7	49.9
Metric	68.8	58.5	63.3	58.4	60.4	56.5
Ours (75 tables)						
TDMS	38.3	20.8	26.3	26.6	19.2	21.3
TDM	68.2	45.3	56.5	49.7	43.1	42.5
Task	70.3	53.7	59.2	60.5	57.3	57.1
Dataset	70.9	52.8	59.3	54.7	55.2	53.9
Metric	63.2	57.9	60.2	56.3	55.1	55.4

Analysis of Human Review We further investigate the effect of the feedback by the number of the annotations. Figure 2 shows the impact of the guided human review system. We see improvement in accuracy over the first 50 annotations with convergence after 50 annotations. We observe that the system struggles to identify the 60+ datasets in Atari Games and all the presentation variations of the Accuracy metric without human feedback. The tables with these entities are always among the first for human review.

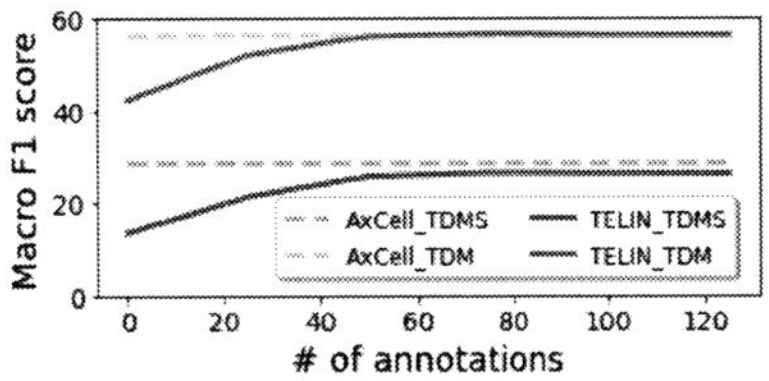

Figure 2: Effect of active learning on the performance. Solid lines are the performance of TELIN on quadruple (Red) and triple (Blue) extraction. Dashed lines are the performance of AxCell as a reference. Human feedback provides performance boost in the first 50 annotations. The performance converges after 50 annotations.

4 Discussion

While TELIN presents promising performance, it still does not exceed the state-of-the-art accuracy in extracting leaderboards from machine learning research papers. Our method relies on the propagation of discoveries from one paper to another. The relatively small data size (731 papers) of PWCLeaderboard dataset limits the capability of TELIN. We will investigate whether introducing more data helps the performance of TELIN. Moreover, unlike existing studies relying on taxonomy of leaderboards known in advance, TELIN operates without any assumptions of taxonomy. We are interested in analyzing the capacity of TELIN for novel taxonomy discovery.

Extracting leaderboards from the scientific papers on the web is an example of integrating artificial intelligence in conceptual modeling (Embley et al., 1998; Olivé, 2007). Conceptual modeling is a vessel for humans to transform the noise in the nature to structured or semi-structured presentations. While automatic machine extraction has been utilized to collect and organize data from a wide variety of sources in conceptual modeling (Embley et al., 1998; Bork, 2022; Nalchigar and Yu, 2018), the role of deep learning and artificial intelligence remains understudied in this field. The design of TELIN is a demonstration of involving artificial intelligence to facilitate conceptual modeling. We hope this effort will invite future studies in this domain.

References

Dominik Bork. 2022. Conceptual modeling and artificial intelligence: Challenges and opportunities for enterprise engineering. In *Enterprise Engineering Working Conference*, pages 3–9. Springer.

Zhiyu Chen, Mohamed Trabelsi, Jeff Heflin, and Brian D Davison. 2020. Towards knowledge acquisition of metadata on ai progress. In *ISWC (Demos/Industry)*, pages 232–237.

Markus Eberts and Adrian Ulges. 2020. Span-based joint entity and relation extraction with transformer pre-training. In *ECAI 2020*, pages 2006–2013. IOS Press.

David W Embley, Douglas M Campbell, YS Jiang, Stephen W Liddle, Y-K Ng, DW Quass, and Randy D Smith. 1998. A conceptual-modeling approach to extracting data from the web. In *International Conference on Conceptual Modeling*, pages 78–91. Springer.

Chungu Guo, Liangwei Yang, Xiao Chen, Duanbing Chen, Hui Gao, and Jing Ma. 2020. Influential nodes identification in complex networks via information entropy. *Entropy*, 22(2):242.

Yufang Hou, Charles Jochim, Martin Gleize, Francesca Bonin, and Debasis Ganguly. 2019. Identification of tasks, datasets, evaluation metrics, and numeric scores for scientific leaderboards construction. In *Proceedings of the 57th Annual Meeting of the Association for Computational Linguistics*, pages 5203–5213.

Marcin Kardas, Piotr Czapla, Pontus Stenetorp, Sebastian Ruder, Sebastian Riedel, Ross Taylor, and Robert Stojnic. 2020. Axcell: Automatic extraction of results from machine learning papers. In *Proceedings of the 2020 Conference on Empirical Methods in Natural Language Processing (EMNLP)*, pages 8580–8594.

Yi Luan, Luheng He, Mari Ostendorf, and Hannaneh Hajishirzi. 2018. Multi-task identification of entities, relations, and coreferencefor scientific knowledge graph construction. In *Proc. Conf. Empirical Methods Natural Language Process. (EMNLP)*.

Soheila Molaei, Reza Farahbakhsh, Mostafa Salehi, and Noel Crespi. 2020. Identifying influential nodes in heterogeneous networks. *Expert Systems with Applications*, 160:113580.

Soroosh Nalchigar and Eric Yu. 2018. Business-driven data analytics: A conceptual modeling framework. *Data & Knowledge Engineering*, 117:359–372.

Antoni Olivé. 2007. *Conceptual modeling of information systems*. Springer Science & Business Media.

Joseph Redmon and Ali Farhadi. 2018. Yolov3: An incremental improvement. *arXiv preprint arXiv:1804.02767*.

Nils Reimers and Iryna Gurevych. 2019. Sentence-bert: Sentence embeddings using siamese bert-networks. In *Proceedings of the 2019 Conference on Empirical Methods in Natural Language Processing and the 9th International Joint Conference on Natural Language Processing (EMNLP-IJCNLP)*, pages 3982–3992.

Mayank Singh, Rajdeep Sarkar, Atharva Vyas, Pawan Goyal, Animesh Mukherjee, and Soumen Chakrabarti. 2019. Automated early leaderboard generation from comparative tables. In *European Conference on Information Retrieval*, pages 244–257. Springer.

Vijay Viswanathan, Graham Neubig, and Pengfei Liu. 2021. Citationie: Leveraging the citation graph for scientific information extraction. *arXiv preprint arXiv:2106.01560*.

Daniel Zhang, Nestor Maslej, Andre Barbe, Helen Ngo, Latisha Harry, Ellie Sakhaee, Benjamin Bronkema-Bekker, et al. 2022. The ai index 2022 annual report.

Xiaohang Zhang, Ji Zhu, Qi Wang, and Han Zhao. 2013. Identifying influential nodes in complex networks with community structure. *Knowledge-Based Systems*, 42:74–84.

PICO Corpus: A Publicly Available Corpus to Support Automatic Data Extraction from Biomedical Literature

Faith Wavinya Mutinda, Kongmeng Liew, Shuntaro Yada, Shoko Wakamiya, Eiji Aramaki
Nara Institute of Science and Technology
{mutinda.faith_wavinya.mz2, liew.kongmeng, s-yada, wakamiya, aramaki}@is.naist.jp

Abstract

We present a publicly available corpus with detailed annotations describing the core elements of clinical trials: Participants, Intervention, Control, and Outcomes. The corpus consists of 1011 abstracts of breast cancer randomized controlled trials extracted from the PubMed database. The corpus improves previous corpora by providing detailed annotations for outcomes to identify numeric texts that report the number of participants that experience specific outcomes. The corpus will be helpful for the development of systems for automatic extraction of data from randomized controlled trial literature to support evidence-based medicine. Additionally, we demonstrate the feasibility of the corpus by using two strong baselines for named entity recognition task. Most of the entities achieve F1 scores greater than 0.80 demonstrating the quality of the dataset.

1 Introduction

Evidence-based medicine (EBM) is an approach where doctors and health care professionals use the best available research evidence to guide them in making clinical decision about the care of patients (Sackett, 1997). Meta-analyses are one of the essential tools in EBM because they provide the highest form of medical evidence (Cook et al., 1997). A meta-analysis is a statistical technique that combines results of different research studies to determine the effectiveness of a treatment. Despite their importance, meta-analyses are labor-intensive and time-consuming as they involve manually reading hundreds of unstructured research articles and extracting data from them (Jonnalagadda et al., 2015). The number of research articles is increasing rapidly making it difficult/impossible for researchers to keep up. For instance, a recent study showed that more than 50,000 research articles related to COVID-19 have been published and more articles are being published every day (Wang and Lo, 2021).

Machine learning and natural language processing (NLP) techniques to automate data extraction from biomedical literature and speed up dissemination of biomedical evidence have been widely studied. Although automatic (or semi-automatic) approaches for extracting data from research articles have been proposed, they are still not ready for practical use (Marshall and Wallace, 2019). This is because data extraction requires high accuracy, which may be difficult for automated systems to achieve. The scarcity of publicly available corpora, which are usually expensive to create, is one barrier to the development of high-performance systems.

This paper presents a publicly available[1] corpus annotated with the core components of clinical trials, i.e., Participants, Intervention, Control, and Outcomes (PICO). We annotate in detail numeric texts especially those that identify the number of participants having certain outcomes. The annotation of the numeric texts is important for statistical analysis to determine the overall effect of an intervention. Currently, the corpus consists of 1011 research abstracts extracted from the PubMed database. The abstracts are of randomized controlled trials (RCTs) related to breast cancer, which is one of the leading causes of deaths in the world[2]. We focus on RCTs as they are considered the gold standard for clinical research methods.

2 Related work

Although there are some corpora with PICO elements annotated in abstracts and full-text articles, most of the corpora are not publicly available. Kiritchenko et al. (2010) developed a dataset containing 182 full-text articles. They annotated 21 entities including treatment dosage, frequency, funding organization, grant number, and so on. Summerscales et al. (2011) created a corpus consisting of 263 abstracts and annotated the treatment groups, out-

[1] https://github.com/sociocom/PICO-Corpus
[2] https://www.who.int/news-room/factsheets/detail/cancer

Proceedings of the 1st Workshop on Information Extraction from Scientific Publications, pages 26–31
Nov 20, 2022.

comes, group sizes, and outcome numbers. Their work is close to our study as they attempted to identify outcome numbers and group sizes for the purpose of calculating summary statistics. The annotations are however less extensive and the corpus is not publicly available.

Since constructing large corpora is expensive, Wallace et al. (2016) employed a distant supervision approach to create a large corpora consisting of full-text articles. They also manually annotated 133 articles for evaluation. Although distant supervision is a cheap way to construct large datasets, the dataset's quality might be low.

Most of these previous datasets are not publicly available. Nye et al. (2018) developed the EBM-NLP corpus, which is one of the largest publicly available corpora. Their annotation was done by crowd-sourcing through Amazon Mechanical Turk and a small part (200 abstracts) was done by medical professionals. The corpus consists of about 5000 abstracts of RCTs mostly related to cardiovascular diseases, cancer, and autism. They however do not annotate numeric texts that identify the number of participants who had certain outcomes.

3 Corpus annotation

3.1 Dataset collection

The corpus in this study consists of abstracts extracted from PubMed[3]. PubMed is a free search engine that provides access to the MEDLINE database[4] that indexes abstracts for biomedical and life sciences articles. We extracted research abstracts related to breast cancer whose study type is RCT, and are not meta-analysis or systematic-reviews. This was achieved by using keywords such as "breast cancer," "randomized controlled," "randomised controlled," "meta-analysis," and "systematic review."

3.2 Annotation process

The research abstracts were manually annotated. The annotator was asked to read and label text spans that identify the PICO elements, i.e., Participants (P), Interventions (I), Control (C), and Outcomes (O). For each PICO category, we developed sub-categories to capture detailed information within each category. The PICO label hierarchy is shown in Figure 2. In total we annotated 26 sub-categories (entities) which are described below.

[3]https://pubmed.ncbi.nlm.nih.gov/

[4]https://www.nlm.nih.gov/medline/medline_overview.html

- **Participants**: we annotate text snippets that describe the characteristics of the participants in a study. We annotate eight entities that include the total number of participants in the study, the number of participants in the intervention group, the number of participants in the control group, condition, eligibility, age, ethnicity, and location. Although breast cancer is the main condition, some studies focus on treating conditions associated with breast cancer such as hair loss, bone loss, depression, and pain.

- **Intervention and Control**: we annotate text snippets that mention the specific intervention

Sub-category	Tag count	Number of abstracts
Participants (P)		
total-participants	1094	847
intervention-participants	887	674
control-participants	784	647
age	231	210
eligibility	925	864
ethinicity	101	83
condition	327	321
location	186	168
Intervention & Control (IC)		
intervention	1067	1011
control	979	949
Outcomes (O)		
outcome	5053	978
outcome-measure	1081	413
iv-bin-abs	556	288
cv-bin-abs	465	258
iv-bin-percent	1376	561
cv-bin-percent	1148	520
iv-cont-mean	366	154
cv-cont-mean	327	154
iv-cont-median	270	140
cv-cont-median	247	133
iv-cont-sd	129	69
cv-cont-sd	124	67
iv-cont-q1	4	3
cv-cont-q1	4	3
iv-cont-q3	4	3
cv-cont-q3	4	3

Table 1: Corpus statistics: The frequency of each entity (sub-category) and the number of abstracts in which each entity is found.

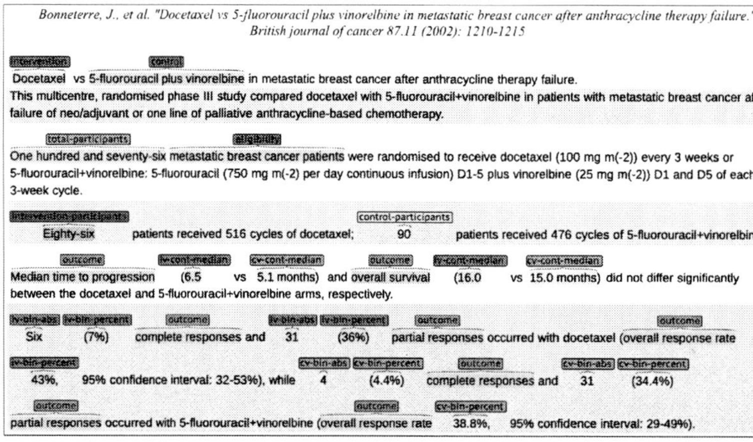

Figure 1: An abstract with PICO elements annotated

and control used in the study. There are only two entities in this category.

- **Outcomes**: we annotate the outcome measures (primary and secondary end-points) and outcomes that were measured. We also aim to capture detailed information for the outcomes especially the numeric texts that identify the number of participants who experienced a particular outcome. In meta-analysis statistical analysis, these numeric texts are important for calculating summary statistics to ascertain the effectiveness of the intervention.

In the annotation, we mainly consider two types of outcomes, i.e, *binary outcomes* and *continuous outcomes*. Binary outcomes take two values such as the treatment was successful or failed, or survival (alive or dead). Continuous outcomes are not as straightforward as binary outcomes. Continuous outcomes such as pain are measured on a numerical scale (for instance, pain scores on a scale of 0 and 10). Continuous outcomes are usually measured at different time points (such as at baseline and at followup) and the results reported as mean, standard deviation, median, or quartiles.

We created labels to capture the various types of numeric texts in the intervention and control groups. We use "*iv*," "*cv*," "*bin*," and "*cont*" to represent intervention group, control group, binary outcome, and continuous outcome, respectively. In addition, binary outcomes numeric texts tend to be absolute values or percentage values. We use "*abs*" and "*percent*" to label absolute and percentage values respectively. Further, for the continuous outcomes, we also designed labels to capture the different types of numeric texts. We use "*mean*," "*sd*," "*median*," "*q1*," and "*q3*" to represent mean, standard deviation, median, first quartile, and third quartile respectively. In total, we have 16 entities for the outcomes. Figure 1 shows an example of an annotated abstract.

Binary outcome example:

- *<iv-bin-abs>*Four*</iv-bin-abs>* patients in the intervention group and *<cv-bin-abs>*two*</cv-bin-abs>* in the control group were *<outcome>*lost to follow-up*</outcome>*.

Continuous outcome example:

- *<outcome>*Depression scores*</outcome>* at follow-up were significantly lower in the exercise group (M = *<iv-cont-mean>*4.78*</iv-cont-mean>*, SD = *<iv-cont-sd>*3.56*</iv-cont-sd>*) compared to the control group (M= *<cv-cont-mean>*6.91*</cv-cont-mean>*, SD =*<cv-cont-sd>*5.86*</cv-cont-sd>*).

3.3 Corpus statistics

The corpus contains 1011 manually annotated abstracts. The annotation was performed using BRAT, an open-source web annotation tool (Stenetorp et al., 2012). The abstracts were annotated by two annotators. One of the annotators was hired from an annotation company and has extensive experience annotating medical documents and the second annotator is one of the authors. The first annotator annotated all the abstracts while the second annotator annotated 45% of the abstracts. The inter-annotator agreement was calculated based on Cohen Kappa and achieved a score of 0.72. Annotator disagreements were mainly found in the *outcome* and *eligibility* entities where the annotators had challenges in determining the start and end spans. How to minimize these disagreements during the annotation process is an important future work. Annotator disagreements for the other entities were minimal since they could be identified by one or two words and these disagreements are easy to resolve.

Currently the corpus has 17,739 entities and the frequencies of the annotated entities are shown in Table 1. The most frequent entity type is *outcome*, which comprises about 28% of all the annotations. Continuous outcomes quartile values (*q1* and *q3*) are the least frequent entity types. Table 1 also shows the number of abstracts containing each of the entities. The entities found in most abstracts are *intervention*, *outcome*, and *control* which are in 100%, 97%, and 94% of the abstracts, respectively. Most abstracts do not contain continuous outcomes values (*mean*, *median*, *sd*, *q1*, *q3*) and *ethnicity*.

4 Baseline experiments

We evaluate the corpus using named entity recognition (NER) task. This task is important for automatic information extraction from RCT research articles. Since deep learning language models have gained a lot of attention in NLP tasks, we adopt Bidirectional Encoder Representations from Transformers (BERT)-based models. BERT-based models have achieved state-of-the-art results in NLP tasks including NER (Devlin et al., 2018). These models are usually pre-trained on huge amounts of unlabeled data and can be fine-tuned to specific tasks. They use the encoder structure of the transformer which is an attention mechanism that learns contextual relations between words (or subwords).

We chose two pre-trained transformer-based baseline models, BioBERT (Lee et al., 2020) and LongFormer (Beltagy et al., 2020). BioBERT is initialized with general domain corpora and further trained on biomedical domain texts (PubMed abstracts and PubMed Central articles). LongFormer is pre-trained on general domain corpora including books, wikipedia, news, stories.

The 1011 abstracts were randomly split into 80% training data and 20% test data. As baseline experiments, we followed the standard BERT practice of formulating NER task as a sequential tagging task. Since neural networks provide different results when initialized with different seeds, we trained the models with five different seeds and averaged the results.

Sub-category	Bio-BERT	Long-Former
total-participants	0.94	**0.95**
intervention-participants	**0.85**	**0.85**
control-participants	**0.88**	**0.88**
age	0.80	**0.87**
eligibility	0.74	**0.88**
ethinicity	**0.88**	0.79
condition	**0.80**	0.79
location	0.76	**0.87**
intervention	**0.84**	**0.84**
control	0.76	**0.81**
outcome	0.81	**0.85**
outcome-measure	0.84	**0.90**
iv-bin-abs	0.80	**0.82**
cv-bin-abs	**0.82**	**0.82**
iv-bin-percent	**0.87**	0.86
cv-bin-percent	**0.88**	0.85
iv-cont-mean	0.81	**0.84**
cv-cont-mean	**0.86**	**0.86**
iv-cont-median	**0.75**	0.69
cv-cont-median	**0.79**	0.73
iv-cont-sd	0.83	**0.89**
cv-cont-sd	0.82	**0.89**
iv-cont-q1	0	0
cv-cont-q1	0	0
iv-cont-q3	0	0
cv-cont-q3	0	0

Table 2: NER models results in terms of F1 score

The performance of the models was evaluated using F1 score. Table 2 shows the results of the NER models. The models achieved satisfactory performance and several sub-categories achieved high F1 scores. *Total-participants* achieved the highest F1 score of 0.95. Most of the sub-categories achieved F1 scores greater than 0.80. The models could not predict for sub-categories with the lowest frequency (F1 score=0).

We performed an error analysis and identified misclassified entities and boundary detection as the common types of errors. In the case of misclassified entities errors, the models identified the correct boundaries but assigned the wrong entities. For example, *iv-bin-abs* was misclassified as *cv-bin-abs* and vice-versa. Boundary detection errors were common in the *outcome* and *eligibility* entities, where the models identified longer or shorter entities than those marked in the gold set.

5 Conclusion

We presented a publicly available corpus with detailed annotation of the PICO elements. The corpus contains 1011 abstracts related to breast cancer RCTs. The corpus provides detailed annotation for outcomes especially numeric texts to identify the number of participants having certain outcomes. This is important for statistical analysis to determine the effectiveness of a treatment. The corpus will facilitate NLP research on automatic information extraction from biomedical literature and contribute towards evidence-based medicine. Since the corpus consists of breast cancer related abstracts, one of the future works is to extend it to include other diseases. The corpus is publicly available at `https://github.com/sociocom/PICO-Corpus`.

Acknowledgment

This work was supported by JST CREST Grant Number: JPMJCR22N1, Japan.

References

Iz Beltagy, Matthew E Peters, and Arman Cohan. 2020. Longformer: The long-document transformer. *arXiv preprint arXiv:2004.05150*.

Deborah J Cook, Cynthia D Mulrow, and R Brian Haynes. 1997. Systematic reviews: synthesis of best evidence for clinical decisions. *Annals of internal medicine*, 126(5):376–380.

Jacob Devlin, Ming-Wei Chang, Kenton Lee, and Kristina Toutanova. 2018. Bert: Pre-training of deep bidirectional transformers for language understanding. *arXiv preprint arXiv:1810.04805*.

Siddhartha R Jonnalagadda, Pawan Goyal, and Mark D Huffman. 2015. Automating data extraction in systematic reviews: a systematic review. *Systematic reviews*, 4(1):1–16.

Svetlana Kiritchenko, Berry De Bruijn, Simona Carini, Joel Martin, and Ida Sim. 2010. Exact: automatic extraction of clinical trial characteristics from journal publications. *BMC medical informatics and decision making*, 10(1):1–17.

Jinhyuk Lee, Wonjin Yoon, Sungdong Kim, Donghyeon Kim, Sunkyu Kim, Chan Ho So, and Jaewoo Kang. 2020. Biobert: a pre-trained biomedical language representation model for biomedical text mining. *Bioinformatics*, 36(4):1234–1240.

Iain J Marshall and Byron C Wallace. 2019. Toward systematic review automation: a practical guide to using machine learning tools in research synthesis. *Systematic reviews*, 8(1):1–10.

Benjamin Nye, Junyi Jessy Li, Roma Patel, Yinfei Yang, Iain J Marshall, Ani Nenkova, and Byron C Wallace. 2018. A corpus with multi-level annotations of patients, interventions and outcomes to support language processing for medical literature. In *Proceedings of the conference. Association for Computational Linguistics. Meeting*, volume 2018, page 197. NIH Public Access.

David L Sackett. 1997. Evidence-based medicine. In *Seminars in perinatology*, volume 21, pages 3–5. Elsevier.

Pontus Stenetorp, Sampo Pyysalo, Goran Topić, Tomoko Ohta, Sophia Ananiadou, and Jun'ichi Tsujii. 2012. Brat: a web-based tool for nlp-assisted text annotation. In *Proceedings of the Demonstrations at the 13th Conference of the European Chapter of the Association for Computational Linguistics*, pages 102–107.

Rodney L Summerscales, Shlomo Argamon, Shangda Bai, Jordan Hupert, and Alan Schwartz. 2011. Automatic summarization of results from clinical trials. In *2011 IEEE International Conference on Bioinformatics and Biomedicine*, pages 372–377. IEEE.

Byron C Wallace, Joël Kuiper, Aakash Sharma, Mingxi Zhu, and Iain J Marshall. 2016. Extracting pico sentences from clinical trial reports using supervised distant supervision. *The Journal of Machine Learning Research*, 17(1):4572–4596.

Lucy Lu Wang and Kyle Lo. 2021. Text mining approaches for dealing with the rapidly expanding literature on covid-19. *Briefings in Bioinformatics*, 22(2):781–799.

A Appendix

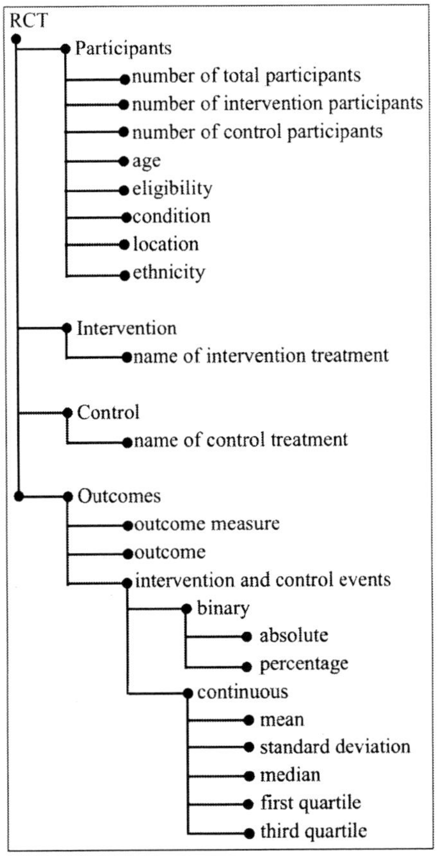

Figure 2: PICO label hierachy

Linking a Hypothesis Network From the Domain of Invasion Biology to a Corpus of Scientific Abstracts: The INAS Dataset

Marc Brinner
Bielefeld University
marc.brinner@uni-bielefeld.de

Sina Zarrieß
Bielefeld University
sina.zarriess@uni-bielefeld.de

Tina Heger
Leibniz Institute of Freshwater Ecology and Inland Fisheries (IGB), Berlin
t.heger@tum.de

Abstract

We investigate the problem of identifying the major hypothesis that is addressed in a scientific paper. To this end, we present a dataset from the domain of invasion biology that organizes a set of 954 papers into a network of fine-grained domain-specific categories of hypotheses. We carry out experiments on classifying abstracts according to these categories and present a pilot study on annotating hypothesis statements within the text. We find that hypothesis statements in our dataset are complex, varied and more or less explicit, and, importantly, spread over the whole abstract. Experiments with BERT-based classifiers show that these models are able to classify complex hypothesis statements to some extent, without being trained on sentence-level text span annotations.

1 Introduction

In many disciplines of science, researchers need to develop specific hypotheses that make it possible to confront general scientific claims with empirical evidence (Lloyd, 1987). For instance, studies in invasion biology, a sub-discipline of biodiversity research, investigate why certain species can establish in new ecosystems and typically formulate hypotheses specific to the species or the forms of invasion success they address (see Figure 2). It is essential for a researcher to be aware of the existing hypotheses in these fields, but, to date, structured information on claims and hypotheses investigated in a field is often hardly available. In some cases, though, valuable resources and overviews are compiled manually by domain experts as, for instance, Jeschke and Heger (2018)'s hierarchical network of hypotheses synthesizing research in the field of invasion biology. In this paper, we propose to leverage this resource as a new dataset for domain-specific information extraction from scientific publications and explore the potential of state-of-the-art off-the-shelf NLP models for automatic hypothesis identification.

Extracting domain-specific information on hypotheses from scientific publications is still a considerable challenge for state-of-the-art approaches in NLP and IE. Research on IE for the biodiversity domain provides many annotated datasets and models with domain-specific labeling schemes for named entities and relations – e.g., species, locations and habitats (Nguyen et al., 2019) – but does not account for more complex entities like claims, research questions or hypotheses. Work on argumentation mining for scientific texts (Fisas et al., 2016; Lauscher et al., 2018) annotate argumentative spans of texts, including claims, but do not link them to domain-specific knowledge. However, the lack of domain-specific categories is a major gap in existing search repositories for biodiversity researchers, as shown by (Löffler et al., 2021).

In this work, we perform initial studies on the automatic extraction of information on hypotheses investigated in scientific publications. We compile a corpus of scientific abstracts, based on metadata in Jeschke and Heger (2018)'s hypothesis network for invasion biology. We release the resulting INAS dataset that links 954 scientific papers (with abstracts and titles) to nodes in a hypothesis network. Similar to datasets in relation extraction (Mintz et al., 2009), the INAS dataset is weakly labeled, as the hypotheses are linked to the abstract as a whole, and not annotated in terms of text spans. We present a pilot analysis on hypothesis statements within the texts and find that they are complex, varied and spread over the whole abstract, challenging existing labeling schemes in IE. We carry out experiments on labeling abstracts with BERT-based

Proceedings of the 1st Workshop on Information Extraction from Scientific Publications, pages 32–42
Nov 20, 2022. ©2022 Association for Computational Linguistics

classifiers and show that these models are able to detect fine-grained hypothesis categories to some extent, without being trained on text span annotations. This shows that domain-specific resources on hypotheses provide a valuable starting point for this complex IE task, and points to some challenges for future research on automatic hypothesis extraction.

2 Related Work

Our work combines ideas from named entity recognition (NER) and relation extraction (RE), which typically targets domain-specific tagging schemes, with ideas of domain-general mining of claims, which aims at discovering complex statements of claims in text. We will briefly discuss related work from these areas in the following.

2.1 Entity and Relation Extraction in Scientific Texts

Extracting information on scientific studies from publications is a well-known problem in IE (Augenstein et al., 2017; Gábor et al., 2018). Within this area, biomedical text is one of the most widely and deeply explored domains, cf. (Demner-Fushman et al., 2022), with many datasets and tools that tag, e.g., diseases (Doğan et al., 2014), drugs and chemicals (Li et al., 2016), or drug-protein relations (Miranda et al., 2021) (among many others). In the domain of biodiversity, NER datasets focus on tagging species (Gerner et al., 2010; Pafilis et al., 2013), specific concepts like bacteria and their locations (Deléger et al., 2016), or combinations of species, habitats, locations (Nguyen et al., 2019). Löffler et al. (2020) present the QEMP benchmark, which further extends the types of entities and links them to existing ontologies in biovdiversity research. The INAS dataset follows a similar direction, as our hypothesis tags are taken from an existing network of hypotheses.

2.2 Mining Claims in Scientific Texts

In argument mining, different annotation schemes for aspects of scientific arguments have been proposed, such as argumentative zones (Teufel et al., 1999, 2009), argumentation schemes (Green, 2015), or argumentative components (Lauscher et al., 2018). Due to the importance of claims in argumentative structures, several studies focus specifically on the detection of claims in a variety of domains (Aharoni et al., 2014; Lippi and Torroni, 2015; Daxenberger et al., 2017; Habernal and Gurevych, 2017), using binary schemes that mark individual sentences or spans of texts as being claims or not. Blake (2010) present a more detailed annotation study for claims in scientific texts, distinguishing between different types of claim formulations (e.g., explicit claim vs. implicit claim) and roles that different parts of the claim fulfill. Accuosto et al. (2021) annotate scientific abstracts from computational linguistics and biomedicine with a variety of tags and relations related to argumentative structure, and Fergadis et al. (2021) annotate claims and topics in scientific abstracts on sustainable development, with both studies performing experiments on automatic prediction of these annotations. None of theses datasets, though, links annotations of claims to domain-specific concepts.

3 The INAS Dataset

We now introduce the INAS dataset[1], which is based on an existing resource that organizes papers from the field of invasion biology into a network of hypotheses. In the following, we will describe this network (Section 3.1), provide an overview of the dataset we created from this resource (Section 3.2, 3.3), present a qualitative and preliminary quantitative analysis of hypothesis statements (Section 3.4) and discuss its intended use (Section 3.5).

3.1 Hi-Knowledge Network of Hypotheses

Invasion biology is concerned with researching the human-induced spread of species outside of their native ranges, caused by factors like global transport and trade. For example, plants are imported as exotic garden plants, and small insects, plant seeds, and even reptiles and mammals are regularly transported as hitchhikers with traded goods around the globe, sometimes leading to an establishment of viable populations in the wild and spread to new locations within the new range (Elton, 1958; Davis, 2009). One aim of invasion biology is to explain why it is possible for these species to establish and often even flourish in areas in which they did not evolve. Over time, many major hypotheses have been developed as potential explanations for this phenomenon. For example, the "enemy release hypothesis" states that the absence of a species' natural enemies in the exotic range can be a cause of invasion success. Other major hypotheses are more concerned with the conditions under which

[1]https://github.com/inas-argumentation/inas-abstracts

an introduced, non-native species will be able to establish amongst the native species as, e.g., the "biotic resistance hypothesis" stating that an ecosystem with high biodiversity is more resistant against non-native species than an ecosystem with lower biodiversity.

Many empirical studies in invasion biology aim to test such major hypotheses. In order to do this, researchers have to decide on a specific study system (i.e., focal organisms and habitat) and a research method (e.g., observational survey, lab experiment), and they often also have to choose which specific aspect of the hypothesis they address. In the case of the enemy release hypothesis, one group of empirical studies tests whether invasive species actually are released from their enemies and a second group studies whether invaders show enhanced performance if they are released from enemies. Each of these groups can be further subdivided into studies focusing on specialist enemies (i.e., species only preying on specific other species) or generalist enemies (i.e., enemies without specific preferences, e.g., slugs). All these decisions progressively instantiate more general concepts from the main hypothesis until a concrete, testable sub-hypothesis is reached.

Jeschke and Heger (2018) identified these specific instantiations of the main hypotheses as well as the underlying decision process and organized them in a hierarchical hypothesis network based on the Hierarchy-of-Hypotheses (HoH) approach (Jeschke et al., 2012; Heger et al., 2013, 2021). Therefore, each node in the hierarchy represents a hypothesis at a certain level of abstraction while links to nodes on higher/lower levels connect each hypothesis to its more abstract or more specific versions, respectively. The underlying decision process of replacing abstract components of hypotheses by more specific instantiations thereby induces a tree structure, meaning that each node can have several child nodes but at most one parent node.

In (Jeschke and Heger, 2018), ten out of the 12 main hypotheses were depicted as such hierarchies of hypotheses, and a large literature survey was conducted to quantify the level of empirical support for each of them. In this process, a list of papers for each main hypothesis was collected, with each paper being annotated with the necessary information to correctly place it in the hierarchy, so that a group of empirical studies that address the

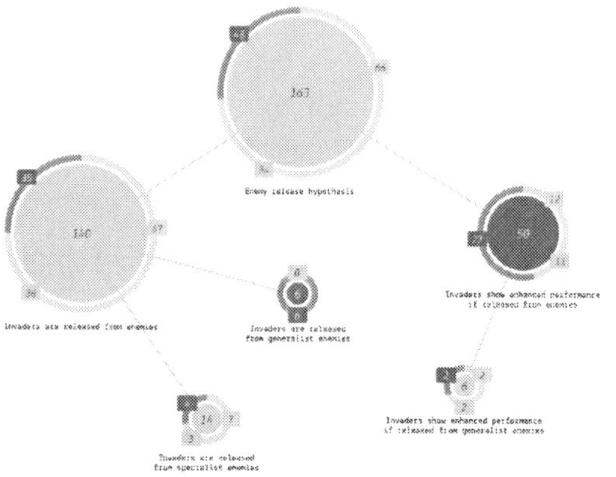

Figure 1: The sub-hypothesis structure for the enemy release hypothesis, one of the ten main hypotheses.

specific hypothesis can be linked to each node in the hierarchy. A visualization of the hierarchical hypothesis network, as well as the underlying data, are available[2] (see Figure 1).

3.2 Dataset for Hypothesis Detection

The basis for the INAS dataset is a collection of Excel files (one for each main hypothesis) containing paper titles from the field of invasion biology in combination with further information about each paper. Since this data is not easily accessible for automatic processing, we extracted the paper titles as well as the information needed to determine the placement of the papers in the hierarchical hypothesis network from the Excel files and subsequently used a web scraper to obtain the corresponding abstracts. This was possible for 954 samples, leading to the final dataset of 954 paper titles, abstracts, and hierarchical hypothesis labels. The dataset also includes written statements of all hypotheses from the hypothesis network to provide the option of introducing general information about the hypotheses in different prediction settings.

Since the basis for this dataset are scientific paper titles and abstracts it is not possible to publish all texts from this dataset due to copyright. Instead, we release the paper titles with corresponding DOIs and links to the websites the papers are published on to allow for easy automated scraping of the necessary data.

Figure 2 shows two example abstracts, one of which is linked to the enemy release hypothesis (Figure 2a) while the second abstract is linked to two hypotheses in the network (Figure 2b).

[2] https://hi-knowledge.org/invasion-biology/

Title: Influence of insects and fungal pathogens on individual and population parameters of Cirsium arvense in its native and introduced ranges

Abstract: Introduced weeds are hypothesized to be invasive in their exotic ranges due to release from natural enemies. Cirsium arvense (Californian, Canada, or creeping thistle) is a weed of Eurasian origin that was inadvertently introduced to New Zealand (NZ), where it is presently one of the worst invasive weeds. We tested the 'enemy release hypothesis' (ERH) by establishing natural enemy exclusion plots in both the native (Europe) and introduced (NZ) ranges of C. arvense. We followed the development and fate of individually labelled shoots and recorded recruitment of new shoots into the population over two years. Natural enemy exclusion had minimal impact on shoot height and relative growth rate in either range. However, natural enemies did have a significant effect on shoot population growth and development in the native range, supporting the ERH. In year one, exclusion of insect herbivores increased mean population growth by 2.1-3.6 shoots m(-2), and in year two exclusion of pathogens increased mean population growth by 2.7-4.1 shoots m(-2). Exclusion of insect herbivores in the native range also increased the probability of shoots developing from the budding to the reproductive growth stage by 4.0x in the first year, and 13.4x in the second year; but exclusion of pathogens had no effect on shoot development in either year. In accordance with the ERH, exclusion of insect herbivores and pathogens did not benefit shoot development or population growth in the introduced range. In either range, we found no evidence for an additive benefit of dual exclusion of insects and pathogens, and in no case was there an interaction between insect and pathogen exclusion. This study further demonstrates the value of conducting manipulative experiments in the native and introduced ranges of an invasive plant to elucidate invasion mechanisms.

(a) Paper title and abstract from (Cripps et al., 2011), linked to the enemy release hypothesis.

Title: Herbivory by an introduced Asian weevil negatively affects population growth of an invasive Brazilian shrub in Florida

Abstract: The enemy release hypothesis (ERH) is often cited to explain why some plants successfully invade natural communities while others do not. This hypothesis maintains that plant populations are regulated by coevolved enemies in their native range but are relieved of this pressure where their enemies have not been co-introduced. Some studies have shown that invasive plants sustain lower levels of herbivore damage when compared to native species, but how damage affects fitness and population dynamics remains unclear. We used a system of co-occurring native and invasive Eugenia congeners in south Florida (USA) to experimentally test the ERH, addressing deficiencies in our understanding of the role of natural enemies in plant invasion at the population level. Insecticide was used to experimentally exclude insect herbivores from invasive Eugenia uniflora and its native co-occurring congeners in the field for two years. Herbivore damage, plant growth, survival, and population growth rates for the three species were then compared for control and insecticide-treated plants. Our results contradict the ERH, indicating that E. uniflora sustains more herbivore damage than its native congeners and that this damage negatively impacts stem height, survival, and population growth. In addition, most damage to E. uniflora, a native of Brazil, is carried out by Myllocerus undatus, a recently introduced weevil from Sri Lanka, and M. undatus attacks a significantly greater proportion of E. uniflora leaves than those of its native congeners. This interaction is particularly interesting because M. undatus and E. uniflora share no coevolutionary history, having arisen on two separate continents and come into contact on a third. Our study is the first to document negative population-level effects for an invasive plant as a result of the introduction of a novel herbivore. Such inhibitory interactions are likely to become more prevalent as suites of previously noninteracting species continue to accumulate and new communities assemble worldwide.

(b) Paper title and abstract from (Bohl Stricker and Stiling, 2012), linked to the invasional meltdown hypothesis (underlined annotations) and the enemy release hypothesis (non-underlined annotations).

Figure 2: Two abstracts from the INAS dataset, annotated with explicit (green) and implicit (blue) hypothesis statements, and hypothesis names (red). The first example is classified correctly by all trained classifiers (Section 4). In the second example, the enemy release hypothesis is always classified correctly again, while the invasional meltdown hypothesis is only recognized by one out of ten trained classifiers (BioBERT base).

3.3 Dataset Analysis

Scientific abstracts are usually short and concise, which is also the case in the INAS dataset: On average, an abstract from the dataset consists of 10.26 sentences, with only 3.1% of samples surpassing the usual limit of 510 tokens for BERT models if the concatenation of paper title and abstract are tokenized using a standard BERT tokenizer. The class distribution among the ten main hypotheses is uneven, mirroring the true distribution of papers addressing the different hypotheses in the literature: The most dominant class contains about 21.8% of the samples (Invasional meltdown hypothesis) while about 1.8% of samples are assigned the most infrequent class (Island susceptibility hypothesis). This uneven distribution is even more pronounced among the sub-hypotheses, with some being assigned only a single sample while the most frequent hypothesis on the lowest level is addressed by 6.8% of papers. Importantly, every paper can address multiple (sub-)hypotheses (5.5% of samples address two main hypotheses) and can also be only assigned to hypotheses that are not on the lowest level in the hierarchy if non of the hypotheses on the next lower level matches the research conducted in it.

3.4 Hypothesis Statements

Since the hypothesis labels for the INAS dataset were created based on the full-text papers, it is unclear whether the titles and abstracts contain enough information to correctly identify every hypothesis that the corresponding papers address. Additionally, different ways of conveying hypothesis information can be more challenging to recognize, with domain knowledge being required regularly. Both these factors potentially affect the performance of automatic hypothesis identification models (compare Section 4), so that gaining insight into the typical ways that hypothesis information is stated in these abstracts is a mandatory basis for many analyses. To this end, together with a domain expert from invasion biology, we carried out a qualitative analysis of hypothesis statements and formulations within abstracts in the INAS dataset. We observe that hypothesis statements are extremely varied, ranging from explicit statements of hypothesis names in the case of some of the most well-known hypotheses to implicit hypothesis statements through, e.g., descriptions of experiments. In this initial analysis, we identified the following types of hypothesis statements:

Hypothesis name Explicit mentions of the hypotheses by their name (see text spans marked in red in Figure 2a). Some hypotheses are named after the main concepts they represent (e.g., *biotic resistance hypothesis*), a mention of these concepts provides almost the same information as an explicit hypothesis name and is therefore also annotated.

Explicit hypothesis statement Sentences stating the general hypothesis addressed in the paper, but without naming it (see green text span in Figure 2b).

Hypothesis fragment Spans of text that contain important parts of the hypothesis that is addressed in the paper but that do not belong to a complete hypothesis statement.

Implicit hypothesis statement Spans of text that reveal the hypothesis that is addressed in the paper without actually formulating it (e.g., descriptions of experiments, see blue text spans in Figure 2a and 2b).

Tag Type	Title	Abstract	Both
Name	.10/0.10	.30/0.64	.34/0.74
Statement	0/0	.42/0.58	.42/0.58
Fragment	.24/0.30	.56/1.08	.60/1.38
Implicit	.28/0.28	.80/1.86	.80/2.14
All	.62/0.68	.96/4.16	.96/4.84

Table 1: Distribution of the different tags in our subset of 50 annotated samples, broken down into presence of the tags in the titles, abstracts, or both (titles and abstracts combined). The statistics provided are the fraction of texts containing the specific tag at least once as well as the average number of annotated spans of the tag per text.

These different types of hypothesis statements we observed correspond to different types of tasks addressed in existing work on IE. While hypothesis names would be covered by NER schemes and systems (though existing NER schemes in biodiversity do not include them), explicit hypothesis statements are more similar to claims annotated in argument mining (Fergadis et al., 2021). Implicit claims are not well covered by both approaches, except in Blake (2010)'s study on claim formulations. Interestingly, the qualitative examples in Figure 2 suggest that implicit hypothesis statements are the most frequent, an observation that will be supported by data analyses that follow.

We conduct a pilot study to evaluate the presence of different types of hypothesis statements in scientific titles and abstracts from the field of invasion biology. To do this, we asked an expert annotator who was familiar with (Jeschke and Heger, 2018)'s hypothesis network to annotate a set of 50 titles and abstracts from the test set of the INAS dataset on span-level with the statement types introduced in Section 3.4. The set of annotated samples allows us insight into several interesting properties of the distribution of information about hypotheses in the dataset: Even though every paper addresses at least one hypothesis from the network, only 42% of titles and abstracts contain an actual hypothesis statement, while 34% state the name of the hypothesis. Accounting for the overlap in these groups, only 56% of samples provide concrete information about the hypothesis that the paper addresses in the title or abstract. Instead, authors often rely on hypothesis fragments (60% of samples) or implicit hypothesis statements (80% of samples) to make clear which hypothesis is addressed in their work. A detailed breakdown of the distribution of hypoth-

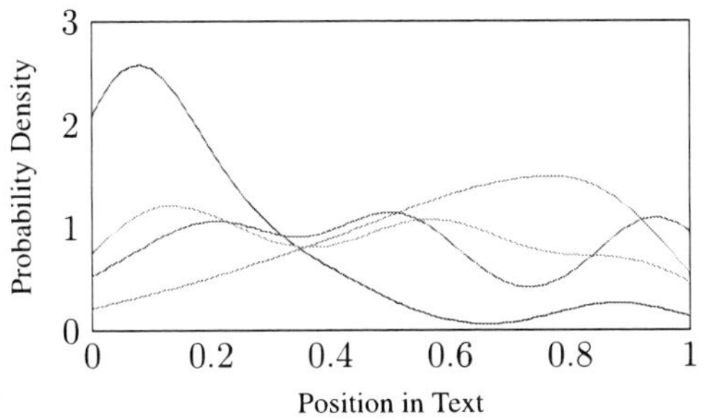

Figure 3: Empirical probability density function of the positionings of hypothesis statements (blue), hypothesis names (red), hypothesis fragments (orange), and implicit hypothesis statements (green) in the abstracts, created using a kernel density estimator using a Gaussian kernel (bandwidth=0.1).

Model	F1(S)	F1(M)
Naive Bayes	.702	-
BERT base	.665 (±.047)	.659 (±.051)
BERT large	.670 (±.045)	.674 (±.032)
BioBERT base	**.758** (±.025)	.751 (±.033)
BioBERT large	.734 (±.020)	.731 (±.065)
PubMedBERT base	**.758** (±.027)	.757 (±.026)

Table 2: Classification F1 scores for all models tested in our study. F1(S) denotes the F1 scores in the single label classification setting while F1(M) refers to the multi-label classification setting.

esis information in the titles and abstracts is given by Table 1, also including the average number of annotated spans of a certain tag in the dataset. The averages of 1.38 hypothesis fragments and 2.14 implicit hypothesis statements per text as well as the average of 4.84 annotated spans of all classes per text here clearly indicate that the information about the hypothesis addressed in a paper can be seldom found in a single sentence: Instead, information from different parts of the text needs to be used for correct identification of the hypothesis.

Additional interesting patterns arise if we analyze the likelihood of specific tags being located at different positions in the abstract. To do this, we define the position of an annotated span as the average token index of all tokens in the span divided by the total number of tokens in the text, resulting in positions in the range $[0, 1]$. We can then plot the empirical probability density function (created using a kernel density estimator) for each tag, as is done in Figure 3. While hypothesis names and hypothesis fragments have a rather uniform probability of appearing at any position in the text, hypothesis statements are made mainly at the beginning, while implicit hypothesis statements are more likely to be made later in the abstract. The reasons for this are that abstracts regularly begin with an explicit description of the hypothesis while ending with details about experiments and observations, which often fall in the category of implicit hypothesis statements.

3.5 Discussion

Current datasets labelling claims in scientific texts mostly focus on a precise span-level annotation instead of providing detailed semantic labels (see Section 2). While studies addressing also the semantic content of claims exist, the claims often address a variety of very distinct topics that can often be easily differentiated by non-experts as, e.g., claims addressing residency vs. claims addressing foreign policy in DebateNet-mig15 (Lapesa et al., 2020). This stands in stark contrast to the INAS dataset, where all of the hypotheses in the hierarchy address the same phenomenon of invasive species being successful in a new domain, which already is a rather narrow subfield of general biology. Therefore, even with respect to the highest level of the hierarchy, the correct identification of the hypothesis addressed in an abstract is a very challenging problem that requires expert knowledge, with many lower levels in the hierarchy representing even more subtle differences that are harder to distinguish. We argue that researchers in the scientific domain will benefit most from tools differentiating on such a precise level because subtle semantic information about the hypothesis addressed in a paper can be of high importance in judging the relation between scientific studies or the relevance with respect to a search query. Therefore, the INAS dataset adds a new and important facet to the general landscape of datasets on IE for scientific text. At the same time, the fine-graininess of the hypothesis network combined with the varied nature of hypothesis formulations in abstracts (Section 3.4) creates challenges for fully supervised labeling of the dataset. A complete annotation of hypothesis statements linked to the network would require experts familiar with the domain as well as linguistic aspects of annotation (which is very unrealistic). For this reason, we now explore whether "weak" abstract-level hypothesis labels in the current dataset provide useful information for state-of-the-art NLP models.

4 Hypothesis Identification as Abstract Classification

In this Section, we report baseline experiments on modeling the automatic identification of hypotheses in the INAS dataset.

4.1 Experimental Set-up

We frame hypothesis detection as a classification problem where the input is the concatenation of title and abstract of a paper and the output is a label of the major hypotheses that are addressed in the corresponding paper, with major hypotheses meaning the ten hypotheses on the highest level of the hierarchical hypothesis network.

We test different models that allow us to gain insight into different properties of the dataset: On the one hand, we test the performance of a naive Bayes classifier working on unigrams after removing stop words and highly frequent/infrequent words, allowing us to explore how much simple word frequency statistics already reveal about the hypothesis that is addressed in a paper. On the other hand, we test more complex neural classifiers in the form of standard BERT classifiers (Devlin et al., 2019) (base and large) as well as BERT classifiers trained on texts from a domain that presumably more closely resembles the domain of invasion biology abstracts: BioBERT models (Lee et al., 2019) (base and large) and the PubMedBERT model (Gu et al., 2022) (base), all trained on scientific abstracts and full-text papers from the biomedical domain. The training is done on a training set comprising 75% of the samples from the dataset, evaluation and testing are done on subsets containing 10% and 15% of the samples, respectively.

Due to the fact that a single paper can address multiple hypotheses, the classification is a multi-label classification problem. The naive Bayes classifier is only applicable to single-label classification, though, so we train it by inserting the samples with multiple labels repeatedly into the training set, once with each label. We proceed in the same way for the test and validation splits, meaning that the classifier will not be able to achieve perfect accuracy. To be able to compare the results, we test the BERT models in the same single-label setting (using a softmax classification layer). Additionally, we test the BERT classifiers in the multi-label setting by predicting an individual probability for each class. In this case, we still force the classifier to predict at least one positive label for each sample since this lead to increased performance. For all BERT classifiers, we reduce the effect of variance during training on our results by training ten classifiers for each model type and classification setting and report the average macro F1 score as well as the standard deviation.

4.2 Results

Table 2 displays the classification results in terms of the macro F1 score for both the single-label and the multi-label classification setting.

Notably, the naive Bayes classifier performs reasonably well and even outperforms the standard BERT classifiers, indicating that simple word frequency statistics provide significant information about the correct label. An analysis of the naive Bayes classifier weights revealed that hypothesis-specific concepts, as well as parts of the hypothesis names, were strong indicators for the specific classes, but also some species and country names that mostly appear in the context of specific hypotheses were used as a basis for the classification. The advantage of the naive Bayes classifier compared to the BERT classifiers might originate in the fact that many domain-specific terms might be unknown to the BERT models and the small training set might not be enough to fully learn these new concepts.

The classifiers based on variants of BERT that are adapted to texts from the biomedical domain consistently outperformed the naive Bayes classifier, which is consistent with earlier results that show that in-domain fine-tuning generally leads to improved performance (Gururangan et al., 2020). Notably, especially the smaller BERT_{base} models show better performance as well as reduced variance, making them the best performing models in our study. We also observe that the ability to do multi-label predictions generally does not yield an improvement, which can be explained by the small number of cases where multi-label prediction is necessary.

Even though the BioBERT and PubMedBERT models show increased performance compared to the naive Bayes classifier, the difference appears to be moderate considering the large difference in complexity. All BERT models should be able to process the same word frequency information as the naive Bayes classifier, meaning that their ability to combine the information from different words and sentences is only responsible for a 7%

performance increase. We believe that this indicates that the BERT classifiers are not able to understand the full semantic content of hypothesis statements, especially if they are only made implicitly. Instead, the increase in performance might simply be caused by the classifier's ability to detect slightly more complex patterns than unigrams (e.g., n-grams) and by its ability to nonlinearly combine the information about the presence of these still simple patterns.

4.3 Ablation Study

We use the domain expert annotations from 3.3 to evaluate which kinds of information are most important for the neural network classifiers. To test this, we perform an ablation study in which we train a classifier (BioBERT base) on: (i) only the title, (ii) the first two sentences from the abstract, or (iii) the last two sentences from the abstract.

The evaluation of the ablated classifiers on the test set yielded an F1 score of 0.61 for the titles and an equal score of 0.53 for the first two and for the last two sentences. Therefore, the title contains on average more information that is useful for the classification, which is to be expected since a good title should clearly indicate the key aspects of the underlying study while it is not necessary that every sentence in the abstract has the same density of information. The equal performance on the first and the last sentences from the abstract is more surprising since it implies that the different types of information that are commonly found at these positions (hypothesis statement vs. implicit hypothesis statement) seem to be equally useful for the classification.

An alternative explanation for this result is that the human annotations do not generally correspond to information that is used by the neural network classifier. To explore this hypothesis, we divide the 50 annotated samples into 10 folds, in a way that, beginning from fold one, each fold progressively contains samples that contain more annotated spans and thus contain more information about the hypotheses according to our annotation. We then measure the performance of BioBERT base on each of these folds and plot the average number of annotations in each fold against the micro F1 score the model achieved on that fold (see Figure 4). To better see the correlation, we also fit a kernel regression model (Nadaraya, 1964; Watson, 1964) to the data, resulting in a clearly visible positive correlation between the number of annotated spans in a sample and the classification performance of the neural classifier. This correlation is mainly caused by two low-scoring batches that both have a low number of annotated spans, which means that samples with few annotated spans have an increased probability of being misclassified while the probability stays relatively constant for samples that have at least four annotated spans. This indicates that our annotations correspond to useful information for the classification and therefore indicates that the general annotation scheme that allows for a distributed annotation of hypotheses is reasonable.

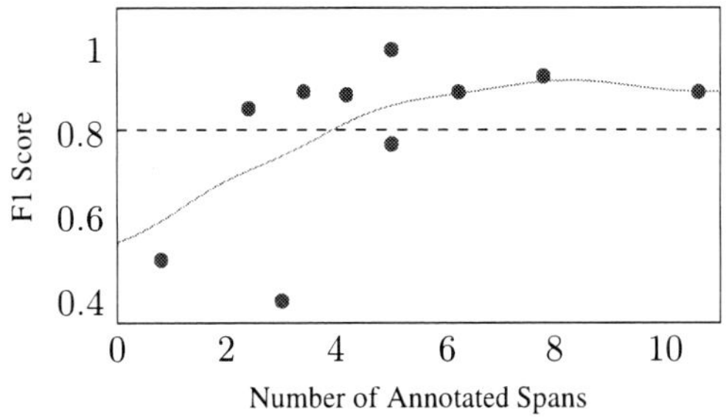

Figure 4: Classification micro F1 score vs. number of annotated spans for ten folds from the test set. The data was split into ten folds so that, beginning from fold one, each fold progressively contains samples with more annotated spans. The dashed line indicates the F1 score on all 50 samples, the red line is fitted to the data via a kernel regression model (Gaussian kernel with bandwidth=2.5).

In combination with the fact that the distributed annotations also correspond to the intuition of the domain expert, our study shows that the annotation of hypotheses and claims as single spans of text is limited and can be insufficient for certain domains like scientific texts. For this reason, our study shifts the focus from the simple, binary classification of sentences as claims to more fine-grained semantic categories, and at the same time, shifts the focus from detailed annotations of text spans to more general abstract- or paragraph-level annotation of hypotheses. We also note that the latter type of annotation may be more intuitive and faster for domain experts, which may not be trained linguistic annotators familiar with the complexities in text annotation.

5 Conclusion

In this work, we proposed and published the INAS dataset and conducted initial analyses and experiments on it. Our studies revealed interesting insights into the availability and distribution of information about the hypotheses in scientific paper titles and abstracts from the field of invasion biology. We believe that there is great potential for a variety of different studies to be performed using this dataset, some of which we plan on conducting in future work. These include further classification experiments like exploring the full hierarchical classification problem, trying to improve classification performance by conducting pretraining on full-texts from the field of invasion biology, or testing one-shot classification leveraging the written hypothesis descriptions. Further, our annotation experiment could enable studies on span-level hypothesis detection, e.g. in a weakly-supervised manner or in a one-shot classification setting. Finally, we also hypothesize that the introduction of human-engineered knowledge (e.g., in the form of ontologies) into, for example, the classification process can help overcome the problem of a lack of domain-knowledge of current language models.

References

Pablo Accuosto, Mariana Neves, and Horacio Saggion. 2021. Argumentation mining in scientific literature: from computational linguistics to biomedicine. Accepted: 2021-05-19T07:47:36Z Publisher: CEUR Workshop Proceedings.

Ehud Aharoni, Anatoly Polnarov, Tamar Lavee, Daniel Hershcovich, Ran Levy, Ruty Rinott, Dan Gutfreund, and Noam Slonim. 2014. A benchmark dataset for automatic detection of claims and evidence in the context of controversial topics. In *Proceedings of the First Workshop on Argumentation Mining*, pages 64–68, Baltimore, Maryland. Association for Computational Linguistics.

Isabelle Augenstein, Mrinal Das, Sebastian Riedel, Lakshmi Vikraman, and Andrew McCallum. 2017. SemEval 2017 task 10: ScienceIE - extracting keyphrases and relations from scientific publications. In *Proceedings of the 11th International Workshop on Semantic Evaluation (SemEval-2017)*, pages 546–555, Vancouver, Canada. Association for Computational Linguistics.

Catherine Blake. 2010. Beyond genes, proteins, and abstracts: Identifying scientific claims from full-text biomedical articles. *Journal of Biomedical Informatics*, 43(2):173–189.

Kerry Bohl Stricker and Peter Stiling. 2012. Herbivory by an introduced asian weevil negatively affects population growth of an invasive brazilian shrub in florida. *Ecology*, 93:1902–11.

Michael Cripps, Graeme Bourdôt, David Saville, Hariet Hinz, Simon Fowler, and Grant Edwards. 2011. Influence of insects and fungal pathogens on individual and population parameters of cirsium arvense in its native and introduced ranges. *Biological Invasions - BIOL INVASIONS*, 13.

Mark A. Davis. 2009. *Invasion Biology*. Oxford University Press.

Johannes Daxenberger, Steffen Eger, Ivan Habernal, Christian Stab, and Iryna Gurevych. 2017. What is the essence of a claim? cross-domain claim identification. *arXiv preprint arXiv:1704.07203*.

Louise Deléger, Robert Bossy, Estelle Chaix, Mouhamadou Ba, Arnaud Ferré, Philippe Bessieres, and Claire Nédellec. 2016. Overview of the bacteria biotope task at bionlp shared task 2016. In *Proceedings of the 4th BioNLP shared task workshop*, pages 12–22.

Dina Demner-Fushman, Kevin Bretonnel Cohen, Sophia Ananiadou, and Junichi Tsujii, editors. 2022. *Proceedings of the 21st Workshop on Biomedical Language Processing*. Association for Computational Linguistics, Dublin, Ireland.

Jacob Devlin, Ming-Wei Chang, Kenton Lee, and Kristina Toutanova. 2019. BERT: Pre-training of Deep Bidirectional Transformers for Language Understanding. Number: arXiv:1810.04805 arXiv:1810.04805 [cs].

Rezarta Islamaj Doğan, Robert Leaman, and Zhiyong Lu. 2014. Ncbi disease corpus: a resource for disease name recognition and concept normalization. *Journal of biomedical informatics*, 47:1–10.

Charles S. Elton. 1958. *The Ecology of Invasions by Animals and Plants*. Methuen & Co. Ltd.

Aris Fergadis, Dimitris Pappas, Antonia Karamolegkou, and Haris Papageorgiou. 2021. Argumentation mining in scientific literature for sustainable development. In *Proceedings of the 8th Workshop on Argument Mining*, pages 100–111, Punta Cana, Dominican Republic. Association for Computational Linguistics.

Beatriz Fisas, Francesco Ronzano, and Horacio Saggion. 2016. A Multi-Layered Annotated Corpus of Scientific Papers. In *Proceedings of the Tenth International Conference on Language Resources and Evaluation (LREC'16)*, pages 3081–3088, Portorož, Slovenia. European Language Resources Association (ELRA).

Kata Gábor, Davide Buscaldi, Anne-Kathrin Schumann, Behrang QasemiZadeh, Haïfa Zargayouna, and Thierry Charnois. 2018. SemEval-2018 task 7: Semantic relation extraction and classification in scientific papers. In *Proceedings of The 12th International Workshop on Semantic Evaluation*, pages 679–688, New Orleans, Louisiana. Association for Computational Linguistics.

Martin Gerner, Goran Nenadic, and Casey M Bergman. 2010. Linnaeus: a species name identification system for biomedical literature. *BMC bioinformatics*, 11(1):1–17.

Nancy Green. 2015. Identifying argumentation schemes in genetics research articles. In *Proceedings of the 2nd Workshop on Argumentation Mining*, pages 12–21.

Yu Gu, Robert Tinn, Hao Cheng, Michael Lucas, Naoto Usuyama, Xiaodong Liu, Tristan Naumann, Jianfeng Gao, and Hoifung Poon. 2022. Domain-Specific Language Model Pretraining for Biomedical Natural Language Processing. *ACM Transactions on Computing for Healthcare*, 3(1):1–23. ArXiv:2007.15779 [cs].

Suchin Gururangan, Ana Marasović, Swabha Swayamdipta, Kyle Lo, Iz Beltagy, Doug Downey, and Noah A. Smith. 2020. Don't stop pretraining: Adapt language models to domains and tasks.

Ivan Habernal and Iryna Gurevych. 2017. Argumentation mining in user-generated web discourse. *Computational Linguistics*, 43(1):125–179.

Tina Heger, Carlos A Aguilar-Trigueros, Isabelle Bartram, Raul Rennó Braga, Gregory P Dietl, Martin Enders, David J Gibson, Lorena Gómez-Aparicio, Pierre Gras, Kurt Jax, Sophie Lokatis, Christopher J Lortie, Anne-Christine Mupepele, Stefan Schindler, Jostein Starrfelt, Alexis D Synodinos, and Jonathan M Jeschke. 2021. The hierarchy-of-hypotheses approach: A synthesis method for enhancing theory development in ecology and evolution. 71(4):337–349.

Tina Heger, Anna T Pahl, Zoltan Botta-Dukát, Francesca Gherardi, Christina Hoppe, Ivan Hoste, Kurt Jax, Leena Lindström, Pieter Boets, Sylvia Haider, et al. 2013. Conceptual frameworks and methods for advancing invasion ecology. *Ambio*, 42(5):527–540.

J. Jeschke, Lorena Gómez Aparicio, S. Haider, Tina Heger, C. Lortie, P. Pyšek, and D. Strayer. 2012. Support for major hypotheses in invasion biology is uneven and declining.

J. M. Jeschke and T. Heger. 2018. Invasion biology: hypotheses and evidence.

Gabriella Lapesa, Andre Blessing, Nico Blokker, Erenay Dayanik, Sebastian Haunss, Jonas Kuhn, and Sebastian Padó. 2020. DEbateNet-mig15:Tracing the 2015 Immigration Debate in Germany Over Time. In *Proceedings of the 12th Language Resources and Evaluation Conference*, pages 919–927, Marseille, France. European Language Resources Association.

Anne Lauscher, Goran Glavaš, and Simone Paolo Ponzetto. 2018. An Argument-Annotated Corpus of Scientific Publications. In *Proceedings of the 5th Workshop on Argument Mining*, pages 40–46, Brussels, Belgium. Association for Computational Linguistics.

Jinhyuk Lee, Wonjin Yoon, Sungdong Kim, Donghyeon Kim, Sunkyu Kim, Chan Ho So, and Jaewoo Kang. 2019. Biobert: a pre-trained biomedical language representation model for biomedical text mining. *CoRR*, abs/1901.08746.

Jiao Li, Yueping Sun, Robin J Johnson, Daniela Sciaky, Chih-Hsuan Wei, Robert Leaman, Allan Peter Davis, Carolyn J Mattingly, Thomas C Wiegers, and Zhiyong Lu. 2016. Biocreative v cdr task corpus: a resource for chemical disease relation extraction. *Database*, 2016.

Marco Lippi and Paolo Torroni. 2015. Context-independent claim detection for argument mining. In *Proc. of IJCAI*.

Elisabeth A Lloyd. 1987. Confirmation of ecological and evolutionary models. *Biology and Philosophy*, 2(3):277–293.

Felicitas Löffler, Nora Abdelmageed, Samira Babalou, Pawandeep Kaur, and Birgitta König-Ries. 2020. Tag me if you can! semantic annotation of biodiversity metadata with the QEMP corpus and the BiodivTagger. In *Proceedings of the 12th Language Resources and Evaluation Conference*, pages 4557–4564, Marseille, France. European Language Resources Association.

Felicitas Löffler, Valentin Wesp, Birgitta König-Ries, and Friederike Klan. 2021. Dataset search in biodiversity research: Do metadata in data repositories reflect scholarly information needs? *PloS one*, 16(3):e0246099.

Mike Mintz, Steven Bills, Rion Snow, and Daniel Jurafsky. 2009. Distant supervision for relation extraction without labeled data. In *Proceedings of the Joint Conference of the 47th Annual Meeting of the ACL and the 4th International Joint Conference on Natural Language Processing of the AFNLP*, pages 1003–1011, Suntec, Singapore. Association for Computational Linguistics.

Antonio Miranda, Farrokh Mehryary, Jouni Luoma, Sampo Pyysalo, Alfonso Valencia, and Martin Krallinger. 2021. Overview of drugprot biocreative vii track: quality evaluation and large scale text mining of drug-gene/protein relations. In *Proceedings of the seventh BioCreative challenge evaluation workshop*.

E. A. Nadaraya. 1964. On estimating regression. *Theory of Probability & Its Applications*, 9(1):141–142.

Nhung TH Nguyen, Roselyn S Gabud, and Sophia Ananiadou. 2019. Copious: A gold standard corpus of named entities towards extracting species occurrence from biodiversity literature. *Biodiversity data journal*, (7).

Evangelos Pafilis, Sune P Frankild, Lucia Fanini, Sarah Faulwetter, Christina Pavloudi, Aikaterini Vasileiadou, Christos Arvanitidis, and Lars Juhl Jensen. 2013. The species and organisms resources for fast and accurate identification of taxonomic names in text. *PloS one*, 8(6):e65390.

Simone Teufel, Jean Carletta, and Marc Moens. 1999. An annotation scheme for discourse-level argumentation in research articles. In *Ninth Conference of the European Chapter of the Association for Computational Linguistics*, pages 110–117, Bergen, Norway. Association for Computational Linguistics.

Simone Teufel, Advaith Siddharthan, and Colin Batchelor. 2009. Towards Domain-Independent Argumentative Zoning: Evidence from Chemistry and Computational Linguistics. In *Proceedings of the 2009 Conference on Empirical Methods in Natural Language Processing*, pages 1493–1502, Singapore. Association for Computational Linguistics.

Geoffrey S. Watson. 1964. Smooth Regression Analysis. *Sankhyā: The Indian Journal of Statistics, Series A (1961-2002)*, 26(4):359–372. Publisher: Springer.

Leveraging knowledge graphs to update scientific word embeddings using latent semantic imputation

Jason Hoelscher-Obermaier[*], Edward Stevinson[*]
Valentin Stauber, Ivaylo Zhelev
Victor Botev[†], Ronin Wu[†], Jeremy Minton[†]
Iris AI, Bekkestua, Norway
jason@iris.ai

Abstract

The most interesting words in scientific texts will often be novel or rare. This presents a challenge for scientific word embedding models to determine quality embedding vectors for useful terms that are infrequent or newly emerging. We demonstrate how latent semantic imputation (LSI) can address this problem by imputing embeddings for domain-specific words from up-to-date knowledge graphs while otherwise preserving the original word embedding model. We use the Medical Subject Headings (MeSH) knowledge graph to impute embedding vectors for biomedical terminology without retraining and evaluate the resulting embedding model on a domain-specific word-pair similarity task. We show that LSI can produce reliable embedding vectors for rare and out of vocabulary (OOV) terms in the biomedical domain.

1 Introduction

Word embeddings are powerful representations of the semantic and syntactic properties of words that facilitate high performance in natural language processing (NLP) tasks. Because these models completely rely on a training corpus, they can struggle to reliably represent words which are infrequent, or missing entirely, in that corpus. The latter will happen for any new terminology emerging after training is complete.

Rapid emergence of new terminology and a long tail of highly significant but rare words are characteristic of technical domains, but these terms are often of particular importance to NLP tasks within these domains. This drives a need for methods to generate reliable embeddings of rare and novel words. At the same time, there are efforts in many scientific fields to construct large, highly specific and continuously updated knowledge graphs that capture information about these exact terms. Can we leverage these knowledge graphs to mitigate the short-comings of word embeddings on rare, novel and domain-specific words?

We investigate one method for achieving this information transfer, latent semantic imputation (LSI) (Yao et al., 2019). In LSI the embedding vector for a given word, w, is imputed as a weighted average of existing embedding vectors, where the weights are inferred from the local neighborhood structure of a corresponding embedding vector, $\mathbf{w}_d$, in a domain-specific embedding space. We study how to apply LSI in the context of the biomedical domain using the Medical Subject Headings (MeSH) knowledge graph (Lipscomb, 2000), but expect the methodology to be applicable to other scientific domains.

2 Related work

Embeddings for rare/out of vocabulary (OOV) words. Early methods for embedding rare words relied on explicitly provided morphological information (Alexandrescu and Kirchhoff, 2006; Sak et al., 2010; Lazaridou et al., 2013; Botha and Blunsom, 2014; Luong and Manning, 2016; Qiu et al., 2014). More recent approaches avoid dependence on explicit morphological information by learning representations for fixed-length character n-grams that do not have a direct linguistic interpretation (Bojanowski et al., 2017; Zhao et al., 2018). Alternatively, the subword structure used for generalization beyond a fixed vocabulary can be learnt from data using techniques such as byte-pair encoding (Sennrich et al., 2016; Gage, 1994) or the WordPiece algorithm (Schuster and Nakajima, 2012). Embeddings for arbitrary strings can also be generated using character-level recurrent networks (Ling et al., 2015; Xie et al., 2016; Pinter et al., 2017). These approaches, as well as transformer-based methods mentioned below, provide some OOV generalization capability but are unlikely to be a general solution since they will struggle with

[*] Co-first authors
[†] Co-PIs

Proceedings of the 1st Workshop on Information Extraction from Scientific Publications, pages 43–53
Nov 20, 2022.

novel terms whose meaning is not implicit in the subword structure such as, *e.g.*, eponyms. Note that we experimented with fastText and it performed worse than our approach.

Word embeddings for the biomedical domain. Much research has focused on how to best generate biomedical-specific embeddings and provide models to improve performance on downstream NLP tasks (Major et al., 2018; Pyysalo et al., 2013; Chiu et al., 2016; Zhang et al., 2019). Work in the biomedical domain has investigated optimal hyperparameters for embedding training (Chiu et al., 2016), the influence of the training corpus (Pakhomov et al., 2016; Wang et al., 2018; Lai et al., 2016), and the advantage of subword-based embeddings (Zhang et al., 2019). Word embeddings for clinical applications have been proposed (Ghosh et al., 2016; Fan et al., 2019) and an overview was provided in Kalyan and Sangeetha (2020). More recently, transformer models have been successfully adapted to the biomedical domain yielding contextual, domain-specific embedding models (Peng et al., 2019; Lee et al., 2019; Beltagy et al., 2019; Phan et al., 2021). Whilst these works highlight the benefits of domain-specific training corpora this class of approaches requires retraining to address the OOV problem.

Improving word embeddings using domain information. Our problem task requires improving a provided embedding model for a given domain, without detrimental effects on other domains.

Zhang et al. (2019) use random walks over the MeSH headings knowledge graph to generate additional training text to be used during the word embedding training. Similar ideas have led to using regularization terms that leverage an existing embedding during training of a new embedding to preserve information from an original embedding during training on a new corpus (Yang et al., 2017). Of course, these methods require the complete training of one or more embedding models.

Faruqui et al. (2014) achieve a similar result more efficiently by defining a convex objective function that balances preserving an existing embedding with decreasing the distance between related vectors, based on external data sources such as a lexicon. This technique has been applied in the biomedical domain (Yu et al., 2016, 2017), but has limited ability to infer new vocabulary because without the contribution from the original embedding this reduces to an average of related vectors.

Another approach is to extend the embedding dimension to create space for encoding new information. This can be as simple as vector concatenation from another embedding (Yang et al., 2017), possibly followed by dimensionality reduction (Shalaby et al., 2018). Alternatively, new dimensions can be derived from existing vectors based on external information like synonym pairs (Jo and Choi, 2018). Again, this has limited ability to infer new vocabulary.

All of these methods change the original embedding, which limits applicability in use-cases where the original embedding quality must be retained or where incremental updates from many domains are required. The optimal alignment of two partially overlapping word embedding spaces has been studied in the literature on multilingual word embeddings (Nakashole and Flauger, 2017; Jawanpuria et al., 2019; Alaux et al., 2019) and provides a mechanism to patch an existing embedding with information from a domain-specific embedding. Unfortunately, it assumes the embedding spaces have the same structure, meaning it is not suitable when the two embeddings encode different types of information, such as semantic information from text and relational information from a knowledge base.

3 Latent Semantic Imputation

LSI, the approach pursued in this paper, represents embedding vectors for new words as weighted averages over existing word embedding vectors with the weights derived from a domain-specific feature matrix (Yao et al., 2019). This process draws insights from Locally Linear Embedding (Roweis and Saul, 2000). Specifically, a local neighborhood in a high-dimensional word embedding space E_s (s for semantic) can be approximated by a lower-dimensional manifold embedded in that space. Hence, an embedding vector $\mathbf{w}_s$ for a word w in that local neighborhood can be approximated as a weighted average over a small number of neighboring vectors.

This would be useful to construct a vector of a new word w if we could determine the weights for the average over neighboring terms. But since, by assumption, we do not know w's word embedding vector $\mathbf{w}_s$, we also do not know its neighborhood in E_s. The main insight of LSI is that we can use the local neighborhood of w's embedding $\mathbf{w}_d$ in a domain-specific space, E_d, as a proxy for that neighborhood in the semantic space of our word-embedding model, E_s. The weights used for constructing an embedding for w in E_s are calculated from the domain space as shown in Fig. 1: a k-nearest-neighbors minimum-spanning-tree (kNN-MST) is built from the domain space features. Then the L2-distance between $\mathbf{w}_d$ and a weighted average over its neighbors in the kNN-MST is minimized using non-negative least squares. The resulting weights are used to impute the missing embedding vectors in E_s using the power iteration method. This procedure crucially relies on the existence of words with good representations in both E_s and E_d, referred to as anchor terms, which serve as data from which the positions of the derived embedding vectors are constructed.

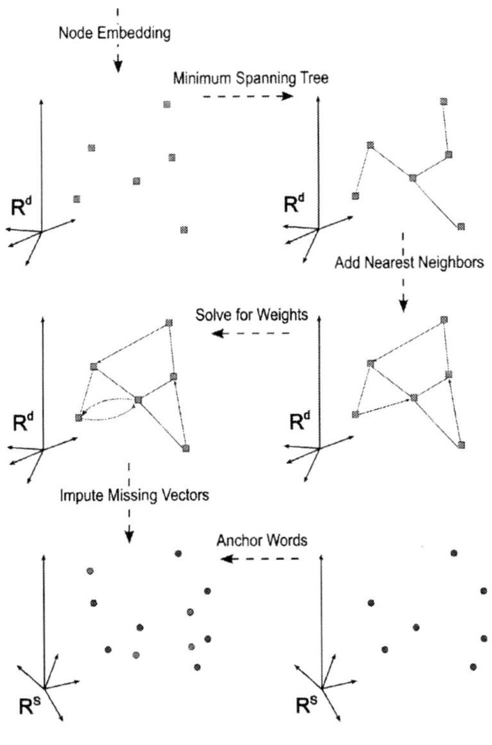

Figure 1: Latent Semantic Imputation. $\mathbb{R}^d$ is the domain space and $\mathbb{R}^s$ is the semantic space.

4 Methodology

We extend the original LSI procedure described above in a few key ways. Instead of using a numeric data matrix as the domain data source of LSI, we use a node embedding model trained on a domain-specific knowledge graph to obtain E_d. As knowledge graphs are used as a source of structured information in many fields, we expect our method to be applicable to many scientific domains. Knowledge graphs are prevalent in scientific fields as they serve as a means to organise and store scientific data, as well as to aid downstream tasks such as reasoning and exploration. Their structure and ability to represent different relationship types makes it relatively easy to integrate new data, meaning they can evolve to reflect changes in a field and as new data becomes available.

We use the 2021 RDF dump of the MeSH knowledge graph (available at `https://id.nlm.nih.gov/mesh/`). The complete graph consists of 2,327,188 nodes and 4,272,681 edges, which we reduce into a simpler, smaller, and undirected graph to be fed into a node embedding algorithm. We extract a subgraph consisting of solely the nodes of type "nsO_TopicalDescriptor" and the nodes of type "nsO_Concept" that are directly connected to the topical descriptors via any relationship type. The relationship types and directionality were removed. This results in 58,695 nodes and 113,094 edges.

We use the node2vec graph embedding algorithm (Grover and Leskovec, 2016) on this subgraph to produce an embedding matrix of 58,695 vectors with dimension 200 (orange squares in Fig. 2). The hyperparameters are given in Appendix 8.1. These node embeddings form the domain-specific space, E_d, as described in the previous section. We note that in preliminary experiments, the adjacency matrix of the knowledge graph was used directly as E_d but this yielded imputed embeddings that performed poorly.

To provide the mapping between the MeSH nodes and the word embedding vocabulary we normalize the human-readable "rdfs_label" node property by replacing spaces with hyphens and lower-casing. The anchor terms are then identified as the normalized words that match between the graph labels and the vocabulary of the word-embedding model; resulting in 12,676 anchor terms. As an example, "alpha-2-hs-glycoprotein" appears as both a node in the reduced graph and in the word-embedding model, along with its neighbors in the kNN-MST, which include "neoglycoproteins" and "alpha-2-antiplasmin". These serve to stabilise the positions of unknown word embedding vectors for domain space nodes which did not have corresponding representations in the semantic

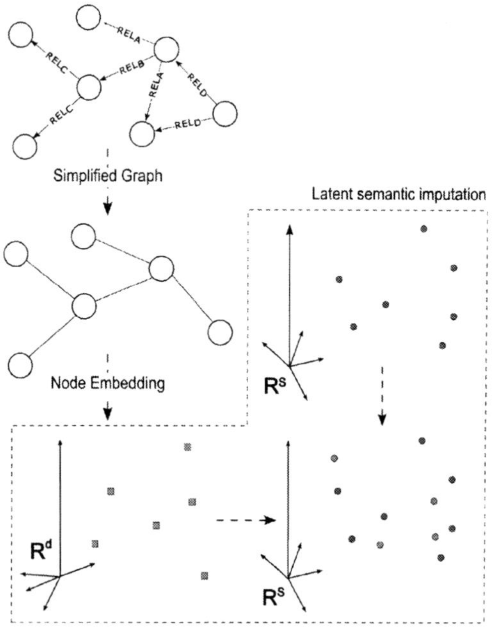

Figure 2: Extended latent semantic imputation pipeline. A knowledge graph is simplified to a smaller, undirected graph. This is used to derive the node embedding model used in LSI (see Fig. 1) to impute missing terms in the semantic space.

space during the LSI procedure.

LSI has one key hyper-parameter: the minimal degree of the kNN-MST graph, k. The stopping criterion of the power iteration method is controlled by another parameter, η, but any sufficiently small value should allow adequate convergence and have minimal impact on the resulting vectors. Following Yao et al. (2019) we set $\eta = 10^{-4}$ but we use a larger $k = 50$ since initial experiments showed a better performance for larger values of k.

5 Experiments

We aim to answer two questions to evaluate our imputation approach: Do the imputed embeddings encode semantic similarity and relatedness information as judged by domain experts? And, can the imputed embeddings be reliably used alongside the original, non-imputed word embeddings?

We use the UMNSRS dataset to answer these questions (Pakhomov et al., 2010). It is a collection of medical word-pairs annotated with a relatedness and similarity score by healthcare professionals, such as medical coders and clinicians; some examples are shown in Table 1. For each word-pair we calculate the cosine similarity between the corresponding word embedding vectors and report the Pearson correlation between these cosine similarities and the human scores.

Term1	Term2	Similarity	Relatedness
Acetylcysteine	Adenosine	256.25	586.50
Anemia	Coumadin	623.75	926.50
Rales	Lasix	742.00	1379.50
Tuberculosis	Hemoptysis	789.50	1338.50

Table 1: Examples of UMNSRS word pairs. Scores range from 0 to 1600 (larger = more similar/related).

To obtain additional insight into the performance of the imputation procedure we split the words in the UMNSRS dataset into two groups of roughly the same size: one group of words (*trained*) which we train directly as part of the word embedding training and another group of words (*imputed*) which we obtain via imputation. This split results in three word-pair subsets that contain *imputed/imputed* word pairs, *trained/trained* word pairs, and *imputed/trained* word pairs. Note that due to an incomplete overlap of the UMNSRS test vocabulary with both the MeSH node labels and our word embedding vocabulary we cannot evaluate on every word pair in UMNSRS (see Table 4 for more details). Applying the UMNSRS evaluation to these three groups of word pairs we aim to measure the extent to which the imputation procedure encodes domain-specific semantic information.

For word embedding training we prepare a corpus of 74.4M sentences from open access publications on PubMed (from `https://ftp.ncbi.nlm.nih.gov/pub/pmc/oa_bulk/`; accessed on 2021-08-30). To simulate the problem of missing words as realistically as possible we then prepare a filtered version of this corpus by removing any sentence containing one of the *imputed* terms (in either singular or plural form). This filtering removes 2.36M of the 74.4M sentences (3.2%).

We then train 200-dimensional skip-gram word embedding models on both the full and the filtered version of the training corpus. In addition, we also train fastText embeddings (Bojanowski et al., 2017) on both the full and the filtered corpus. For details on the hyper-parameters see Appendix 8.2. Since fastText, which represents words as n-grams of their constituent characters, has been shown to give reasonable embedding vectors for words which are rare or missing in the training corpus it represents a suitable baseline to which we can compare our imputation procedure.

We check that the embedding models (both skip-gram and fastText) trained on the filtered corpus perform roughly on par with those trained on the full corpus when evaluated using the *trained/trained* subset of the UMNSRS test data. We also check that the skip-gram model trained on the full corpus performs comparable to the BioWordVec model (Zhang et al., 2019) across all subsets of UMNSRS. See Appendix 8.3 for details.

LSI is a means of leveraging the domain space to create OOV embedding vectors. As a simple alternative baseline, we directly use the domain space embeddings for the OOV words. We need to align the domain space onto the semantic space, which we do with a rotation matrix derived from the anchor term embeddings in the two spaces via singular value decomposition.

5.1 Results

The main results are displayed in Fig. 3 which shows the Pearson correlation between cosine similarities and human annotator scores for UMNSRS similarity and relatedness. The error bars are standard deviations across 1,000 bootstrap resamples of the test dataset. From left to right we show results for the *trained/trained*, *imputed/trained*, and *imputed/imputed* subsets.

We compare two models trained on the filtered corpus (which does not contain any mentions of the *imputed* words): a skip-gram model extended by LSI and a fastText model. For reference we also show the correlation strengths obtained when directly using the MeSH node embeddings which form the basis of the imputation. Note that for this last model, the test cases we evaluate are different, since the MeSH model cannot represent all word pairs in UMNSRS (see appendix 8.3 for details). Uncertainties on the MeSH model are high for the *trained/trained* subset due to the limited overlap of the MeSH model with the words in the *trained* subset (see Table 4).

In Fig. 3 the *imputed/trained* group also includes the performance of the simple baseline, *Skip-gram (filtered) + MeSH*, formed of a mixture of aligned embeddings. We do not show the performance of this baseline on the other two groups since, by construction, it is identical to that of *Skip-gram (filtered) + LSI* for *trained/trained* and that of *MeSH node2vec* for *imputed/imputed*.

(a) UMNSRS similarity.

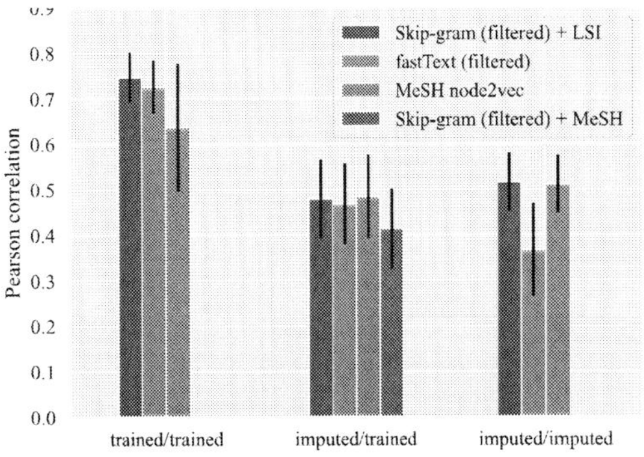

(b) UMNSRS relatedness.

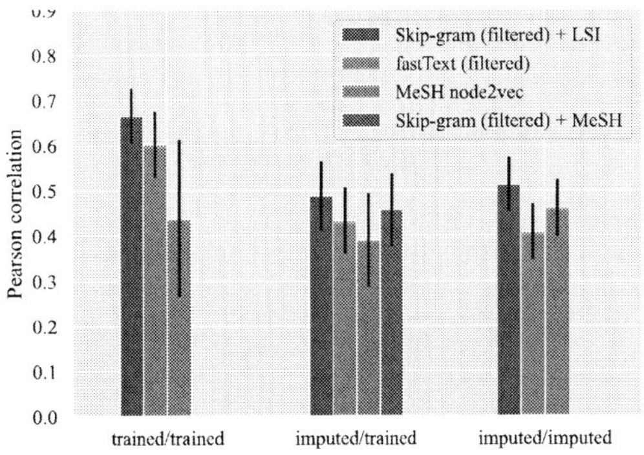

Figure 3: Correlation with UMNSRS scores.

Three things stand out:

1. The LSI-based model is competitive on novel vocabulary: it performs significantly better than the fastText model on word pairs containing only imputed terms (*imputed/imputed*) and modestly better on mixed word pairs (*imputed/trained*). It also outperforms the simple but surprisingly strong baseline, *Skip-gram (filtered) + MeSH*.

2. There is a significant difference in Pearson correlation between the different word pair categories. Note that the same trend in correlation across word pair categories can be seen in the word embedding model trained on the full corpus without imputation (see Fig. 4).

3. The LSI-based model obtains better scores than the underlying MeSH node embeddings across most categories. This proves that the similarity and relatedness information directly encoded in the domain embedding does not limit the similarity and relatedness information encoded in the resulting imputed model.

5.2 Discussion

In this paper we use a significantly larger subset of the MeSH graph compared to related work on MeSH-based embeddings (Guo et al., 2021; Zhang et al., 2019) by including more than just the topical descriptor nodes. Using a larger graph for the imputation allows us to impute a wider variety of words and evaluate the imputation procedure on a larger subset of UMNSRS. The graph we use for imputation is also much larger than the domain data used in previous work on LSI (Yao et al., 2019). This shows that LSI can apply to knowledge graphs and scale to larger domain spaces which is crucial for real-world applications.

We observe that the UMNSRS similarity and relatedness correlations of the MeSH node embedding models do not constitute an upper bound on the correlations obtained for the imputed word embeddings. This is intuitively plausible since LSI combines the global structure of the trained word embedding vectors with the local structure of the domain embeddings. This is in contrast to the original LSI paper in which the domain data alone was sufficient to obtain near perfect scores on the evaluation task and, as such, could have been used directly which obviates the need for LSI. This observation reduces the pressure for an optimal knowledge graph and associated embedding, although a systematic search for better subgraphs to use is likely to yield improved imputation results.

It is also of note that most of the trends displayed by the LSI model hold for both the similarity and relatedness scores, despite these being distinctly separate concepts. Relatedness is a more general measure of association between two terms whilst similarity is a narrower concept tied to their likeness. This might not be the case if the graph construction had been limited to particular relationship types or if direction of the relations had been retained.

There are noteworthy differences between our experiment and the use cases we envisage for LSI. The words we impute in our experiment are taken from the constituent words of the UMNSRS word pairs rather than being solely defined by training corpus statistics. This is a necessary limitation of our evaluation methodology. It remains a question for further research to establish ways of evaluating embedding quality on a larger variety of OOV words and use this for a broader analysis of the performance of LSI.

6 Strengths and weaknesses of LSI

Our experiments highlight several beneficial features of LSI. It is largely independent of the nature of the domain data as long as embeddings for the domain entities can be inferred. It does not rely on retraining the word embedding and is therefore applicable to cases where retraining is not an option due to limitations in compute or because of lack of access to the training corpus. It allows word embeddings to be improved on demand for specific OOV terms, thus affording a high level of control. In particular, it allows controlled updates of word embeddings in light of new emerging research.

The current challenges we see for LSI are driven by limited research in the constituent steps of the imputation pipeline. Specifically, there is not yet a principled answer for the optimal selection of a subgraph from the full knowledge graph or the optimal choice of node embedding architecture. The answer to these may depend on the domain knowledge graph. Also, there are not yet generic solutions for quality control of LSI. This problem is likely intrinsically hard since the words which are most interesting for imputation are novel or rare and thus exactly the words for which little data is available.

7 Conclusion

In this paper, we show how LSI can be used to improve word embedding models for the biomedical domain using domain-specific knowledge graphs. We use an intrinsic evaluation task to demonstrate that LSI can yield good embeddings for domain-specific out of vocabulary words.

We significantly extend the work of Yao et al. (2019) by showing that LSI is applicable to scientific text where problems with rare and novel words are particularly acute. Yao et al. (2019) assumed a small number of domain entities and a numeric domain data feature matrix. This immediately yields the metric structure required to determine the nearest neighbors and minimum spanning tree graph used in LSI. We extend this to a much larger number of domain entities and to domain data which does not have an a priori metric structure but is instead given by a graph structure. We demonstrate that LSI can also work with relational domain data thus opening up a broader range of data sources. The metric structure induced by node embeddings trained on a domain knowledge graph provides an equally good starting point for LSI.

This shows that LSI is a suitable methodology for controlled updates and improvements of scientific word embedding models based on domain-specific knowledge graphs.

8 Future work

We see several fruitful directions for further research on LSI and would like to see LSI applied to other scientific domains, thereby testing the generalizability of our methodology. This would also provide more insight on how the domain knowledge graph as well as the node embedding architecture impact the imputation results.

The use of automatic methods for creating medical term similarity datasets (Schulz and Juric, 2020) would facilitate the creation of large-scale test sets. The UMNSRS dataset, along with the other human-annotated, biomedical word pair similarity test sets used in the literature, all consist of fewer than one thousand word pairs (Pakhomov et al., 2016, 2010; Chiu et al., 2018). The use of larger test sets would remove the aforementioned evaluation limitations.

Further research could elucidate how to best utilize the full information of the domain knowledge graph in LSI. This includes information about node and edge types, as well as literal information such as human-readable node labels and numeric node properties (such as measurement values). It also remains to be studied how to optimally choose the anchor terms (to be used in the imputation step) to maximize LSI performance. Our methodology could also be generalized from latent semantic imputation to what might be called latent semantic information fusion where domain information is used for incremental updates instead of outright replacement of word embedding vectors.

Finally, LSI could also be extended to provide alignment between knowledge graphs and written text by using the spatial distance between imputed vectors of knowledge graph nodes and trained word embedding vectors as an alignment criterion.

Acknowledgements

This paper was supported by the AI Chemist funding (Project ID: 309594) from the Research Council of Norway (RCN). We thank Shibo Yao for helpful input and for sharing raw data used in (Yao et al., 2019) and Dr. Zhiyong Lu and Dr. Yijia Zhang of the National Institute of Health for sharing their word embedding models. We thank the three anonymous reviewers for their careful reading and helpful comments.

References

Jean Alaux, Edouard Grave, Marco Cuturi, and Armand Joulin. 2019. Unsupervised Hyperalignment for Multilingual Word Embeddings.

Andrei Alexandrescu and Katrin Kirchhoff. 2006. Factored Neural Language Models. In *Proceedings of the Human Language Technology Conference of the NAACL, Companion Volume: Short Papers*, pages 1–4, New York City, USA. Association for Computational Linguistics.

Iz Beltagy, Kyle Lo, and Arman Cohan. 2019. SciBERT: A Pretrained Language Model for Scientific Text. In *Proceedings of the 2019 Conference on Empirical Methods in Natural Language Processing and the 9th International Joint Conference on Natural Language Processing (EMNLP-IJCNLP)*, pages 3615–3620, Hong Kong, China. Association for Computational Linguistics.

Piotr Bojanowski, Edouard Grave, Armand Joulin, and Tomas Mikolov. 2017. Enriching Word Vectors with Subword Information. *Transactions of the Association for Computational Linguistics*, 5:135–146.

Jan A. Botha and Phil Blunsom. 2014. Compositional Morphology for Word Representations and Language Modelling.

Billy Chiu, Gamal Crichton, Anna Korhonen, and Sampo Pyysalo. 2016. How to Train good Word Embeddings for Biomedical NLP. In *Proceedings of the 15th Workshop on Biomedical Natural Language Processing*, pages 166–174, Berlin, Germany. Association for Computational Linguistics.

Billy Chiu, Sampo Pyysalo, Ivan Vulić, and Anna Korhonen. 2018. Bio-simverb and bio-simlex: wide-coverage evaluation sets of word similarity in biomedicine. *BMC Bioinformatics*, 19(1):33.

Yadan Fan, Serguei Pakhomov, Reed McEwan, Wendi Zhao, Elizabeth Lindemann, and Rui Zhang. 2019. Using word embeddings to expand terminology of dietary supplements on clinical notes. *JAMIA Open*, 2(2):246–253.

Manaal Faruqui, Jesse Dodge, Sujay K. Jauhar, Chris Dyer, Eduard Hovy, and Noah A. Smith. 2014. Retrofitting word vectors to semantic lexicons. *arXiv preprint arXiv:1411.4166*.

Philip Gage. 1994. A new algorithm for data compression. *The C Users Journal archive*, 12:23–38.

Saurav Ghosh, Prithwish Chakraborty, Emily Cohn, John S. Brownstein, and Naren Ramakrishnan. 2016. Characterizing diseases from unstructured text: A vocabulary driven word2vec approach. In *Proceedings of the 25th ACM International on Conference on Information and Knowledge Management*, CIKM '16, page 1129–1138, New York, NY, USA. Association for Computing Machinery.

Aditya Grover and Jure Leskovec. 2016. node2vec: Scalable feature learning for networks.

Zhen-Hao Guo, Zhu-Hong You, De-Shuang Huang, Hai-Cheng Yi, Kai Zheng, Zhan-Heng Chen, and Yan-Bin Wang. 2021. MeSHHeading2vec: A new method for representing MeSH headings as vectors based on graph embedding algorithm. *Briefings in Bioinformatics*, 22(2):2085–2095.

Pratik Jawanpuria, Arjun Balgovind, Anoop Kunchukuttan, and Bamdev Mishra. 2019. Learning Multilingual Word Embeddings in Latent Metric Space: A Geometric Approach. *Transactions of the Association for Computational Linguistics*, 7:107–120.

Hwiyeol Jo and Stanley Jungkyu Choi. 2018. Extrofitting: Enriching Word Representation and its Vector Space with Semantic Lexicons. *arXiv:1804.07946 [cs]*.

Katikapalli Subramanyam Kalyan and S. Sangeetha. 2020. SECNLP: A survey of embeddings in clinical natural language processing. *Journal of Biomedical Informatics*, 101:103323.

Siwei Lai, Kang Liu, Shizhu He, and Jun Zhao. 2016. How to generate a good word embedding. *IEEE Intelligent Systems*, 31(6):5–14.

Angeliki Lazaridou, Marco Marelli, Roberto Zamparelli, and Marco Baroni. 2013. Compositional-ly Derived Representations of Morphologically Complex Words in Distributional Semantics. In *Proceedings of the 51st Annual Meeting of the Association for Computational Linguistics (Volume 1: Long Papers)*, pages 1517–1526, Sofia, Bulgaria. Association for Computational Linguistics.

Jinhyuk Lee, Wonjin Yoon, Sungdong Kim, Donghyeon Kim, Sunkyu Kim, Chan Ho So, and Jaewoo Kang. 2019. BioBERT: A pre-trained biomedical language representation model for biomedical text mining. *Bioinformatics*, page btz682.

Wang Ling, Chris Dyer, Alan W Black, Isabel Trancoso, Ramón Fermandez, Silvio Amir, Luís Marujo, and Tiago Luís. 2015. Finding Function in Form: Compositional Character Models for Open Vocabulary Word Representation. In *Proceedings of the 2015 Conference on Empirical Methods in Natural Language Processing*, pages 1520–1530, Lisbon, Portugal. Association for Computational Linguistics.

Carolyn E. Lipscomb. 2000. Medical Subject Headings (MeSH). *Bulletin of the Medical Library Association*, 88(3):265–266.

Minh-Thang Luong and Christopher D. Manning. 2016. Achieving Open Vocabulary Neural Machine Translation with Hybrid Word-Character Models. In *Proceedings of the 54th Annual Meeting of the Association for Computational Linguistics (Volume 1: Long Papers)*, pages 1054–1063, Berlin, Germany. Association for Computational Linguistics.

Vincent Major, Alisa Surkis, and Yindalon Aphinyanaphongs. 2018. Utility of General and Specific Word Embeddings for Classifying Translational Stages of Research. *AMIA Annual Symposium Proceedings*, 2018:1405–1414.

Ndapandula Nakashole and Raphael Flauger. 2017. Knowledge Distillation for Bilingual Dictionary Induction. In *Proceedings of the 2017 Conference on Empirical Methods in Natural Language Processing*, pages 2497–2506, Copenhagen, Denmark. Association for Computational Linguistics.

Serguei V. S. Pakhomov, Greg Finley, Reed McEwan, Yan Wang, and Genevieve B. Melton. 2016. Corpus domain effects on distributional semantic modeling of medical terms. *Bioinformatics (Oxford, England)*, 32(23):3635–3644.

Serguei V. S. Pakhomov, Bridget T. McInnes, T. Adam, Y. Liu, Ted Pedersen, and G. Melton. 2010. Semantic Similarity and Relatedness between Clinical Terms: An Experimental Study. In *AMIA ... Annual Symposium Proceedings. AMIA Symposium*.

Yifan Peng, Shankai Yan, and Zhiyong Lu. 2019. Transfer Learning in Biomedical Natural Language Processing: An Evaluation of BERT and ELMo on Ten Benchmarking Datasets.

Long N. Phan, James T. Anibal, Hieu Tran, Shaurya Chanana, Erol Bahadroglu, Alec Peltekian, and Grégoire Altan-Bonnet. 2021. SciFive: A text-to-text transformer model for biomedical literature.

Yuval Pinter, Robert Guthrie, and Jacob Eisenstein. 2017. Mimicking Word Embeddings using Subword RNNs. In *Proceedings of the 2017 Conference on Empirical Methods in Natural Language Processing*, pages 102–112, Copenhagen, Denmark. Association for Computational Linguistics.

Sampo Pyysalo, Filip Ginter, Hans Moen, Tapio Salakoski, and Sophia Ananiadou. 2013. Distributional Semantics Resources for Biomedical Text Processing. In *Proceedings of LBM 2013*, page 5.

Siyu Qiu, Qing Cui, Jiang Bian, Bin Gao, and Tie-Yan Liu. 2014. Co-learning of Word Representations and Morpheme Representations. In *Proceedings of COLING 2014, the 25th International Conference on Computational Linguistics: Technical Papers*, pages 141–150, Dublin, Ireland. Dublin City University and Association for Computational Linguistics.

Sam T. Roweis and Lawrence K. Saul. 2000. Nonlinear dimensionality reduction by locally linear embedding. *Science*, 290(5500):2323–2326.

Haşim Sak, Murat Saraçlar, and Tunga Güngör. 2010. Morphology-based and sub-word language modeling for Turkish speech recognition. In *2010 IEEE International Conference on Acoustics, Speech and Signal Processing*, pages 5402–5405.

Claudia Schulz and Damir Juric. 2020. Can embeddings adequately represent medical terminology? new large-scale medical term similarity datasets have the answer! *Proceedings of the AAAI Conference on Artificial Intelligence*, 34(05):8775–8782.

Mike Schuster and Kaisuke Nakajima. 2012. Japanese and korean voice search. In *2012 IEEE International Conference on Acoustics, Speech and Signal Processing (ICASSP)*, pages 5149–5152.

Rico Sennrich, Barry Haddow, and Alexandra Birch. 2016. Neural Machine Translation of Rare Words with Subword Units. *arXiv:1508.07909 [cs]*.

W. Shalaby, Wlodek Zadrozny, and Hongxia Jin. 2018. Beyond word embeddings: Learning entity and concept representations from large scale knowledge bases. *Information Retrieval Journal*.

Yanshan Wang, Sijia Liu, Naveed Afzal, Majid Rastegar-Mojarad, Liwei Wang, Feichen Shen, Paul Kingsbury, and Hongfang Liu. 2018. A comparison of word embeddings for the biomedical natural language processing. *Journal of Biomedical Informatics*, 87:12–20.

Ruobing Xie, Zhiyuan Liu, Jia Jia, Huanbo Luan, and Maosong Sun. 2016. Representation Learning of Knowledge Graphs with Entity Descriptions.

Wei Yang, Wei Lu, and Vincent Zheng. 2017. A Simple Regularization-based Algorithm for Learning Cross-Domain Word Embeddings. In *Proceedings of the 2017 Conference on Empirical Methods in Natural Language Processing*, pages 2898–2904, Copenhagen, Denmark. Association for Computational Linguistics.

Shibo Yao, Dantong Yu, and Keli Xiao. 2019. Enhancing Domain Word Embedding via Latent Semantic Imputation. *Proceedings of the 25th ACM SIGKDD International Conference on Knowledge Discovery & Data Mining*, pages 557–565.

Zhiguo Yu, Trevor Cohn, Byron C. Wallace, Elmer Bernstam, and Todd Johnson. 2016. Retrofitting word vectors of mesh terms to improve semantic similarity measures. In *Proceedings of the Seventh International Workshop on Health Text Mining and Information Analysis*, pages 43–51.

Zhiguo Yu, Byron C. Wallace, Todd Johnson, and Trevor Cohen. 2017. Retrofitting concept vector representations of medical concepts to improve estimates of semantic similarity and relatedness. *Studies in health technology and informatics*, 245:657.

Yijia Zhang, Qingyu Chen, Zhihao Yang, Hongfei Lin, and Zhiyong Lu. 2019. BioWordVec, improving biomedical word embeddings with subword information and MeSH. *Scientific Data*, 6(1):52.

Jinman Zhao, Sidharth Mudgal, and Yingyu Liang. 2018. Generalizing Word Embeddings using Bag of Subwords.

Appendix

8.1 Hyper-parameters for MeSH node2vec

We train node2vec (`https://github.com/thibaudmartinez/node2vec`) embeddings with the hyperparameters shown in Table 2 from a subgraph of MeSH containing 58,695 nodes and 113,094 edges.

Hyperparameter	Variable name	Value
Training epochs	epochs	50
No. of random walks	n_walks	10
Return parameter	p	0.5
Inout parameter	q	0.5
Context window	context_size	15
Dimension	dimension	200

Table 2: Hyperparameters for MeSH node2vec training

8.2 Hyper-parameters for word embeddings

We use gensim (`https://radimrehurek.com/gensim`; version 4.1.2.) for training skipgram and fastText word embedding models with the hyperparameters provided in Table 3. All other hyperparameters are set to the default values of the gensim implementation. For the skipgram model we use the hyperparameters from Chiu et al. (2016), which are reported to be optimal for the biomedical domain. For fastText we are not aware of literature on optimal hyperparameters for the biomedical domain so we use the default values except for the embedding dimension which we set to 200 to ease comparison with the skipgram model. We trained the fastText models for 10 epochs but found that the performance of the fastText model on UMNSRS saturates after epoch 1. We use the fastText model after the first epoch for the remainder of our experiments and analysis.

Variable name	fastText	skipgram
epochs	1	10
negative	5	10
vector_size	200	200
alpha	0.025	0.05
sample	1E-03	1E-04
window	20	30

Table 3: Hyperparameters for skipgram and fastText training. See the gensim documentation for the definition of the hyperparameters.

(a) UMNSRS similarity. (b) UMNSRS relatedness.

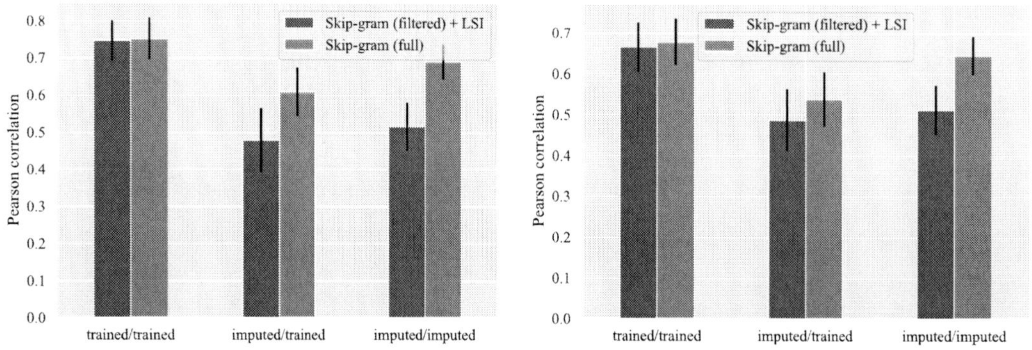

Figure 4: UMNSRS correlations for skipgram models.

(a) UMNSRS similarity. (b) UMNSRS relatedness.

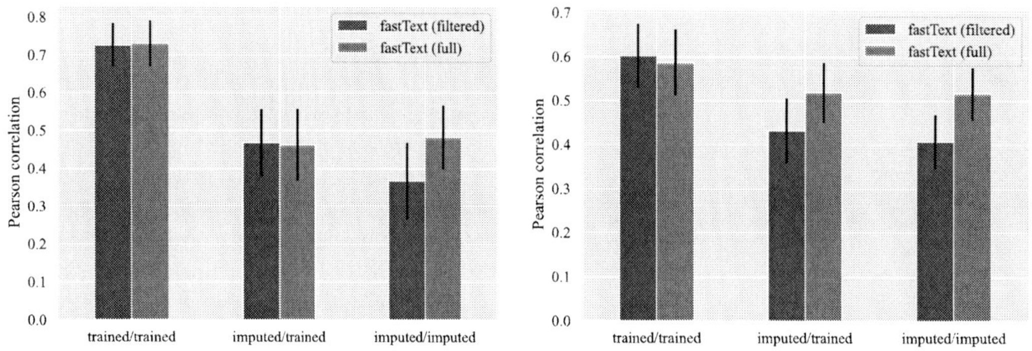

Figure 5: UMNSRS correlations for fastText models.

(a) UMNSRS similarity. (b) UMNSRS relatedness.

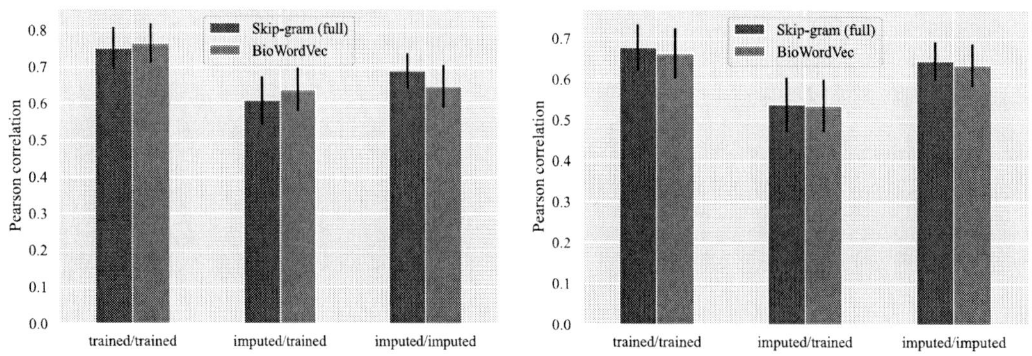

Figure 6: UMNSRS correlations for BioWordVec.

Model	UMNSRS relatedness trained/ trained	imputed/ trained	imputed/ imputed	UMNSRS similarity trained/ trained	imputed/ trained	imputed/ imputed
MeSH node2vec	28	70	133	30	72	135
all other models	83	99	124	84	101	126

Table 4: Number of test cases per model and test set split for UMNSRS evaluation.

8.3 Details on the UMNSRS evaluation

Table 4 shows the number of test cases per model and UMNSRS test data split. All models have been evaluated on the same subsets of UMNSRS except for the MeSH node embeddings model where limited overlap with the UMNSRS test vocabulary prevents us from evaluating on exactly the same subsets.

The embedding models (both skip-gram and fastText) trained on the filtered corpus perform roughly on par with those trained on the full corpus when evaluated using the *trained/trained* subset of the UMNSRS test data (see Fig. 4 and 5). When comparing the performance of the filtered skipgram model + LSI to the full skipgram model on the subset of test data involving imputed words (*imputed/trained* and *imputed/imputed*) the full model outperforms LSI (see Fig. 4). This suggests that, if training text for the OOV words were available, we should make use of it. Similarly, and as expected, when comparing the performance of the filtered and full fastText models on the subset of test data involving imputed words (*imputed/trained* and *imputed/imputed*) the full model again outperforms the filtered model (see Fig. 5).

As a sanity check, we also compare the skip-gram model trained on the full corpus to BioWordVec, a recent state-of-the-art word embedding model for the biomedical domain (Zhang et al., 2019) and find similar performance across all subsets of UMNSRS (see Fig. 6).

Full-Text Argumentation Mining on Scientific Publications

Arne Binder[1] **Bhuvanesh Verma**[2] **Leonhard Hennig**[1]
[1]German Research Center for Artificial Intelligence (DFKI)
[2]University of Potsdam
[1]{*arne.binder, leonhard.hennig*}*@dfki.de*
[2]*bhuvanesh.verma@uni-potsdam.de*

Abstract

Scholarly Argumentation Mining (SAM) has recently gained attention due to its potential to help scholars with the rapid growth of published scientific literature. It comprises two subtasks: argumentative discourse unit recognition (ADUR) and argumentative relation extraction (ARE), both of which are challenging since they require e.g. the integration of domain knowledge, the detection of implicit statements, and the disambiguation of argument structure (Al Khatib et al., 2021). While previous work focused on dataset construction and baseline methods for specific document sections, such as abstract or results, full-text scholarly argumentation mining has seen little progress. In this work, we introduce a sequential pipeline model combining ADUR and ARE for full-text SAM, and provide a first analysis of the performance of pretrained language models (PLMs) on both subtasks. We establish a new SotA for ADUR on the Sci-Arg corpus, outperforming the previous best reported result by a large margin (+7% F1). We also present the first results for ARE, and thus for the full AM pipeline, on this benchmark dataset. Our detailed error analysis reveals that non-contiguous ADUs as well as the interpretation of discourse connectors pose major challenges and that data annotation needs to be more consistent.

1 Introduction

Argumentation Mining (AM) is concerned with the detection of the argumentative structure of text (Stede and Schneider, 2018). It is commonly organized into two subtasks: 1) Recognition of argumentative discourse units (ADUs), i.e. detecting argumentative spans of text and classifying them into types such as *claim* or *premise*, and 2) determining which ADUs have a relationship to each other and of what kind, e.g. *support* or *attack*. Consider the following example, where the premise P supports the claim C:

> Dot-product attention is much faster than additive attention$_C$, since it can be implemented using highly optimized matrix multiplication code$_P$.[1]

Since the amount of published scientific literature is growing exponentially (Fortunato et al., 2018), there is recently an increased interest in scholarly argumentation mining (SAM). Understanding the argumentative structure is key, not just to efficiently digest such work, but also to assess its quality (Walton, 2001). Solving scholarly AM is challenging, because it requires, among other things, the use of domain knowledge, the detection of implicit statements, and the disambiguation of argument structure (Al Khatib et al., 2021). This is even harder when handling full-text that is often less concise and standardized, than, for example, abstracts.

Previous work in SAM has focused on dataset construction (Teufel and Moens, 1999; Lauscher et al., 2018b), ADU recognition (Lauscher et al., 2018a; Li et al., 2021), and the analysis of specific document sections, such as abstract or results (Dasigi et al., 2017; Accuosto and Saggion, 2019; Mayer et al., 2020). However, to get a thorough understanding of a scientific publication, all parts of the document matter. Ideally, they back up the main argumentation and usually contain details that are relevant for the knowledgeable reader, thus, they should not be neglected. However, since the task is very complex, also for humans, there is not much training data for full-text SAM available.

Pretrained Language Models (PLMs) such as SciBERT (Beltagy et al., 2019) may help to address the above challenges because they contain a lot of linguistic and domain knowledge and have better long-range capabilities, allowing for improved contextualisation, especially when training data is rare. We hence propose a PLM based model for full-text

[1]replicated from Vaswani et al. (2017)

Proceedings of the 1st Workshop on Information Extraction from Scientific Publications, pages 54–66
Nov 20, 2022.

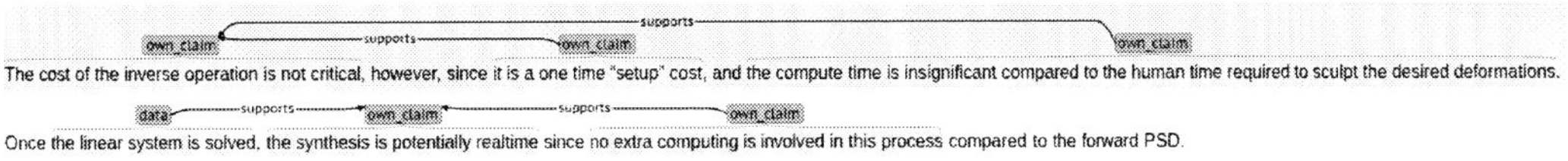

Figure 1: Example with argumentative structure from the Sci-Arg dataset.

SAM. To summarize, our contributions in this work are:

- We are the first to investigate PLMs for full-text SAM, and to present a sequential pipeline for both ADU recognition and argumentative RE on full-text scientific publications (Section 3).
- Our experimental results show that a SciBERT-based ADU recognition model improves over the state-of-the-art by $+7\%$ F1-score. We present the first relation extraction baseline for the Sci-Args corpus and achieve strong 0.74 F1 (Section 5.1).
- Our detailed error analysis reveals open challenges and possible ways of improvements (Section 5.2).

2 Preliminaries

We first define the two tasks of ADUR and ARE, and discuss differences to the standard Information Extraction (IE) tasks of Named Entity Recognition (NER) and Relation Extraction (RE).

An Argumentative Discourse Unit (ADU) can be defined as "span of text that plays a single role for an argument being analyzed and is demarcated by neighboring text spans that play a different role, or none at all" (Stede and Schneider, 2018). It is the smallest unit of argumentation, and may span anything from an in-sentence clause up to multiple full sentences. ADU recognition requires both detecting argumentative spans, as well as classifying them into predefined categories. Typically, this is realised as sequence tagging task similar to NER, where a sequence of tokens $X = \{t_1, t_2, ..., t_N\}$ is assigned with a corresponding N-length sequence of labels $Y = \{l_1, l_2, ..., l_N\}$ with $l_i \in C$ where C is the set of tags that result from converting the ADU types into a tagging scheme like BIO2.[2] In scholarly AM, common ADU classes are *(Own / Background) Claim*, and *Evidence*, *Data*, or *Warrant* (Green, 2014; Lauscher et al., 2018b).

[2]BIO2: **B**egin, **I**nside, **O**utside of an entity

In contrast to NER, ADUs typically vary much more in length than named entities. They are also highly context dependent and often discontinuous. ADUR is also related to discourse segmentation, but depends more on broader context and semantics instead of linguistic structure. Elementary Discourse Units (EDUs), the building blocks in the context of Rethorical Structure Theory (Mann and Thompson, 1988), are more fine-grained, of shorter length and usually cover the complete text which is less the case for argumentative units.

Argumentative Relation Extraction is usually defined as classifying a pair of ADUs, *head* and *tail*, as either an instance of one of the target types or the artificial NO-RELATION type. In other words, the task is to assign a label $Y \in C \cup \{\text{NO-RELATION}\}$ to a given input $X = \{T, h, t\}$, where C is the set of relation types, T is the text and $h = (s_h, e_h, l_h)$ and $t = (s_t, e_t, l_t)$ describe the candidate head and tail entities where s and e are the start and end indices with respect to T and l is the entity type. Typical relation types for SAM are *Supports*, *Mentions*, *Attacks*, *Contradicts*, and *Contrasts* (Lauscher et al., 2018b; Accuosto and Saggion, 2019; Nicholson et al., 2021).

ARE is very similar to standard RE, but SAM relations are often marked by syntactic cues such as connectors, e.g. "because", "however", or "but", whereas in common RE, content words like verbs and nouns are typical relation triggers. This makes ARE challenging because these connectors do not always realise argumentative structure, but also mark other aspects of discourse. Consider, for example, the different meanings of "while" in the following example:

1. While I love a romantic dinner, I also like fast food.
2. While I prepare dinner, I watch a movie.

Here, the "while" in sentence 1) has a contrastive meaning, whereas sentence 2) denotes a temporal aspect.

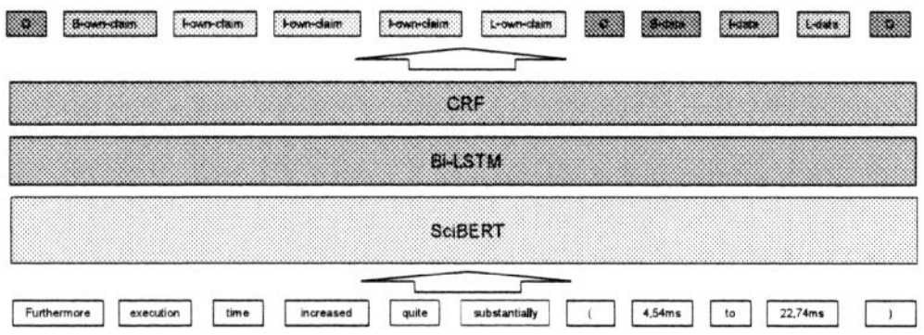

(a) **ADU Recognition.** Tokens are embedded with a frozen PLM, further contextualized with a trained LSTM followed by a CRF to calculate the tag sequence.

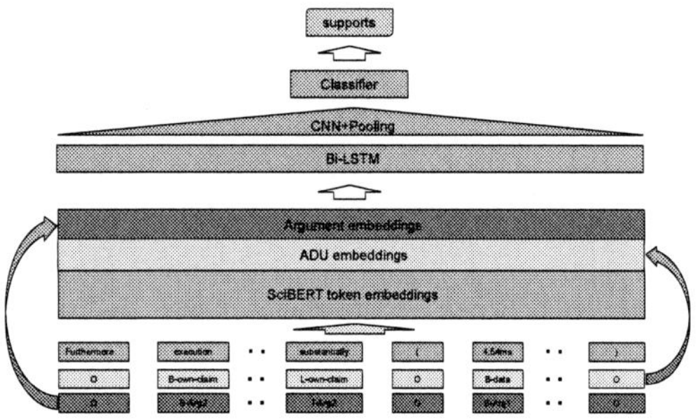

(b) **Argumentative RE.** Tokens are embedded with a frozen PLM, ADU tags and argument tags are embedded with simple embedding matrices. Embeddings are concatenated, contextualized with a LSTM and converted into a single vector that gets classified by a single fully connected layer.

Figure 2: Model setup for (a) ADUR (top) and (b) ARE (bottom).

3 Models

We propose a pipeline of two distinct models, one for each subtask, that are described in the following.

ADU Recognition (ADUR). The architecture of the ADUR model is visualized in Figure 2a. We first embed the token sequence with a frozen PLM encoder. For sequences that exceed the maximum input length of the embedding model, we process the sequence piece-wise and concatenate the result afterwards. The embedded tokens are then fed into a BiLSTM (Schuster and Paliwal, Nov./1997). Finally, a Conditional Random Field (CRF) (Lafferty et al., 2001) is used to obtain the label probabilities for each token. We use a combination of a frozen PLM with a trainable contextualization (LSTM) on top because its training requires less resources than fine-tuning the PLM and initial tests have shown similar performance.[3]

Argumentative RE (ARE). The model architecture for the relation extraction subtask is shown in Figure 2b. ARE is implemented as a classification task, where a pair of candidate ADUs is selected and marked in the input token sequence. To reduce combinatorial complexity, only ADU pairs with a distance smaller than some threshold `d` are considered. Similar to ADU recognition, we first embed the token sequence in a window of `k` tokens around the candidate entity pair with a frozen PLM model. We also create non-contextualized embeddings for the ADU- and argument-tags of the tokens within the window. As argument tags we simply use *head* and *tail* labels to mark the candidate entity tokens. All three embedding sequences are concatenated token-wise and fed into a BiLSTM. The result is converted into a single vector using a Convolutional Neural Network (CNN) and max-pooling, which then is classified as one of the relation labels by a linear projection with softmax.

[3]Note that the training dataset is relative small, so restricting the number of trainable parameters seems to mitigate overfitting.

	Train	Test	Total
ADUs			
background claim	2563	661	3224
own claim	4608	1241	5849
data	3346	858	4204
Relations			
supports	4426	1260	5686
contradicts	551	133	684
semantically same	36	3	39
parts of same	1000	269	1269

Table 1: Label counts for the Sci-Arg dataset.

4 Experimental Setup

Dataset. We use the Sci-Arg dataset (Lauscher et al., 2018b) for model training and evaluation. It is the only available full text argumentation mining dataset for scientific publications. It contains 40 full text publications annotated with ADUs and argumentative relations. Figure 1 shows an example excerpt, and Table 1 summarizes the main dataset statistics. The PARTS OF SAME relation type is used to model non-contiguous spans. The label counts differ slightly from values published in Lauscher et al. (2018b), because annotations in one file (A28) caused parsing errors and were excluded. Furthermore, non-contiguous spans are not merged. We create a train/test split by using the first 30 documents for training and the remaining 9 for evaluation.

system	span based		token based
	exact	weak	
Lauscher 2018c	-	-	0.447
ours	0.532	0.668	0.518
human	0.602	0.729	-

Table 2: **ADU Recognition Performance** as F1 macro average over classes. For *weak* metrics, the gold and the predicted span have to match for at least the half of the characters of the longer span.

Preprocessing. We preprocess the documents by removing the initial XML headers. To decrease the sequence length of the input, we also split the documents into sections, e.g. *introduction* or *conclusion*. This is important to lower computational resource consumption since recent PLMs like SciBERT (Beltagy et al., 2019) usually scale quadratic with the input length and are restricted to a certain max input size, e.g. 512 tokens. Unfortunately, this leads to the removal of all relations labeled with SEMANTICALLY SAME, since these connect ADUs from different sections. However, this affects only 0.6% of the argumentative relations instances.

Data Augmentation. If the pair of ADUs (A, B) is part of an argumentative relation, it is wrong to assume that B is argumentatively unrelated with A, i.e. (B, A) should not be in the NO RELATION class. Thus, we add reversed instances for each available relation in the dataset with the special label SUPPORTS REV in the case of SUPPORTS and keep the labels for CONTRADICTS and PARTS OF SAME since these relations are symmetric. In addition to the positive training instances, we also sample negative relation instances from all possible ADU pairs that are no instances of any argumentative relation.

Training Objective. We use the the cross entropy loss (Rubinstein, 1999) as the training objective for both models f_{ADU} and f_{RE}:

$$\mathcal{L}_{CE}(y, \hat{y}; \boldsymbol{\theta}) := -f_{\boldsymbol{\theta}}(y) \cdot \log f_{\boldsymbol{\theta}}(\hat{y})$$

where y and $\hat{y}$ are the target and predicted probabilities for the token or relation labels, respectively, and $\boldsymbol{\theta}$ is the set of trainable model parameters. In the case of ADU recognition, we obtain the best tagging sequence via Viterbi Decoding (Viterbi, 1967), as usual for CRF-based models.

	F1-exact	F1-weak
@gold ADUs	0.739	
@predicted ADUs	0.210	0.310
human	0.341	0.469

Table 3: **Argumentative RE Performance** as micro average over classes with provided gold ADUs (@gold ADUS) or ADUs predicted with our entity recognition model (@predicted ADUs), i.e. the full relation extraction pipeline. *human* indicates inter-annotator-agreement for the corpus data (Lauscher et al., 2018c) which is comparable to *@predicted ADUs*. For *weak* metrics, best weakly matching ADUs are calculated first, then predicted relations are mapped to these and finally metrics are calculated as usual.

Metrics. Since we compare against evaluation results from Lauscher et al. (2018d), we adopt their metrics for ADU recognition, namely a token-based F1-score that is macro-averaged over classes. However, we also compute *span-based* macro-F1 scores in two variants as described in Lauscher et al. (2018b): For *exact* span-based metrics, the recognized ADU has to match exactly for start and end indices, as well as ADU type. For *weak* matches, the ADU has to match in type, but the target and predicted spans only have to overlap by at least the half of the length of the shorter span. Weak match evaluation is motivated by considerable length and variance of ADU expressions, which makes exact matches difficult, and also allows for comparison with human annotator agreement scores as presented in Lauscher et al. (2018c).

For the relation recognition task, we follow the literature and present micro-averaged F1 scores. Similar to ADU recognition metrics, we calculate weak metrics by first determining target ADUs that can be assigned to predicted ADUs in the way of weak ADU matching as described above, and then calculate F1 scores as usual (Lauscher et al., 2018b). Note that PARTS OF SAME is just a helper relation, so we merge ADUs connected by this relation type first, and then compute scores over the remaining relation types.

Training Details & Hyperparameters. For both tasks, we first conduct a hyperparameter search. We use token-based macro-F1 as the optimization target for ADU recognition and micro-F1 as the target for relation classification. Final hyperparameter values are listed in Appendix A.2.

		P	R	F1
exact	background claim	0.56	0.44	0.49
	own claim	0.48	0.55	0.51
	data	0.57	0.62	0.60
weak	background claim	0.77	0.60	0.68
	own claim	0.63	0.73	0.67
	data	0.62	0.69	0.65

Table 4: **ADUR Performance per Class.** Macro averaged precision (P), recall (R), and F1.

Since there is no dev split, we perform 5-fold cross validation for each subtask on the train split with the best hyperparameter settings and different random seeds for parameter initialization. The best of these 5 models are used for the final evaluation. Detailed training configurations, logs and statistics for the ADU recognition and the ARE subtasks are collected within the Weights & Biases framework.[4] We make these and our source code publicly available for better reproducibility of our experiments.[5]

5 Results and Discussion

This section presents our experimental results. First, we compare against the ADU recognition baseline as provided by Lauscher et al. (2018c). Then, we present findings about prominent error cases and close with an ablation study.

5.1 Results

Table 2 presents the macro-F1 scores of the ADUR baseline, our approach, and human performance in terms of inter-annotator agreement, as reported in Lauscher et al. (2018c). Our model achieves 0.518 token-based F1, significantly outperforming the baseline by 7%. The gap to the human performance is also narrow, especially when looking at the weak metrics with relaxed boundary constraints, where our model achieves 92% of to the human score. For exact metrics, the model reaches only 88% of the human performance, suggesting that exact ADU boundary detection is more challenging. The performance of the model for argumentative RE is a strong 0.739 micro-F1. Note, that we need to merge non-contiguous ADUs first before calculating the ARE scores. We do this via predicted PARTS OF SAME relations, which are recognized with a F1-score of 0.860. For the full pipeline, the model achieves a respectable 0.210 micro-F1 score, which corresponds to 62% of the human performance.

[4]see https://wandb.ai

[5]For ADU recognition, see https://wandb.ai/sam_dfki/best_adu_uncased, for argumentative RE, see https://wandb.ai/sam_dfki/best_rel_uncased, and for the source code, see https://github.com/DFKI-NLP/sam.

	P	R	F1
contradicts	0.505	0.724	0.595
supports	0.739	0.774	0.756

Table 5: **ARE Performance per Class.** Micro averaged precision (P), recall (R), and F1 on gold ADUs. Note that non contiguous ADUs linked via predicted PARTS OF SAME relations are merged first before calculating the scores.

5.2 Error Analysis

ADUR Error Analysis. The decrease in performance when comparing weak with exact metrics is high for the classes BACKGROUND CLAIM (−28%) and OWN CLAIM (−24%), but low for class DATA (−8%), see Figure 4. This may be because the latter is mainly about references or mentions of concise facts where boundaries are much easier to detect.

Most of the errors originate from *detecting* ADUs, i.e. deciding if a text span is an ADU from any type, in comparison to *classifying* a detected ADU span into one of types. The exact span-based macro-F1 for the subtask of ADU *classification* is 0.854, whereas the respective score for ADU *detection* is only 0.617. This difference is even larger for the RE subtask where the micro-F1 is 0.749 for relation *detection* and 0.992 (!) for relation *classification*. Figure 3 shows the confusion matrices for the ADUR and ARE subtasks.

Interestingly, many of ADU classification errors (48%) are instances of type BACKGROUND CLAIM, where the model predicts OWN CLAIM instead, indicated by low precision for OWN CLAIM and low recall for BACKGROUND CLAIM as shown in Table 4. Looking into these misclassifications revealed the following main challenges (in order of decreasing frequency): 1) an island of one or two background claims surrounded by many own claims or located at the border between regions of these two types, 2) the ADU is linked via the structural PARTS OF SAME relation, i.e. it is split by some other content and at least one part of the complete ADU is

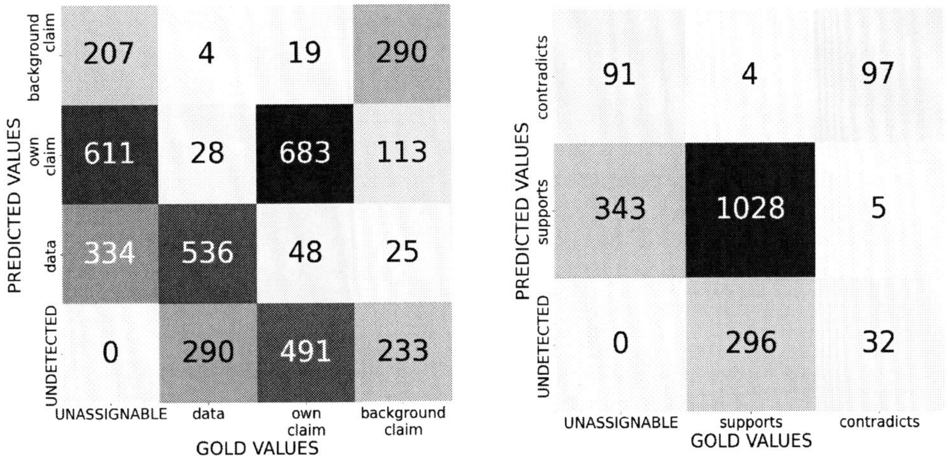

Figure 3: Confusion matrices for ADU recognition (left) and argumentative RE (right).

not detected correctly, and 3) mentions of the author in a background claim (e.g. "[A] drawback of this model for *our* application is [...]" or "It enables *us* to model [...]"). Issues 1) and 2) may suggest that looking at the sequence of ADU types or linguistic surface features is not enough and a deeper "understanding" and/or domain knowledge are required, especially since the training data is very limited. Lauscher et al. (2018c); Accuosto and Saggion (2019) analyse the impact of SAM to related tasks, suggesting to train on these may mitigate this issue. Finally, issue 2) may be improved by using a joint ADUR+ARE model or an ADUR model that allows to predict non-contiguous spans. Note that we tackle ADU detection in fact with both models in combination because we require the PARTS OF SAME predictions to merge the respective ADUs. This poses a challenge for both models: The ADUR model is trained to predict incomplete instances and the ARE model needs to handle instances from conceptional different types of classes, i.e. argumentative and structural relations.

ARE Error Analysis. For the relation extraction subtask, the general performance is higher than for ADUR with approximately only one third of false negatives or false positives with respect to true positive. However, the performance for CONTRADICTS is much lower than for SUPPORTS, see Figure 5. On reason appears to be the class imbalance. There are substantially less training instances for that class (ratio of $1 : 8$, see Figure 1). Furthermore, the model significantly overpredicts the CONTRADICTS relations (see confusion matrix in Figure 3). To unravel this phenomenon, we manually analysed 255 relation candidates from different error categories (true positives, false positives, and false negatives). This revealed, that most of the instances falsely predicted as CONTRADICTS can be associated with specific linguistic surface features, especially occurrences of discourse connectors like “however” that are commonly used to express contrastive ideas, but not in this case (see the example in the end of Section 2). Apparently, the model overfits on these shallow markers which is further supported by the fact that all analysed correctly predicted relation instances of that type could be associated with entries of a small set of connectors.[6]

Regarding the SUPPORTS relation, the analysis revealed that sentence boundaries seem to be a very strong signal. An over-proportional amount (85%) of correct predictions has both arguments in the same sentence compared to 20% and 15% for false positives and false negatives, respectively. This is even stronger when taking the argument types into account: SUPPORTS relations that are in the same sentence and connect a DATA ADU with any claim ADU make up for 88% true positives, but only for 19% and 12% of false positives and false negatives. Note, that per definition of the Sci-Arg annotation scheme[7] DATA never participates in a CONTRAST relation which may be one reason why

[6]Consisting of (in decreasing order of frequency): “however”, “but”, “while”, “in contrast”, “though”, “despite”, and “even though”.

[7]The original annotation guidelines can be found here: `http://data.dws.informatik.uni-mannheim.de/sci-arg/annotation_guidelines.pdf`

relation classification performance is so high. More detailed results of the manual analysis can be found in Figure 5 in the Appendix.

During our analysis we noticed a reasonable amount of potentially mislabeled relation instances (16%), especially missing support relations between OWN CLAIMs. Table 6 shows some examples where relations were correctly detected by the ARE model, but they do not exist in the gold data.

5.3 Ablation Study

We analysed the effect of our approach to add reversed relations. We trained another set of models in a 5-fold cross validation setting with same hyperparameters, but without the augmentation. The resulting mean bootstrapped micro F1 is 0.601, significantly lower than the mean result with augmentation enabled which is 0.762 with $p <$ 1e-10. We gather bootstrapped scores by randomly sampling 10 test document sections, calculate the scores for both model variants as usual and repeat that process for 100 times. Note that there are 114 document sections in total after preprocessing the test set.

6 Related Work

AM is intensively studied for domains like public debates, essays, or legal texts (Lawrence and Reed, 2019). As one of the earliest work for the scientific domain, Teufel and Moens (1999) proposed Argumentative Zoning (AZ) where sentences are classified as AIM, CONTRAST, TEXTUAL, OWN, BACKGROUND, BASIS, or OTHER. The authors created a corpus of 80 annotated full-text papers. They trained Naive-Bayes (NB) and Support-Vector-Machine (SVM) models with hand crafted features and achieved a performance of 0.442 macro-F1. Later work defines similar concepts like "zone of conceptualization" (Liakata, 2010) with classes like EXPERIMENT, BACKGROUND, or MODEL, and trained CRF based models on that (Liakata et al., 2012) (0.18 to 0.76 F1 depending on classes). Guo et al. (2010) compares these schemes with abstract section name detection and trains NB and SVM models. Dasigi et al. (2017) studied the problem of scientific discourse parsing and annotated the result sections of 75 papers with a seven label taxonomy described in de Waard and Pander Maat (2012) like GOAL, FACT, or HYPOTHESIS. They use an LSTM based model augmented with Attention (Vaswani et al., 2017) to obtain sentence representations and present 0.74 F1 performance. In their follow-up work (Li et al., 2021) they achieve a strong 0.841 F1 by using a combination of transfer learning from discourse annotated abstracts (PubMedRCT, Dernoncourt and Lee (2017)) and a model consisting of SciBERT, Attention, BiLSTM, and CRF. In that respect, their approach is similar to ours for ADUR, however, they apply their methods only on the results section of a document and detect full sentence ADUs only. In a similar vein, Achakulvisut et al. (2019) propose a sentence based claim extraction model consisting of BiLSTM and a CRF that they pre-trained on the PubMedRCT dataset. They achieve a performance of 0.790 F1 on a dataset of 1500 abstracts from the Medline dataset. Lauscher et al. (2018a) proposes a tool for automatic ADU recognition and other tasks. Their models are trained on the Sci-Arg dataset and consist of pre-trained word embeddings and a BiLSTM for token classification tasks (e.g. ADUR) and an additional Attention mechanism to obtain sentence representations for the other tasks.

All work mentioned above focuses primarily on the detection and classification of argumentative components. Stab et al. (2014) argues for the need to also analyse argumentative structure, e.g. to automate knowledge base population or reasonable validate claims because that requires to link the respective premises. They also highlight that discourse theory and data is not suited out of the box for argumentative analysis because discourse relations do not cover relevant argumentative relation types and connect primarily neighboring elements which does not reflect argumentative structure. However, Accuosto and Saggion (2019) propose to derive argumentative structure information from discourse data. They annotate a subset of 60 abstracts from the SciDTB scientific discourse dataset (Yang and Li, 2018) with argumentative units and relations. Then, they train models consisting of a BiLSTM, CRF, contextualized word embeddings (ELMo, Peters et al. (2018)) and an encoder pre-trained on the discourse data. They show that adding the encoder significantly improves the performance up to 0.40 F1 argumentative attachment scores, which subsumes argumentative component and relation recognition. Kirschner et al. (2015) created a new corpus by annotating the introduction and discussion sections of 24 scientific articles. The authors consider two argumentative relations, SUPPORT and ATTACK, and also two discourse relations, DETAIL and SEQUENCE borrowed from RST (Mann

Text with ADUs	Annotated	Correction
As the calculations of the wrinkling coefficients are done on a per triangle basis$^{A}_{\text{DATA}}$, the computational time is linear with respect to number of triangles$^{B}_{\text{OWN CLAIM}}$.	$A \leftarrow_S B$	$A \rightarrow_S B$
There are several possibilities to deal with this restriction$^{A}_{\text{OWN CLAIM}}$. One could decide to restrict the simulations to small deformations where the approximation is valid$^{B}_{\text{OWN CLAIM}}$.	-	$A \leftarrow_S B$
As stated in Section 3.3$^{A}_{\text{DATA}}$, two different wrinkle patterns give different wrinkling coefficients for the same triangle geometry$^{B}_{\text{OWN CLAIM}}$. Hence, for the same deformation of the triangle$^{C}_{\text{DATA}}$, corresponding to each pattern, the modulation factors will be different$^{D}_{\text{OWN CLAIM}}$.	$A \rightarrow_S B$ $C \rightarrow_S D$	$A \rightarrow_S B$ $C \rightarrow_S D$ $B \rightarrow_S D$
If a pattern is orthogonal to the deformation direction$^{A}_{\text{OWN CLAIM}}$ (as compared to the other), corresponding modulation factor will be small$^{B}_{\text{OWN CLAIM}}$. In other words, the direction of the deformation favors one pattern over the other$^{C}_{\text{OWN CLAIM}}$.	$A \rightarrow_S B$	$A \rightarrow_S B$ $B \rightarrow_S C$

Table 6: Examples for potentially mislabeled relation instances. $A \rightarrow_S B$ means that the pair of ADUs (A, B) is an instance of the SUPPORTS relation. All proposed corrections are predicted by our model.

and Thompson, 1988), annotated on the sentence level. Recently, Mayer et al. (2020) proposed an argumentation mining pipeline for ADUR and ARE on a new dataset. They annotate 500 Medline abstracts with CLAIM and EVIDENCE ADUs as well as SUPPORT and ATTACK relations. The authors trained and analysed the performance of different models consisting of encoders, like word embeddings, contextualized word embeddings and BERT variants, in combination with a Gated Recurrent Unit (GRU) or LSTM and a CRF. They present a strong micro-F1 of up to 0.92 for ADUR and a performance of up to 0.69 for the full pipeline and conclude that Transformers, especially domain specific ones like SciBERT, work best for SAM at Medline abstracts. Note that, similar to our weak measures, they count predictions as true positive when 75% of the tokens[8] overlap. Another work (Fergadis et al., 2021) that analyses the performance of Transformers for SAM proposes a new corpus of 1000 abstracts with sentence level annotations for CLAIM and EVIDENCE. The authors use a SciBERT applied sentence wise with a BiLSTM over the CLS token embeddings as contextualizer and present a 0.624 macro-F1.

[8]This differs from our weak measures in two ways: Following Lauscher et al. (2018b), we require 50% overlap in means of characters, not tokens.

7 Conclusion and Future Work

In this paper, we presented a pipeline based approach to handle full-text argumentation mining on scientific publications and showed its effectiveness by establishing new state-of-the-art performance on the Sci-Arg corpus. However, there is still a significant gap to human performance. We used PLM based models for both subtasks, argumentative discourse unit recognition (ADUR) and argumentative relation extraction (ARE), and found similar improvements gains (+7%) as reported elsewhere when using Transformers over traditional approaches without Attention mechanism, even without fine-tuning the PLMs.

Our detailed error analysis revealed several findings. First, recognizing instances is much harder than assigning the correct label, which is true for both tasks, but especially for ARE. The performance suffers from shallow processing, i.e. the models are tricked by linguistic surface features like author referencing pronouns in background claims or non-argumentative discourse connectors. Furthermore, ADUR detection struggles a lot in the context of non-contiguous elements which is reasonable because it is trained with incomplete information. This calls for conceptional better modeling of the task, for instance with a joined model for ADUR and ARE. Finally, we could confirm that SAM is a complex problem that is even hard for humans. However, the low inter-annotator-agreement reported by the Sci-Arg authors and our finding that a significant amount (16%) of the manually analysed ARE instances are questionable labeled raises the need for even more annotation rounds, maybe with multiple domain experts, or a simplified annotation scheme.

Acknowledgments

We would like to thank Aleksandra Gabryszak and the anonymous reviewers for their valuable comments and feedback on the paper. This work has been supported by the German Federal Ministry of Education and Research as part of the projects CORA4NLP (01IW20010) and Software Campus 2.0 (01IS17043).

References

Pablo Accuosto and Horacio Saggion. 2019. Transferring knowledge from discourse to arguments: A case study with scientific abstracts. In *Proceedings of the 6th Workshop on Argument Mining*, pages 41–51, Florence, Italy. Association for Computational Linguistics.

Titipat Achakulvisut, Chandra Bhagavatula, Daniel E. Acuna, and Konrad P. Körding. 2019. Claim extraction in biomedical publications using deep discourse model and transfer learning. *CoRR*, abs/1907.00962.

Khalid Al Khatib, Tirthankar Ghosal, Yufang Hou, Anita de Waard, and Dayne Freitag. 2021. Argument Mining for Scholarly Document Processing: Taking Stock and Looking Ahead. In *Proceedings of the Second Workshop on Scholarly Document Processing*, pages 56–65, Online. Association for Computational Linguistics.

Iz Beltagy, Kyle Lo, and Arman Cohan. 2019. SciBERT: A pretrained language model for scientific text. In *Proceedings of the 2019 Conference on Empirical Methods in Natural Language Processing and the 9th International Joint Conference on Natural Language Processing (EMNLP-IJCNLP)*, pages 3615–3620, Hong Kong, China. Association for Computational Linguistics.

Pradeep Dasigi, Gully A. P. C. Burns, Eduard H. Hovy, and Anita de Waard. 2017. Experiment segmentation in scientific discourse as clause-level structured prediction using recurrent neural networks. *CoRR*, abs/1702.05398.

Anita de Waard and Henk Pander Maat. 2012. Verb form indicates discourse segment type in biological research papers: Experimental evidence. *Journal of English for Academic Purposes*, 11(4):357–366.

Franck Dernoncourt and Ji Young Lee. 2017. PubMed 200k RCT: a dataset for sequential sentence classification in medical abstracts. In *Proceedings of the Eighth International Joint Conference on Natural Language Processing (Volume 2: Short Papers)*, pages 308–313, Taipei, Taiwan. Asian Federation of Natural Language Processing.

Aris Fergadis, Dimitris Pappas, Antonia Karamolegkou, and Haris Papageorgiou. 2021. Argumentation mining in scientific literature for sustainable development. In *Proceedings of the 8th Workshop on Argument Mining*, pages 100–111, Punta Cana, Dominican Republic. Association for Computational Linguistics.

Santo Fortunato, Carl T. Bergstrom, Katy Börner, James A. Evans, Dirk Helbing, Staša Milojević, Alexander M. Petersen, Filippo Radicchi, Roberta Sinatra, Brian Uzzi, Alessandro Vespignani, Ludo Waltman, Dashun Wang, and Albert-László Barabási. 2018. Science of science. *Science*, 359(6379):eaao0185.

Nancy Green. 2014. Towards creation of a corpus for argumentation mining the biomedical genetics research literature. In *Proceedings of the First Workshop on Argumentation Mining*, pages 11–18, Baltimore, Maryland. Association for Computational Linguistics.

Yufan Guo, Anna Korhonen, Maria Liakata, Ilona Silins, Lin Sun, and Ulla Stenius. 2010. Identifying the information structure of scientific abstracts: An investigation of three different schemes. In *Proceedings of the 2010 Workshop on Biomedical Natural Language Processing*, pages 99–107, Uppsala, Sweden. Association for Computational Linguistics.

Diederik P. Kingma and Jimmy Ba. 2014. Adam: A Method for Stochastic Optimization. *arXiv:1412.6980 [cs]*. ArXiv: 1412.6980.

Christian Kirschner, Judith Eckle-Kohler, and Iryna Gurevych. 2015. Linking the thoughts: Analysis of argumentation structures in scientific publications. In *Proceedings of the 2nd Workshop on Argumentation Mining*, pages 1–11, Denver, CO. Association for Computational Linguistics.

John D. Lafferty, Andrew McCallum, and Fernando C. N. Pereira. 2001. Conditional random fields: Probabilistic models for segmenting and labeling sequence data. In *Proceedings of the Eighteenth International Conference on Machine Learning (ICML 2001), Williams College, Williamstown, MA, USA, June 28 - July 1, 2001*, pages 282–289. Morgan Kaufmann.

Anne Lauscher, Goran Glavaš, and Kai Eckert. 2018a. ArguminSci: A tool for analyzing argumentation and rhetorical aspects in scientific writing. In *Proceedings of the 5th Workshop on Argument Mining*, pages 22–28, Brussels, Belgium. Association for Computational Linguistics.

Anne Lauscher, Goran Glavaš, and Simone Paolo Ponzetto. 2018b. An argument-annotated corpus of scientific publications. In *Proceedings of the 5th Workshop on Argument Mining*, pages 40–46, Brussels, Belgium. Association for Computational Linguistics.

Anne Lauscher, Goran Glavaš, Simone Paolo Ponzetto, and Kai Eckert. 2018c. Investigating the role of argumentation in the rhetorical analysis of scientific publications with neural multi-task learning models. In *Proceedings of the 2018 Conference on Empirical Methods in Natural Language Processing*, pages 3326–3338, Brussels, Belgium. Association for Computational Linguistics.

Anne Lauscher, Goran Glavaš, Simone Paolo Ponzetto, and Kai Eckert. 2018d. Investigating the Role of Argumentation in the Rhetorical Analysis of Scientific Publications with Neural Multi-Task Learning Models. In *Proceedings of the 2018 Conference on Empirical Methods in Natural Language Processing*, pages 3326–3338, Brussels, Belgium. Association for Computational Linguistics.

John Lawrence and Chris Reed. 2019. Argument mining: A survey. *Computational Linguistics*, 45(4):765–818.

Xiangci Li, Gully Burns, and Nanyun Peng. 2021. Scientific discourse tagging for evidence extraction. In *Proceedings of the 16th Conference of the European Chapter of the Association for Computational Linguistics: Main Volume*, pages 2550–2562, Online. Association for Computational Linguistics.

Maria Liakata. 2010. Zones of conceptualisation in scientific papers: a window to negative and speculative statements. In *Proceedings of the Workshop on Negation and Speculation in Natural Language Processing*, pages 1–4, Uppsala, Sweden. University of Antwerp.

Maria Liakata, Shyamasree Saha, Simon Dobnik, Colin Batchelor, and Dietrich Rebholz-Schuhmann. 2012. Automatic recognition of conceptualization zones in scientific articles and two life science applications. *Bioinformatics (Oxford, England)*, 28(7):991–1000.

William C. Mann and Sandra A. Thompson. 1988. Rhetorical Structure Theory: Toward a functional theory of text organization. *Text - Interdisciplinary Journal for the Study of Discourse*, 8(3).

Tobias Mayer, Elena Cabrio, and Serena Villata. 2020. Transformer-based argument mining for healthcare applications. In *ECAI 2020 - 24th European Conference on Artificial Intelligence, 29 August-8 September 2020, Santiago de Compostela, Spain, August 29 - September 8, 2020 - Including 10th Conference on Prestigious Applications of Artificial Intelligence (PAIS 2020)*, volume 325 of *Frontiers in Artificial Intelligence and Applications*, pages 2108–2115. IOS Press.

Josh M. Nicholson, Milo Mordaunt, Patrice Lopez, Ashish Uppala, Domenic Rosati, Neves P. Rodrigues, Peter Grabitz, and Sean C. Rife. 2021. Scite: A smart citation index that displays the context of citations and classifies their intent using deep learning. *Quantitative Science Studies*, 2(3):882–898.

Matthew E. Peters, Mark Neumann, Mohit Iyyer, Matt Gardner, Christopher Clark, Kenton Lee, and Luke Zettlemoyer. 2018. Deep contextualized word representations. In *Proceedings of the 2018 Conference of the North American Chapter of the Association for Computational Linguistics: Human Language Technologies, Volume 1 (Long Papers)*, pages 2227–2237, New Orleans, Louisiana. Association for Computational Linguistics.

Reuven Rubinstein. 1999. The Cross-Entropy Method for Combinatorial and Continuous Optimization. *Methodology And Computing In Applied Probability*, 1(2):127–190.

M. Schuster and K.K. Paliwal. Nov./1997. Bidirectional recurrent neural networks. *IEEE Transactions on Signal Processing*, 45(11):2673–2681.

Christian Stab, Christian Kirschner, Judith Eckle-Kohler, and Iryna Gurevych. 2014. Argumentation mining in persuasive essays and scientific articles from the discourse structure perspective. In *Proceedings of the Workshop on Frontiers and Connections between Argumentation Theory and Natural Language Processing, Forlì-Cesena, Italy, July 21-25, 2014*, volume 1341 of *CEUR Workshop Proceedings*. CEUR-WS.org.

Manfred Stede and Jodi Schneider. 2018. Argumentation Mining. *Synthesis Lectures on Human Language Technologies*, 11(2):1–191.

Simone Teufel and Marc Moens. 1999. Discourse-level argumentation in scientific articles: human and automatic annotation. In *Towards Standards and Tools for Discourse Tagging*.

Ashish Vaswani, Noam Shazeer, Niki Parmar, Jakob Uszkoreit, Llion Jones, Aidan N. Gomez, Lukasz Kaiser, and Illia Polosukhin. 2017. Attention Is All You Need. *arXiv:1706.03762 [cs]*. ArXiv: 1706.03762.

A. Viterbi. 1967. Error bounds for convolutional codes and an asymptotically optimum decoding algorithm. *IEEE Transactions on Information Theory*, 13(2):260–269. Conference Name: IEEE Transactions on Information Theory.

Douglas Walton. 2001. *Informal Logic: A Pragmatic Approach*, 2 edition. Cambridge University Press.

An Yang and Sujian Li. 2018. SciDTB: Discourse dependency TreeBank for scientific abstracts. In *Proceedings of the 56th Annual Meeting of the Association for Computational Linguistics (Volume 2: Short Papers)*, pages 444–449, Melbourne, Australia. Association for Computational Linguistics.

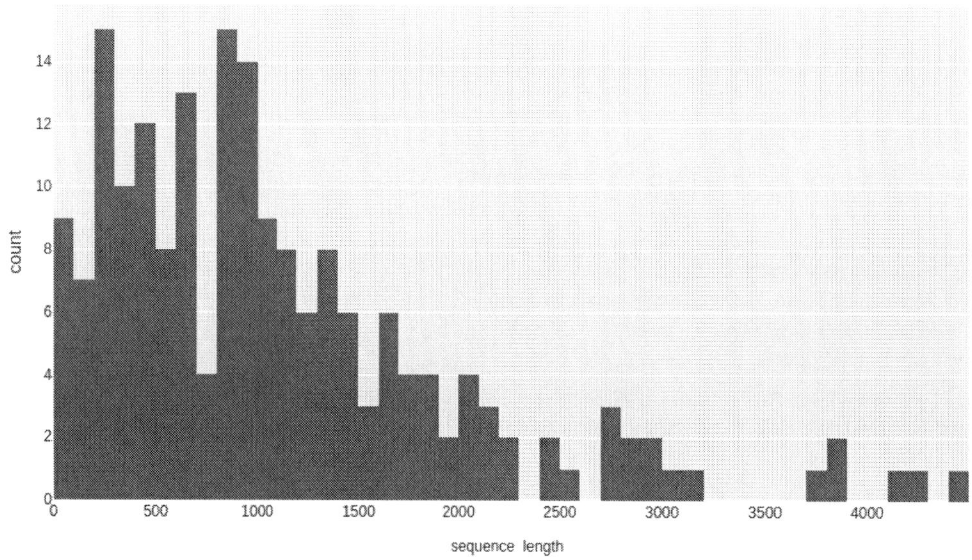

Figure 4: **Distribution of input sequence lengths.** This is after splitting the document text into sections and tokenization. Note that this is primarily relevant for the ADU model since we use a much smaller token window size k to restrict the input for the ARE model.

A Appendix

A.1 Preprocessing

We use the following regular expression pattern to match content in the beginning of the files that we remove: "`<\?xml[^>]*>[^<]*<Document xmlns:gate="http://www.gate.ac.uk"[^>]*>[^<]*`" (without the outer quotes). Main sections are marked by `<h1>SECTION_HEADING</h1>` in the Sci-Arg corpus where `SECTION_HEADING` is any text, so we use this regular expression pattern to split the texts: "`<H1>`"(without the quotes). Note, that we keep that content in the input. The input sequence lengths for the ADU model reaches still values > 4000. Figure 4 shows its distribution.

A.2 Experimental Setup and Hyperparameters

We use the AllenNLP framework to implement the models and execute the training. As PLM, we use the uncased variant of SciBERT (Beltagy et al., 2019) as provided by AllenAI[9]. ADAM (Kingma and Ba, 2014) is used as optimizer. We use batch sizes of 8 and 128 for ADU recognition and RE, respectively, that are derived from resource constraints. The ADU tags are encoded with the BIOUL tagging scheme. For the RE subtask, we hand-picked embedding sizes of 13 and 3 for the ADU-tags and argument-tags, respectively, that are derived form the number of classes.[10]

As a result of the hyperparameter search, we use the following parameters for the ADU recognition task: a learning rate of 0.005, dropout probability of 0.5 before and after the PLM and 0.4394 in the LSTM, a gradient normalization threshold of 7.0, a patience of 20 epochs for early stopping, two layers for the LSTM with a hidden size of 300. In the case of RE, we got the following values: a learning rate of 0.0005, a dropout probability of 0.3061 before and after the PLM and 0.4394 in the LSTM, a gradient normalization threshold of 4.12, 4 layers for the LSTM with a hidden size of 430, 193 filters for the CNN (with ngram sizes of 3, 5, 7, and 10), a hidden size of 860 for the final projection layer, a token window size `k` of 479 tokens around the center of the candidate argument pair, a max inner token distance `d` between the arguments of 177[11], and finally, we use a factor

[9]see `https://huggingface.co/allenai/scibert_scivocab_uncased`

[10]Note, the three ADU-tags are each BIOUL encoded and the argument types, *head* and *tail*, are BIO encoded.

[11]This causes a loss of 0.23% of SUPPORT instances and 0.5% of PARTS OF SAME instances, which is neglectable.

of three for the amount of negative examples, i.e. we add three times as many existing argumentative ADU pairs as NO RELATION instances which we sample from all available pairs without a relation label and within the distance constraint.

A.3 Training Resources

The hyperparameter search was performed on a single Nvidia RTX A6000 (48GB). The training of the final models, i.e. 5 for each subtask, and inference was calculated on single Nvidia GeForce GTX 1080 Ti (12GB). The total training time for all final models was 5h51m for ADUR and 40h17m for ARE.

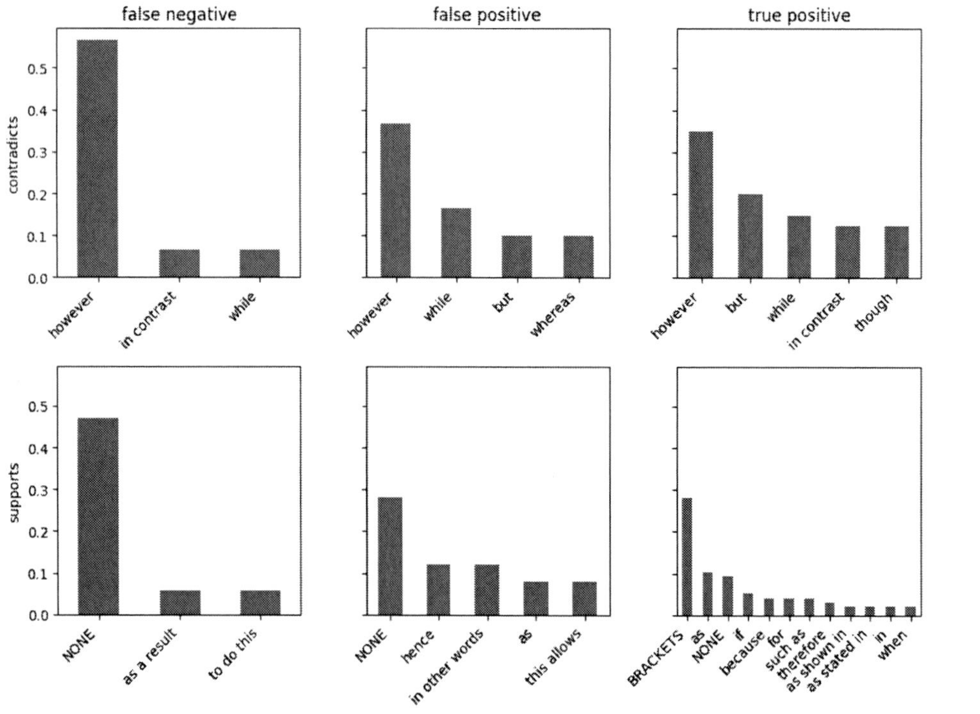

(a) Distribution of **connecting phrases**. Despite being no real discourse connectors, we also collected markers like BRACKETS that seem to be important surface features. NONE indicates that no connective element was found.

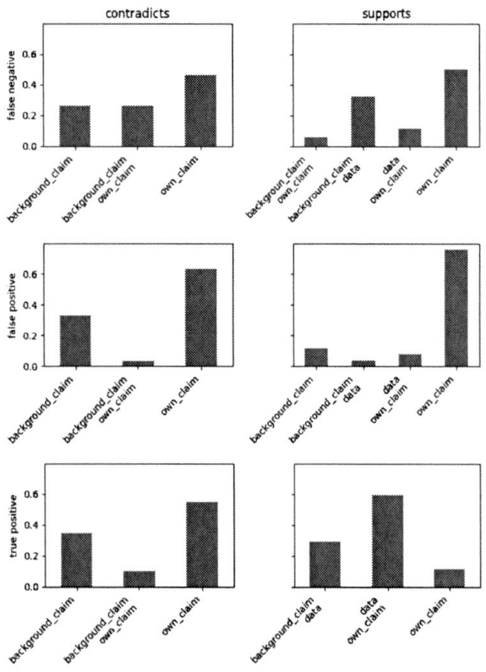

(b) Distribution of **relation arguments** (sorted and mentioned only once if both arguments are the same).

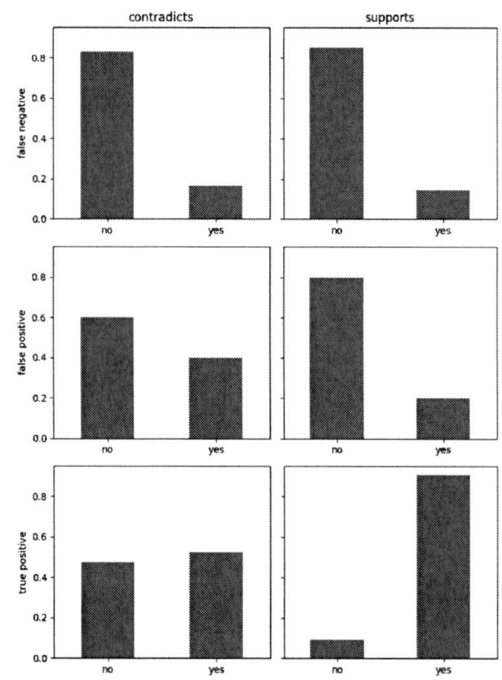

(c) Distribution of the feature that both arguments are **in the same sentence**.

Figure 5: Results of the manual error analysis for argumentative relation extraction. The figures show proportions of different features (connectors, arguments, and same sentence feature) at different subsets by error type (false negative, false positive, or true positive). The lowest entries per category are excluded. Values are calculated on a manually collected subset of 255 relation instances in total.

On the portability of extractive Question-Answering systems on scientific papers to real-life application scenarios

Chyrine Tahri [♣,◇] **Xavier Tannier** [♣] **Patrick Haouat** [◇]
[♣] Sorbonne Université, Inserm, Université Sorbonne Paris-Nord, LIMICS, Paris, France
[◇] ERDYN, Paris, France
{chyrine.tahri, xavier.tannier}@sorbonne-universite.fr
patrick.haouat@erdyn.fr

Abstract

There are still hurdles standing in the way of faster and more efficient knowledge consumption in industrial environments seeking to foster innovation. In this work, we address the portability of extractive Question Answering systems from academic spheres to industries basing their decisions on thorough scientific papers analysis. Keeping in mind that such industrial contexts often lack high-quality data to develop their own QA systems, we illustrate the misalignment between application requirements and cost sensitivity of such industries and some widespread practices tackling the domain-adaptation problem in the academic world. Through a series of extractive QA experiments on QASPER, we adopt the pipeline-based retriever-ranker-reader architecture for answering a question on a scientific paper and show the impact of modeling choices in different stages on the quality of answer prediction. We thus provide a characterization of practical aspects of real-life application scenarios and notice that appropriate trade-offs can be efficient and add value in those industrial environments.

1 Introduction

It is widely recognized today that the most advanced countries have moved to the so-called knowledge-based economy. In the industrial field, including service providers, this new paradigm has particular consequences for most players in R&D and innovation activities where decisions are based on the analysis of huge corpora of documents (scientific papers, patents, reports, etc). The thorough exploitation of this pre-existing knowledge by highly-skilled workers is costly and time-consuming, but such costs can be significantly reduced by NLP technologies that make exploitation and consumption of textual content faster and more efficient. For instance, Information-Seeking Question-Answering is of particular interest to industrial environments conducting scientific monitoring, but there still remain significant hurdles to efficiently adopt such systems in those environments, predominantly the complexity and accessibility of the data landscape.

As a matter of fact, extracting information from scientific publications is a cognitively complex process and requires domain expertise, but obtaining and ensuring such high-quality annotations could become unreasonably expensive and unreliable. The *scarcity of in-house annotation efforts*, *frequent domain shifts*, and *lack of deep understanding of data-model interaction and evaluation* make these technologies inaccessible especially for industrial environments lacking computational resources. One direction would be to entirely rely on models' transfer learning capabilities and make use of the knowledge they learn on academic benchmarks that meet the size requirement. However, zero and few-shot settings successes, *i.e,* when few to no annotations are available, seem to be largely dominated by large-scale autoregressive models (Chowdhery et al., 2022), which are accessible only to a handful of researchers and practitioners with enormous compute power.

In this paper, we take on extractive information-seeking QA on scientific papers from an industrial point of view. We identify the hurdles standing in the way of adopting such systems and show through a simulation of such context that some modeling and evaluation practices might not align with a suitable return on investment sought by such industries. Our contributions can be summarized as follows: First, we explore the portability challenges of QA models toward scientific content-consuming industrial environments and split them into three major long-standing issues. Second, we simulate through a series of experiments on QASPER (Dasigi et al., 2021) the context where information is sought in research papers and thus illustrate the identified portability issues. Third, we discuss based on the results the relevance of modeling and evaluation choices when compared to the goal of adequately

Proceedings of the 1st Workshop on Information Extraction from Scientific Publications, pages 67–77
Nov 20, 2022.

solving the task in a cost-effective way.

2 The portability challenge in industrial environments

For small and medium-sized enterprises (SMEs) interested in Information-Seeking QA on scientific publications, the question of work to be done compared to the benefit of it is very important as it informs the way resources are allocated. When bringing advancements like QA systems into real-world applications suffering data scarcity issues, choosing a benchmark representative of contexts, questions, and answers one would expect in their application remains the most widely adopted practice for maximizing accuracy. Unfortunately, due to the fact that meeting an information need is a hard concept to quantify, adopting such technologies can fall short of quantitatively measuring the impact and the business value created. We discuss hereafter three major inter-connected long-standing issues that restrain from successful portability:

Issue 1: Modeling real-world problems is challenging. Question Answering aims at meeting an information need and providing a user with relevant answers to their questions. However, in domains with high levels of expertise, assisting professionals in such complex processes requires, depending on the nature of the query, cognitive abilities that AI systems have not yet matured to (Chollet, 2019). The AI community has factually been benchmarking intelligence by comparing the defined skill exhibited by AI and humans at specific tasks, and building special-purpose systems capable of handling narrow, well-described tasks, more and more above human-level performance. This created a plethora of QA benchmarks/tasks measuring very specific skills (Rogers et al., 2021) as opposed to the complex processes one would long for in intelligent systems. Further, annotating the required amount of quality data to build such systems can be unaffordable for many industries and organizations. The question that arises here is whether to favor quantity in task format adequacy and thus potentially model performance, or limited content representativeness with complexity that guarantees quality and better alignment with real-world applications.

Issue 2: There is a real need for transparency and confidence not only in predictions but also in the whole predictive process in a way that allows users to assess how well-informed their decisions would be. However, there still remains insufficient understanding of the capabilities and limitations of models and the way they interact with data during the different stages of their training (Ramnath et al., 2020; Zhou and Srikumar, 2021). Up until recently, there has been little guidance on the suitability of which models for which cases in Question Answering (Luo et al., 2022). Tremendous work continues to be done on modeling and exploring new model architectures and training schemes, however interpretation and explanation of models' behaviors that inform modeling choices in adopting such technologies, have not developed at the same pace. This makes it challenging for adopters to select their models for real-world settings, whether the intended use is at early stages or later in production. The obvious issue here is to identify what makes a certain model a trustworthy fit for the project motivation rather than another.

Issue 3: A good performance metric is not synonymous with how well application requirements are met. While current evaluation schemes contribute to overly specializing solutions for performance benchmarks, adopters and end-users are not only more sensitive to the plus-value models provide, but also the costs of developing and deploying such systems. Extractive QA systems are mainly evaluated using the F-measure, but a token-overlap metric is not informative on how well the system is assisting the user and providing relevant answers. For this reason, misaligning what is measured and what is intended and desired might lead in certain cases to misallocating resources, and although progress has been made towards user-centered evaluation (Chen et al., 2022), real-world applications still have more complexity and demands whereas models' evaluation is lagging behind.

These issues impact different phases of the development cycle of QA systems in real-world expert applications. For instance, issue 1 impacts problem definition and adequate data collection, which are the backbone of the whole cycle. Issue 2 introduces hurdles to experiment design and model training, while issue 3 directly impacts evaluation and complicates the path to successful model deployment. In the rest of the paper, we simulate a scenario of seeking information in research papers and consider our end-user to be an expert in decision support based on scientific publications analysis. We particularly focus on the extractive QA setting where the goal is to provide the user with answers to a particular question on a given paper. This translates to the following formulation of the issues mentioned above: 1. What kind of task and data should we use, given the complexity and the level of expertise present both in the questions and the context? 2. What models would solve this task and would interact well with such data, peculiarly since we need as much transparency as possible in the process of identifying the answers? 3. How does the performance of the chosen model on the chosen task and data reflect the return on investment for deploying such systems?

3 Related work

3.1 Information-Seeking Question Answering

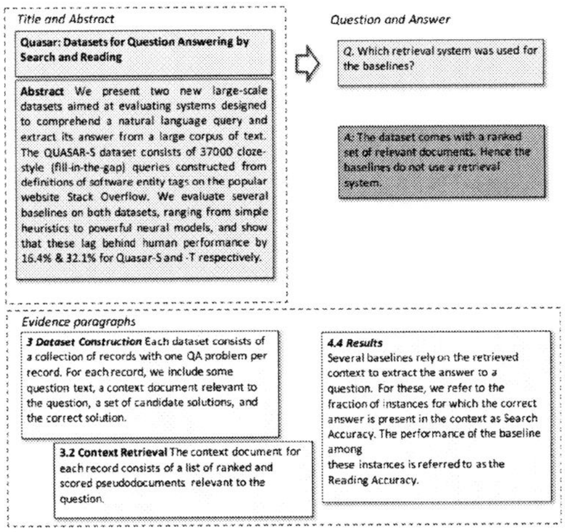

Figure 1: Example instance taken from QASPER as presented in Dasigi et al. (2021)

Rogers et al. (2021) make the distinction between information-seeking and probing questions based on the communicative intent of the user. We are more interested in information-seeking questions that aim to bring forth answers that are unknown at the time of formulating the query. There exists conversational information-seeking datasets such as QuAC (Choi et al., 2018), and grounded-in-documents datasets such as Natural Questions (Kwiatkowski et al., 2019) and QASPER (Dasigi et al., 2021).

3.2 Domain Adaptation for Question Answering

QA systems are often considered to be reliable when they have been trained on enough in-domain data, which is typically around 100k question and answer training examples. However, it is well known that such data is not abundant in specialized and restricted domains that require high-levels of expertise. Sparked industrial interest in QA use-cases has given rise to a line of work on Domain-Adaptation (Hazen et al., 2019; Miller et al., 2021; Yue et al., 2021) hoping to build robust systems for domains with limited data.

Overall, the general approach to domain adaptation of Question-Answering models is to synthesize question-answer pairs (Shinoda et al., 2021; Yue et al., 2022). Nevertheless, in the case of information-seeking QA on research papers, such approaches fall short of producing high-quality questions and are so far unable to efficiently deal with complex question and answer generation from long context dependencies (Luu et al., 2020). Therefore, domain adaptation of QA techniques cannot yet deal with generating synthetic, high-quality, and representative question-answer pairs of information sought in research papers.

3.3 Modular pipelined systems for Question Answering

Although modular pipelined QA systems are mainly developed and used in Open-Domain QA (Zhu et al., 2021), their components can be also beneficial for tackling in-context QA. Figure 2 shows the way we adopt retriever-ranker-reader architecture for answering a question on a scientific paper. We favor such building blocks of a solution rather than complex *do-it-all* models to increase our chances of understanding and trusting the system.

Retriever

A retriever aims at retrieving passages from a corpus that are relevant w.r.t. a given query. Its goal is to filter out irrelevant context and therefore it can be used in QA grounded in documents when these are very long sequences of text like research papers. The granularity of passages to be retrieved depends on the application and the type of answers sought.

State-of-the-art retrievers are mostly dense retrievers (Luan et al., 2021), *i.e,* they extract dense representations of a question and a context by feeding them into a language model and using the dot-product of these representations as a similarity score to rank and select most relevant passages.

Re-ranker

In information-seeking QA, especially on research papers, the end-user might not always employ the terms in their query as they appear in context, whether for lexical reasons like specific terminology or simply because the terms themselves are sought by the query. To this end, in order to improve retrieval quality, a common strategy is to process the retrieved passages or answers using a re-ranking module. Rankers post-retrieval in particular are useful when retrievers have a high recall but fail to rank documents according to relevance, sometimes due to the semantic similarity between questions and passages being very low (Lin et al., 2020).

Reader

A reader infers the answer to the question from a set of ordered documents it receives in a pipelined QA system. Readers are generally regarded as either extractive or generative. Extractive readers mainly assume the correct answer is present in the context and usually focus on learning to predict the start and end position of the answer, while the generative ones generate the answers from their vocabulary. The choice of reader type depends on the nature of questions and context and therefore evaluation procedures differ (Zhang et al., 2020).

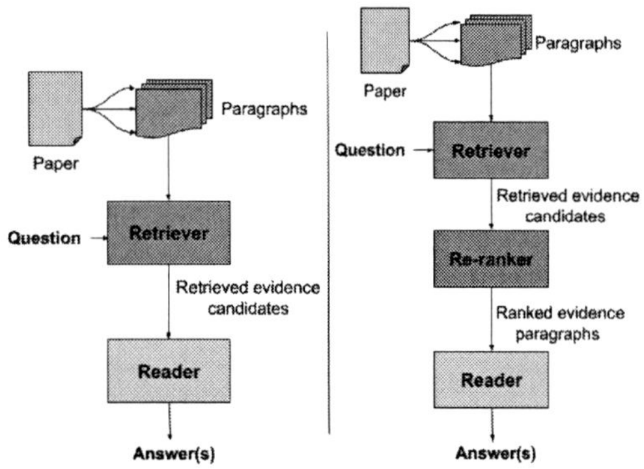

Figure 2: Modular pipeline for Information-Seeking Question Answering grounded in research papers. Left is a retriever-reader pipeline (referred to as pipeline **R**); Right is retriever-ranker-reader (**R-2**).

4 Experimental Setup

4.1 Datasets

QASPER for simulation

In restricted domains with high level of expertise, users tend to ask questions that are naturally different from those in open and general domains. For instance, the distribution of Google Search queries is not representative of all questions an astrophysicist or an economist routinely ask in a work-day. Such big datasets, arising from real-world use cases, might contain microscopic fractions of those specialized distributions one seeks, but will not be representative if regarded as a whole general domain. Therefore, we chose to focus our simulation on a dataset that drifts away from those general and "natural" distributions. To this end, QASPER (Dasigi et al., 2021) is an information-seeking dataset of questions and answers anchored in research papers whose main topic is NLP: it compromises 5,049 questions over 1,585 papers. The dataset is challenging in nature because of the long context requiring reading entire papers and the multiple types of questions (extractive, abstractive, yes/no, and unanswerable). Its task is formally defined as determining the answerability of the question and outputting an answer that can have different formats (span(s), free-form, yes/no).

We consider QASPER to be a good dataset for simulating an industrial environment seeking information in scientific text as the nature of the context, as well as the annotation strategy, are suitable and equivalent to our use-case. At the time of writing, it is currently the only existing benchmark focusing on entire research papers and not just abstracts.

The official baseline for QASPER is Longformer Encoder-Decoder (LED) (Beltagy et al., 2020). LED was trained in a multi-task setup for evidence identification and answer generation and chosen because of its ability to handle the variety of answer types as well as encoding papers' full text.

SQuAD

The Stanford Question Answering Dataset (Rajpurkar et al., 2016, 2018) has been widely used in QA tasks since its creation. It compromises over $100k$ crowd-sourced question-answer pairs derived from Wikipedia. Questions in SQuAD are diverse but answers are very short spans and require less expertise than QASPER to produce.

Natural Questions

Natural Questions (Kwiatkowski et al., 2019) introduced user queries issued to the Google search engine paired with high-quality annotations in the form of (*question, Wikipedia page, long answer, short answer*) quadruples. Additionally, Natural Questions is compromised of 323k examples, making it 64 times the size of QASPER.

4.2 Evidence Retrieval

For identifying relevant evidence paragraphs, we use Dense Passage Retrieval (DPR) (Karpukhin et al., 2020), a highly efficient dual-encoder using two BERT (Devlin et al., 2019) based models to encode documents and queries separately. Both the question encoder and context encoder have been trained on Natural Questions (Kwiatkowski et al., 2019). We use Haystack[1] as a framework and retrieval is performed using ElasticSearch.

Instead of encoding the entire long-context papers that cannot be handled with BERT-like encoders, and building on the definition of the task itself, *i.e,* identifying evidence paragraphs, we chose to deal with paragraphs as units of passages (Figure 2). Furthermore, 55% of the answers to questions with text-only evidence in QASPER have multiple evidence paragraphs. For this reason, and because retriever results could serve as explanations for the end-user and thus increase their confidence in predictions, we experiment with returning k candidate paragraphs with $k \in \{1, 3, 5, 10\}$. We chose these values to be "human-readable": an end-user is not visually bothered by having such $k \geq 1$ returned paragraphs highlighting answer elements.

Finally, because the semantic similarity between questions and passages can be very low (Figure 1), we experiment with re-ranking paragraphs using cross-encoders (Hofstätter et al., 2020) based on two models: MiniLM (Wang et al., 2020) and ELECTRA (Clark et al., 2020), trained on the MS Marco Passage Ranking[2] (Microsoft Machine Reading Comprehension) task. We choose to pass the minimum between the top-50 ranked paragraphs and the total number of paragraphs in the article[3] to the re-ranker because of its computational cost.

4.3 Answer Prediction

QASPER is composed of questions with multiple evidence and answer types. We focus on text-only evidence excluding tables and figures. We further limit experiments to extractive questions as we mentioned before (roughly 51.8% of the dataset) because we prioritized our focus on accessible and extensively-studied models as well as the extractive evaluation scheme. Finally, because we use a pipelined system with paragraphs as units of passages, we are able to fit candidate evidence in all readers[4]. We conduct two sets of experiments:

- Zero-shot settings on a few selected models that are known for robustness, generalization ability, and efficiency among others. This scenario is the closest to a real-world setting where no annotated data is available and the application is quite different from existing benchmarks. Such experiments lay the ground for what can be expected in a least-available resources scenario and it is interesting to see if there is value in those settings.

- Fine-tuned settings where all models are fine-tuned on the extractive set of questions in QASPER. We are particularly interested in seeing how models adapt their answers to better suit the answers' nature in QASPER. Since there would intuitively be improvements over the zero-shot setting when fine-tuning, this kind of scenario gives hints about the relevance of investing in expert annotations when considering the nature of such improvements.

The readers we chose to experiment with are the following: **RoBERTa** (Liu et al., 2019) offering a great trade-off between performance and inference speed, **SciBERT** (Beltagy et al., 2019) trained on scientific text, **deBERTaV3** (He et al., 2021) particularly performing on NLU tasks, **UnifiedQA** (Khashabi et al., 2020) for its strong generalization abilities and **Longformer** (Beltagy et al., 2020) which, although we do not need long-range models as the pipeline deals with paragraphs as units, has the ability to produce longer answer spans if needed.

We choose to have RoBERTa, SciBERT, deBERTa and Longformer trained on SQuAD v2.0 (Rajpurkar et al., 2018) because it is a simple and accessible starting point, *i.e,* a widely used dataset and trained models are open-sourced. UnifiedQA has been trained on other datasets with other formats in addition to SQuAD.

5 Results

We present in this section the results of the different stages of the pipeline when adding components or using different training strategies.

[1] https://github.com/deepset-ai/haystack

[2] https://github.com/microsoft/MSMARCO-Passage-Ranking

[3] Articles in QASPER have a number of paragraphs ranging from ≈ 20 to a maximum of ≈ 230

[4] For readers with 512 tokens limit, one passage exceeded the maximum length so we truncated the input.

		Evidence Span (F_1)				Top-k retrieval accuracy (%)			
LED		32.28				-			
Retriever ↓	Ranker ↓	k = 1	k = 3	k = 5	k = 10	k = 1	k = 3	k = 5	k = 10
DPR	w/o	37.68	54.73	66.68	79.38	23.23	40.69	55.57	71.86
	ELECTRA	52.63	72.07	80.28	89.17	39.08	62.63	73.45	85.60
	MiniLM	**54.65**	**74.05**	**81.76**	**90.91**	**41.54**	**65.31**	**75.48**	**87.97**

Table 1: Evidence F_1 and top-k retrieval accuracy on extractive questions in QASPER test.

5.1 Evidence retrieval

We show in Table 1 the results of the evidence retrieval stage with and without the use of a re-ranker for $k \in \{1, 3, 5, 10\}$ where k is the number of retrieved paragraphs. For $k > 1$, evidence-span (F_1) refers to the maximum overlap found between the gold evidence and the k retrieved paragraphs, whereas top-k retrieval accuracy (%) considers the case where an exact match is found within the top-k retrieved elements. We chose to report this metric because it is more informative to the end-user.

The retriever adequately improves with greater values of k, which is expected since the more it retrieves the more chances of finding a relevant paragraph. However, the use of the re-ranker considerably enhances the evidence retrieval step, with an average gain of $13.92 F_1$ points with ELECTRA, and $15.73 F_1$ points with MiniLM for the different values of k. In terms of retrieval accuracy, re-ranking adds on average 17.35% accuracy with ELECTRA and 19.74% with MiniLM. If we want to avoid overloading the end-user with irrelevant/incomplete evidence, using a ranker with a smaller k can be a very good option.

5.2 Answer identification

We select the best performing retrieval pipeline, i.e, DPR and MiniLM, and test different readers for end-to-end answer selection. We report the results in Table 2: for pipelines where $k > 1$, the reader produces an answer a_i for each retrieved (ranked) paragraph p_i. The results show the maximum overlap between $\{a_i\}_{i \leq k}$ and gold answers[5].

In both zero-shot and fine-tuned settings, all models surpass the LED baseline when returning $k \geq 3$ with ranking (note that LED does not return multiple candidates). When seeing QASPER for the first time, deBERTa outperforms the rest of the models, widening the gap with greater values of k. It is interesting to see that RoBERTa, UnifiedQA, Longformer and SciBERT have very close scores to each other.

Further, finetuning on QASPER does not preserve the performance ranking of models: UnifiedQA outperforms $\forall k \in \{1, 3, 5, 10\}$ all other models, both with and without ranking. This is to be expected with such generalization abilities. Unsurprisingly, models do not all benefit the same from re-ranking and fine-tuning as discussed in Issue 2. We present hereafter the differences in end-to-end performance gain for each model.

Effect of re-ranking

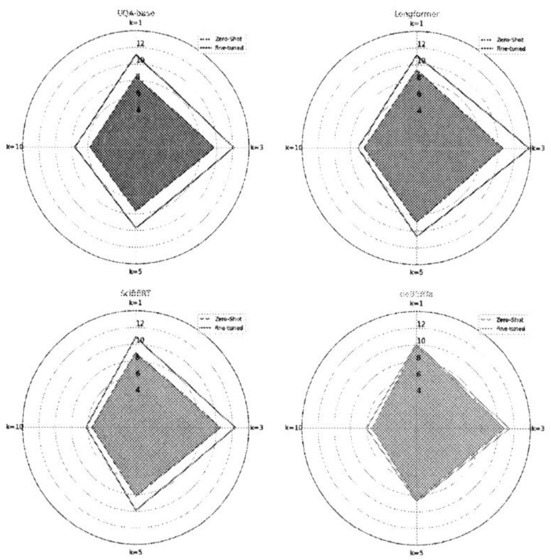

Figure 3: Gain in Answer-Span (F_1) when reranking

Figure 3 shows how much performance UnifiedQA, Longformer, SciBERT and deBERTa gain from re-ranking. The cross-encoder pre-reading helps improve answer identification in all scenarios: $\forall k \in \{1, 3, 5, 10\}$, with and without fine-tuning. The most significant gains are observed for $k = 1$ (a model average of $9.2 F_1$(*zero-shot*) and $10.73 F_1$(*fine-tuned*)) and $k = 3$ ($10.45 F_1$ and $12.33 F_1$ respectively). This is a sign of the ranker

[5]In QASPER, many questions have multiple annotators and therefore many answers. In v0.3, the answers have the same nature, *i.e,* all extractive in our case.

	Answer-span (F_1) end-to-end							
LED	32.0 (29.97*)							
DocHopper	36.4$^{\diamond}$							
	k = 1		k = 3		k = 5		k = 10	
	R	R-2	R	R-2	R	R-2	R	R-2
RoBERTa-base	13.01	22.08	25.05	35.75	32.28	40.52	40.10	45.82
UnifiedQA-base	13.58	22.03	25.31	35.02	32.47	40.09	40.61	46.35
Longformer	11.96	21.49	24.59	35.12	31.30	40.20	39.36	45.73
SciBERT	13.23	22.24	25.24	35.74	32.21	40.49	40.89	46.33
deBERTa	12.87	*22.79*	25.70	**36.53**	33.57	**42.15**	42.76	**48.15**
RoBERTa-base$_{ft}$	15.57	26.00	28.42	40.37	36.58	45.62	45.59	51.52
UnifiedQA-base$_{ft}$	16.41	*27.54*	30.30	**42.42**	38.14	**47.84**	47.47	**55.08**
Longformer$_{ft}$	15.66	26.80	28.32	42.13	36.58	47.22	45.60	52.70
SciBERT$_{ft}$	15.80	26.62	28.79	41.13	36.71	46.60	46.42	52.62
deBERTa$_{ft}$	16.34	26.45	30.01	41.42	38.14	46.87	47.12	53.19

Table 2: Answer-span predictions on extractive questions in QASPER test using DPR and MiniLM for retrieval. ft stands for further fine-tuning on QASPER. (* reported in Dasigi et al. (2021), $^{\diamond}$ reported in Sun et al. (2021))

propelling better context at the top. For all values of k, Longformer benefits most from re-ranking.

Effect of fine-tuning

Similarly, Figure 4 shows the gain in performance that the two pipelines benefit from when fine-tuning readers on QASPER. In all scenarios, fine-tuning enhances performance, with UnifiedQA having the largest gains (an average of $4F1$(*without-ranking*) and $7.35F1$(*with-ranking*)). The greater the value of k, the more models benefit from fine-tuning. This is due to the retrieval stage providing more relevant context.

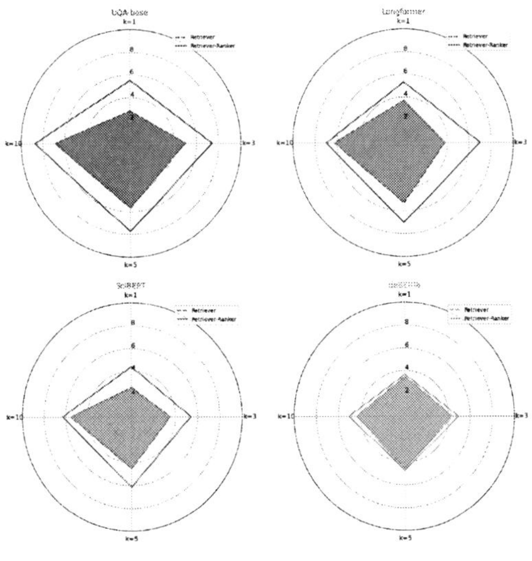

Figure 4: Gain in Answer-Span (F_1) when fine-tuning

6 Discussion

We discuss hereafter the sources of improvements and their alignment with the portability challenges.

6.1 Retrieval stage

Intuitively, we suspect that LED is under-optimized not only due to the size of QASPER but also because it treats evidence selection as a classification task (which is probably good for dealing with multiple evidence). DPR on the other hand has an appropriate training dataset size and the approach is done in a contrastive learning setting that might be better aligned with identifying how close a passage is to a query. If we consider the modeling issue (1) in this case, Natural Questions is one of the benchmarks that have the most similarities with QASPER: different levels of granularity (long and short answers), different types of answers, and no observation bias. With DPR being trained on NQ, this offers an adequate trade-off between task format adequacy and content representativeness.
The remaining issue would be the low semantic similarity faced in Information-Seeking QA grounded in research papers, which we try to circumvent with the use of a re-ranker. The latter very significantly enhances the evidence selection stage. As research papers are themed and specific, and throughout an article, information is redundant with varying degrees of detail, a bi-encoder might not be enough to relevantly score those differences. Additionally, top-k retrieval accuracy is

Paper	Question	Zero-Shot	Fine-Tuned	Gold Answer
1602.03483	Which unsupervised representation-learning objectives do they introduce?	Sequential Denoising Autoencoders	Sequential Denoising Autoencoders (SDAEs) and FastSent, a sentence-level log-linear bag-of-words model	Sequential Denoising Autoencoders (SDAEs) and FastSent
1606.07043	On which corpora do they evaluate on?	20 Newsgroup	20 Newsgroups and the i2b2 2008 Obesity Challenge BIBREF22 data set	20 Newsgroups, i2b2 2008 Obesity Challenge BIBREF22 data set
1602.04341	What was the margin their system outperformed previous ones?	15.6/16.5	The margin between our best-performing ABHCNN-TE and NR is 15.6/16.5 (accuracy/NDCG) on MCTest-150 and 7.3/4.6 on MCTest-500	15.6/16.5 (accuracy/NDCG) on MCTest-150 and 7.3/4.6 on MCTest-500
1707.07212	What are the components of the classifier?	context words, distance between entities	context words, distance between entities, presence of punctuation, dependency paths, and negated keyword	log-linear model, five feature templates: context words, distance between entities, presence of punctuation, dependency paths, and negated keyword

Table 3: Longformer's predictions where the fine-tuned model produces longer spans over the zero-shot prediction.

more informative than span-F_1: for instance with an appropriate retriever and ranker, the user can expect to have 3 questions over 4 where a correct evidence paragraph is placed within 5 suggestions.

6.2 Reading stage

Having models that are fine-tuned with large general-domain datasets before fine-tuning on QASPER is helpful. However, It has to be kept in mind that higher performance is not necessarily a sign of different and thus better answer identification, as the $F1$ metric does not faithfully reflect the actual performance (especially if the difference is about very few points): greater (lesser) non-zero values of $F1$ are not systematic indicators of better (worse) candidate answers (Bulian et al., 2022). The fact that many models have extremely small differences of performance in zero-shot emphasizes the need to look for other preferences than performance when selecting readers before considering investing in their improvement; for instance an ability to return longer answers. To this end, we examined Longformer's predictions in the case $k = 1$, *i.e,* either it receives correct evidence or not, to see how faithful the performance gain is to the improvement of predictions. When investigating the questions where fine-tuning improved the zero-shot prediction, we surprisingly noticed that the gained performance in the pipeline R is due in 36.36% of cases to longer answers containing the string of the zero-shot prediction. Similarly for pipeline R-2, 43.78% of the improved answers are merely longer spans. This might be a sign of completeness, but how necessary is it really compared to the cost of attaining such gains if the answer is visually located in its context? We provide examples of such predictions in Table 3.

6.3 Implications for the portability issues

In real-world settings, a user seeking information in scientific publications might face very frequent topic change. It is well known, both in academia and industry, that QA annotations on scientific papers is extremely scarce: QASPER is the current only benchmark on entire papers. Further, its subset of extractive questions compromises over 1000 expert-annotated questions. As this is very expensive to obtain, users will be tempted to focus on zero-shot settings performance. We discuss hereafter the implications for the portability issues from what we observed on QASPER:

Issue 1: Current benchmarks do not faithfully translate the complexity of tasks humans carry in their quests for innovation and knowledge consumption and there is a tendency to criticize how far real-world data can be from such datasets. Because obtaining high-quality and representative annotations in such environments is way too costly, there can be a plus-value in trading-off content representativeness with task format adequacy. For instance, Natural Questions accounts for a great "similar" task for the retrieval stage.

Issue 2: In some cases, accessible models trained on adequate benchmarks can provide satisfying zero-shot results without incurring the need to invest in having a greater reported F1. To this end, building simple and fast to deploy blocks of a solution does not imply jeopardizing performance since design complexity is not necessarily the groundlaying part of accuracy: LED is outperformed by simpler pipelines offering more transparency of the whole predictive process.

Issue 3: Users should align their application needs with models' characteristics rather than solely focusing on performance metrics and the processes of improving it. Not only enhancing model performance by fine-tuning on domain-specific data might not align well with the cost sensitivity of adopters, but also experts seeking to more efficiently consume scientific content are not to be withdrawn from the information-seeking process the greater the reported performance metric is. For instance, a user visually locating the answer span in a paper accounts for 43% of Longformer's performance improvement with fine-tuning (and the related costs).

6.4 Limitations of this work

We did not experiment on few-shot settings, eventhough such scenarios are anchored in real-world settings. The reason for this is that such scenarios heavily rely on data augmentation techniques; but these approaches fall short of producing the quality we seek in such annotations as we explained in Section 3.2. Therefore we are left with large autoregressive models with stunning few-shot abilities, but those are not yet accessible options either. Another limit is that we restrained our experiments to the extractive questions only. We made this choice because evaluation schemes would be more complex and it would be harder to interpret performance variations (Gehrmann et al., 2022). It is also not mandatory from the industrial point of view at this time to go beyond extractive models, as these already have a plus-value for the workers.

7 Conclusion

Information-seeking QA on scientific content is gaining popularity in a world of knowledge-based economies. In this paper, we identified the hurdles that stand in the way of efficient portability of such systems into industrial environments suffering data scarcity. We revealed through a series of experiments on extractive QA anchored in research papers, that bridging the gap between academic benchmarks along with their models' performance, and concrete user needs that are most often hindered by resource allocation constraints in business can be done with appropriate trade-offs and that caution needs be taken when investing in widespread but costly practices.

Acknowledgements

This work has been funded by the ANRT CIFRE convention N°2019/1314 and ERDYN. We would like to thank the reviewers for their valuable and insightful comments.

References

Iz Beltagy, Kyle Lo, and Arman Cohan. 2019. Scibert: A pretrained language model for scientific text. In *EMNLP*. Association for Computational Linguistics.

Iz Beltagy, Matthew E. Peters, and Arman Cohan. 2020. Longformer: The long-document transformer. *CoRR*, abs/2004.05150.

Jannis Bulian, Christian Buck, Wojciech Gajewski, Benjamin Börschinger, and Tal Schuster. 2022. Tomayto, tomahto. beyond token-level answer equivalence for question answering evaluation. *CoRR*, abs/2202.07654.

Yuyan Chen, Yanghua Xiao, and Bang Liu. 2022. Grow-and-clip: Informative-yet-concise evidence distillation for answer explanation.

Eunsol Choi, He He, Mohit Iyyer, Mark Yatskar, Wentau Yih, Yejin Choi, Percy Liang, and Luke Zettlemoyer. 2018. QuAC: Question answering in context. In *Proceedings of the 2018 Conference on Empirical Methods in Natural Language Processing*, pages 2174–2184, Brussels, Belgium. Association for Computational Linguistics.

François Chollet. 2019. On the measure of intelligence.

Aakanksha Chowdhery, Sharan Narang, Jacob Devlin, Maarten Bosma, Gaurav Mishra, Adam Roberts, Paul Barham, Hyung Won Chung, Charles Sutton, Sebastian Gehrmann, Parker Schuh, Kensen Shi, Sasha Tsvyashchenko, Joshua Maynez, Abhishek Rao, Parker Barnes, Yi Tay, Noam Shazeer, Vinodkumar Prabhakaran, Emily Reif, Nan Du, Ben Hutchinson, Reiner Pope, James Bradbury, Jacob Austin, Michael Isard, Guy Gur-Ari, Pengcheng Yin, Toju Duke, Anselm Levskaya, Sanjay Ghemawat, Sunipa Dev, Henryk Michalewski, Xavier Garcia, Vedant Misra, Kevin Robinson, Liam Fedus, Denny Zhou, Daphne Ippolito, David Luan, Hyeontaek Lim, Barret Zoph, Alexander Spiridonov, Ryan Sepassi, David Dohan, Shivani Agrawal, Mark Omernick, Andrew M. Dai, Thanumalayan Sankaranarayana Pillai, Marie Pellat, Aitor Lewkowycz, Erica Moreira, Rewon Child, Oleksandr Polozov, Katherine Lee, Zongwei Zhou, Xuezhi Wang, Brennan Saeta, Mark Diaz, Orhan Firat, Michele Catasta, Jason Wei, Kathy Meier-Hellstern, Douglas Eck, Jeff Dean, Slav Petrov, and Noah Fiedel. 2022. Palm: Scaling language modeling with pathways.

Kevin Clark, Minh-Thang Luong, Quoc V. Le, and Christopher D. Manning. 2020. ELECTRA: pre-training text encoders as discriminators rather than generators. In *8th International Conference on Learning Representations, ICLR 2020, Addis Ababa, Ethiopia, April 26-30, 2020*. OpenReview.net.

Pradeep Dasigi, Kyle Lo, Iz Beltagy, Arman Cohan, Noah A. Smith, and Matt Gardner. 2021. A dataset of information-seeking questions and answers anchored in research papers. In *Proceedings of the 2021 Conference of the North American Chapter of the Association for Computational Linguistics: Human Language Technologies, NAACL-HLT 2021, Online, June 6-11, 2021*, pages 4599–4610. Association for Computational Linguistics.

Jacob Devlin, Ming-Wei Chang, Kenton Lee, and Kristina Toutanova. 2019. BERT: pre-training of deep bidirectional transformers for language understanding. In *Proceedings of the 2019 Conference of the North American Chapter of the Association for Computational Linguistics: Human Language Technologies, NAACL-HLT 2019, Minneapolis, MN, USA, June 2-7, 2019, Volume 1 (Long and Short Papers)*, pages 4171–4186. Association for Computational Linguistics.

Sebastian Gehrmann, Elizabeth Clark, and Thibault Sellam. 2022. Repairing the cracked foundation: A survey of obstacles in evaluation practices for generated text.

Timothy J. Hazen, Shehzaad Dhuliawala, and Daniel Boies. 2019. Towards domain adaptation from limited data for question answering using deep neural networks.

Pengcheng He, Jianfeng Gao, and Weizhu Chen. 2021. Debertav3: Improving deberta using electra-style pretraining with gradient-disentangled embedding sharing.

Sebastian Hofstätter, Sophia Althammer, Michael Schröder, Mete Sertkan, and Allan Hanbury. 2020. Improving efficient neural ranking models with cross-architecture knowledge distillation.

Vladimir Karpukhin, Barlas Oguz, Sewon Min, Patrick Lewis, Ledell Wu, Sergey Edunov, Danqi Chen, and Wen-tau Yih. 2020. Dense passage retrieval for open-domain question answering. In *Proceedings of the 2020 Conference on Empirical Methods in Natural Language Processing (EMNLP)*, pages 6769–6781, Online. Association for Computational Linguistics.

Daniel Khashabi, Sewon Min, Tushar Khot, Ashish Sabharwal, Oyvind Tafjord, Peter Clark, and Hannaneh Hajishirzi. 2020. UNIFIEDQA: Crossing format boundaries with a single QA system. In *Findings of the Association for Computational Linguistics: EMNLP 2020*, pages 1896–1907, Online. Association for Computational Linguistics.

Tom Kwiatkowski, Jennimaria Palomaki, Olivia Redfield, Michael Collins, Ankur Parikh, Chris Alberti, Danielle Epstein, Illia Polosukhin, Jacob Devlin, Kenton Lee, Kristina Toutanova, Llion Jones, Matthew Kelcey, Ming-Wei Chang, Andrew M. Dai, Jakob Uszkoreit, Quoc Le, and Slav Petrov. 2019. Natural questions: A benchmark for question answering research. *Transactions of the Association for Computational Linguistics*, 7:452–466.

Jimmy Lin, Rodrigo Nogueira, and Andrew Yates. 2020. Pretrained transformers for text ranking: Bert and beyond.

Yinhan Liu, Myle Ott, Naman Goyal, Jingfei Du, Mandar Joshi, Danqi Chen, Omer Levy, Mike Lewis, Luke Zettlemoyer, and Veselin Stoyanov. 2019. Roberta: A robustly optimized BERT pretraining approach. *CoRR*, abs/1907.11692.

Yi Luan, Jacob Eisenstein, Kristina Toutanova, and Michael Collins. 2021. Sparse, dense, and attentional representations for text retrieval. *Transactions of the Association for Computational Linguistics*, 9:329–345.

Man Luo, Kazuma Hashimoto, Semih Yavuz, Zhiwei Liu, Chitta Baral, and Yingbo Zhou. 2022. Choose your QA model wisely: A systematic study of generative and extractive readers for question answering. In *Proceedings of the 1st Workshop on Semiparametric Methods in NLP: Decoupling Logic from Knowledge*, pages 7–22, Dublin, Ireland and Online. Association for Computational Linguistics.

Anh Tuan Luu, Darsh J. Shah, and Regina Barzilay. 2020. Capturing greater context for question generation. In *AAAI*.

Timothy Miller, Egoitz Laparra, and Steven Bethard. 2021. Domain adaptation in practice: Lessons from a real-world information extraction pipeline. In *Proceedings of the Second Workshop on Domain Adaptation for NLP*, pages 105–110, Kyiv, Ukraine. Association for Computational Linguistics.

Pranav Rajpurkar, Robin Jia, and Percy Liang. 2018. Know what you don't know: Unanswerable questions for SQuAD. In *Proceedings of the 56th Annual Meeting of the Association for Computational Linguistics (Volume 2: Short Papers)*, pages 784–789, Melbourne, Australia. Association for Computational Linguistics.

Pranav Rajpurkar, Jian Zhang, Konstantin Lopyrev, and Percy Liang. 2016. SQuAD: 100,000+ questions for machine comprehension of text. In *Proceedings of the 2016 Conference on Empirical Methods in Natural Language Processing*, pages 2383–2392, Austin, Texas. Association for Computational Linguistics.

Sahana Ramnath, Preksha Nema, Deep Sahni, and Mitesh M. Khapra. 2020. Towards interpreting BERT for reading comprehension based QA. In *Proceedings of the 2020 Conference on Empirical Methods in Natural Language Processing (EMNLP)*, pages 3236–3242, Online. Association for Computational Linguistics.

Anna Rogers, Matt Gardner, and Isabelle Augenstein. 2021. Qa dataset explosion: A taxonomy of nlp resources for question answering and reading comprehension.

Kazutoshi Shinoda, Saku Sugawara, and Akiko Aizawa. 2021. Improving the robustness of QA models to challenge sets with variational question-answer pair generation. In *Proceedings of the 59th Annual Meeting of the Association for Computational Linguistics and the 11th International Joint Conference on Natural Language Processing: Student Research Workshop*, pages 197–214, Online. Association for Computational Linguistics.

Haitian Sun, William W. Cohen, and Ruslan Salakhutdinov. 2021. Iterative hierarchical attention for answering complex questions over long documents.

Wenhui Wang, Furu Wei, Li Dong, Hangbo Bao, Nan Yang, and Ming Zhou. 2020. Minilm: Deep self-attention distillation for task-agnostic compression of pre-trained transformers.

Xiang Yue, Ziyu Yao, and Huan Sun. 2022. Synthetic question value estimation for domain adaptation of question answering.

Zhenrui Yue, Bernhard Kratzwald, and Stefan Feuerriegel. 2021. Contrastive domain adaptation for question answering using limited text corpora. In *Proceedings of the 2021 Conference on Empirical Methods in Natural Language Processing (EMNLP)*.

Zhuosheng Zhang, Hai Zhao, and Rui Wang. 2020. Machine reading comprehension: The role of contextualized language models and beyond. *ArXiv*, abs/2005.06249.

Yichu Zhou and Vivek Srikumar. 2021. A closer look at how fine-tuning changes bert.

Fengbin Zhu, Wenqiang Lei, Chao Wang, Jianming Zheng, Soujanya Poria, and Tat-Seng Chua. 2021. Retrieving and reading: A comprehensive survey on open-domain question answering.

Detecting Entities in the Astrophysics Literature: A Comparison of Word-based and Span-based Entity Recognition Methods

Xiang Dai and **Sarvnaz Karimi**
CSIRO Data61
Sydney, NSW, Australia
{dai.dai;sarvnaz.karimi}@csiro.au

Abstract

Information Extraction from scientific literature can be challenging due to the highly specialised nature of such text. We describe our entity recognition methods developed as part of the DEAL (Detecting Entities in the Astrophysics Literature) shared task. The aim of the task is to build a system that can identify Named Entities in a dataset composed by scholarly articles from astrophysics literature. We planned our participation such that it enables us to conduct an empirical comparison between word-based tagging and span-based classification methods. When evaluated on two hidden test sets provided by the organizer, our best-performing submission achieved F_1 scores of 0.8307 (validation phase) and 0.7990 (testing phase).

1 Introduction

A large body of scientific literature is published in different domains, making it difficult for researchers in their respective fields to find information or keep up-to-date. Automatic information extraction, in particular Named Entity Recognition (NER), is one of the core methods from the NLP community to assist researchers. It finds mentions of entities of interest in a given text, such as in medicine (Rybinski et al., 2021), astronomy (Murphy et al., 2006), geology (Consoli et al., 2020), chemistry (Corbett and Boyle, 2018), materials (Friedrich et al., 2020) or even finance (Loukas et al., 2022).

Astrophysics scientific literature has its own unique properties, raising some specific challenges for handling of the text. For example, it contains ambiguous names chosen based on the scientists names responsible for a mission or a facility name. While it is not the first time that NER for astrophysics has been studied (Murphy et al., 2006), it is rather under-studied. DEAL (Detecting Entities in the Astrophysics Literature) shared task introduced as part of the AACL-IJCNLP 2022 conference has challenged the community with the release of an annotated dataset to pave the way for advancing information extraction methods in this field.

We investigate two different NER methods, word-based tagging and span-based classification, on astrophysics data provided by the organisers of the DEAL shared task. In particular, we examine their effectiveness in extracting 31 different types of entities of interest, such as *ComputingFacility* and *Wavelength*, and report our experimental results, which led our team to an overall third ranking among 12 teams.

2 Related Work

Information extraction, and in particular NER, on scientific literature has attracted substantial research (Augenstein et al., 2017; Luan et al., 2018; Jain et al., 2020). NER refers to the task of identifying mentions of different types of entities in free-text. Types of entities of interest depend on the domain of the text; for example disease names in biomedical text (Islamaj Doğan et al., 2014; Dai, 2021) or numbers in finance (Loukas et al., 2022). Methods to recognise such entities should also handle different types of the text, including both formal and informal text , such as social media posts (Karimi et al., 2015; Basaldella et al., 2020).

For astronomy, there are two existing annotated datasets. Hachey et al. (2005) created *The Astronomy Bootstrapping Corpus (ABC)* which is a corpus of 209 annotated article abstracts in English from the radio astronomical papers from the NASA Astrophysics Data System archive. It also includes a further unannotated 778 abstracts used for bootstrapping. Hachey et al. experimented with active learning for NER on a then novel domain of astronomy. Murphy et al. (2006) annotated 200, 000 words of text from astronomy articles published on arXiv. The dataset is manually annotated with approximately 40 entity types of such as galaxy,

Proceedings of the 1st Workshop on Information Extraction from Scientific Publications, pages 78–83
Nov 20, 2022.

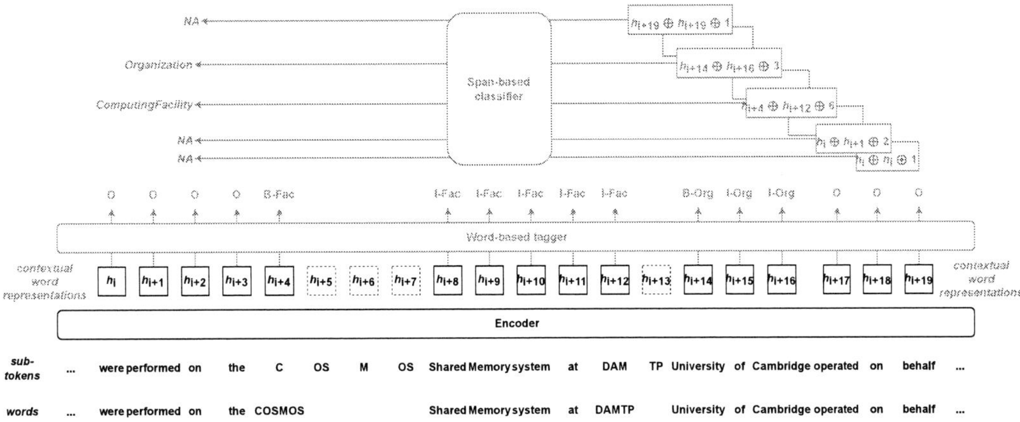

Figure 1: A high-level illustration of word-based and span-based entity recognition methods. These two methods use the same encoder and differ in their classifiers. We use 'Fac' to replace 'ComputingFacility' for brevity purposes.

star and particle. Murphy et al. also propose a maximum entropy-based NER method on this dataset, reporting an F_1 score of approximately 87%.

Grezes et al. (2021) created *astroBERT*, a language model for astronomical text provided by the NASA Astrophysics Data System (ADS). [1] It is pre-trained on 395,499 English documents from ADS, and is benchmarked for NER, showing improvements over BERT (Devlin et al., 2019).

3 Method

We start from splitting a long document into sentences $\mathcal{S}_1\mathcal{S}_2\cdots\mathcal{S}_D$ using a heuristic rule. That is, every full stop is used to mark the end of a sentence if the current sentence consists of more than 10 words. Given a sentence $\mathcal{S}_i$, two neural entity recognition models are employed to recognize all entity mentions. They use the same encoder (i.e., Transformers (Vaswani et al., 2017)) and differ in their classifiers,

A high-level illustration of these two models is shown in Figure 1. We describe the encoder in Section 3.1 and two classifiers—word-based tagger and span-based—in Section 3.2 and Section 3.3, respectively.

3.1 Encoder

Sentence words are further split into sub-tokens which can be directly found in the vocabulary (Sennrich et al., 2016). Token embeddings added with position embeddings are taken as input of a stack of Transformer layers (Vaswani et al., 2017). Transformer layer, which consists of self-attention and feed-forward networks, is designed to let tokens interact with each other and thus builds contextual token representations. In the era of Transformer-based models, model weights (e.g., embeddings, Transformer layers) are usually initialized using publicly available pre-trained models, such as RoBERTa (Liu et al., 2019), in this work.

[1] `https://ui.adsabs.harvard.edu/`

3.2 Word-based Tagger

Once we get the contextual representations from the encoder: a list of vectors $h_0, h_1, \cdots, h_n$, where n is the number of sub-tokens in the sentence. We use the vector corresponding to the first sub-token with each word to represent the word (e.g., h_{i+4} and h_{i+12} in Figure 1). The word-based tagger takes as input a vector representing one word and outputs a tag which is usually composed of a position indicator and an entity type. We use BIO position indicators, where B stands for the beginning of a mention, I for the intermediate of a mention, O for outside a mention. For example, *COSMOS* in Figure 1 is assigned a tag *B-ComputingFacility*, indicates it is a beginning word of an entity name and its entity type is e ComputingFacility.

3.3 Span-based Classifier

We obtain the vector representations for each word in a similar way as described above and then use them to build span representations. The vectors representing two boundary words and the span length—embedded as a dense vector—are concatenated and taken as input of the span-based classifier. Note that we use the number of words within the span as span length. For example, the span length of

Method	Encoder	Development F_1	Development P	Development R	Development MCC	Validation F_1	Validation P	Validation R	Validation MCC	Testing F_1	Testing P	Testing R	Testing MCC
Word-based	base	0.8158	0.8080	0.8238	0.9124	0.8138	0.8047	0.8230	0.9064	0.7910	0.7958	0.7862	0.8921
		(0.0069)	(0.0092)	(0.0053)	(0.0026)	(0.0039)	(0.0059)	(0.0019)	(0.0016)	(0.0038)	(0.0052)	(0.0030)	(0.0018)
	large	0.8342	0.8261	0.8424	0.9167	0.8242	0.8191	**0.8294**	**0.9106**	0.7985	0.8082	**0.7890**	**0.8959**
		(0.0032)	(0.0006)	(0.0065)	(0.0030)	(0.0048)	(0.0052)	(0.0044)	(0.0013)	(0.0040)	(0.0048)	(0.0034)	(0.0016)
Span-based	base	0.8264	0.8302	0.8227	0.9057	0.8223	0.8326	0.8123	0.8907	0.7996	**0.8238**	0.7768	0.8760
		(0.0125)	(0.0123)	(0.0130)	(0.0068)	(0.0027)	(0.0013)	(0.0042)	(0.0032)	(0.0004)	(0.0024)	(0.0014)	(0.0015)
	large	**0.8490**	**0.8499**	**0.8482**	**0.9169**	**0.8267**	**0.8328**	0.8210	0.8999	**0.8034**	0.8229	0.7849	0.8837
		(0.0125)	(0.0050)	(0.0200)	(0.0127)	(0.0019)	(0.0088)	(0.0113)	(0.0042)	(0.0015)	(0.0092)	(0.0101)	(0.0036)
1st		—	—	—	—	0.8364	0.8296	0.8434	0.9129	0.8057	0.8137	0.7979	0.8954
2nd		—	—	—	—	0.8262	0.8145	0.8382	0.9139	0.7993	0.8013	0.7972	0.8978
3rd (ours)		—	—	—	—	0.8307	0.8249	0.8366	0.9138	0.7990	0.8076	0.7906	0.8946

Table 1: A comparison between word-based and span-based entity recognition models. We report mean scores and standard deviations (in brackets), averaged over three repeats. Shared task results, shown in the bottom, are retrieved from the shared task leaderboard at the end of shared task scoring period. Bold indicates highest number among word- and span-based methods.

	Training	Development	Validation	Testing
# Documents	1,753	20	1,366	2,505
# Tokens	573,132	7,454	447,366	794,739
# Mentions	41,159	628	32,916	61,623

Table 2: The descriptive statistics of the DEAL dataset.

'COSMOS Shared Memory system at DAMTP' is 6, and the boundary word representations are h_{i+4} and h_{i+12}, shown in Figure 1. The classifier determines whether a span is a valid entity name and what is its entity type.

4 Dataset and Experimental Setup

The DEAL shared task organisers released one labelled training set ($1,753$ documents) and one labelled development set (20 documents), on which participants can develop their NER systems. Two holdout labelled sets (validation and testing) were used to score submissions, and the labels of these holdout sets were not available to participants until the official scoring period ends.

The dataset has 31 entity types, with entity 'Organization' comprising 16.3% as highest and entity 'TextGarbage', lowest with 0.1%. A descriptive statistics of the dataset is shown in Table 2.

We train our models on the first $1,578$ documents of the training set, and the remaining 175 documents are used for hyper-parameter tuning and best checkpoint selection. We use the Micro-average string match F_1 score to evaluate the effectiveness of the models. The model which is most effective on these 175 documents is finally evaluated on the development, validation, and testing sets. We repeat all experiments three times using different random seeds, and the mean scores and standard deviations are reported.

In addition to the F_1 score, we report precision (P), recall (R) and Matthew's correlation coefficient (MCC) (Matthews, 1975) metrics, calculated using the scripts provided by the shared task organizers.

5 Results and Discussion

We compare word-based and span-based entity recognition models using both RoBERTa-base and RoBERTa-large models. Results in Table 1 show that span-based model outperforms word-based model by 0.011 F_1 when RoBERTa-base is used, while 0.015 F_1 when RoBERTa-large is used. From Table 1, we also observe modest benefit of using RoBERTa-large over RoBERTa-base (0.019 with word-based and 0.023 with span-based).

Task-adaptive pre-training does not guarantee better performance Some studies have shown that pre-trained language models are more effective when pre-training data is similar to downstream task data (Dai et al., 2019). Task-adaptive pre-training (Howard and Ruder, 2018; Gururangan et al., 2020)—continue pre-training on the unlabeled training set for a given task—is a cheap adaptation technique that aims to reduce the disparities between models pre-trained on generic data and domain-specific task data.

We continue pre-training RoBERTa-large on the DEAL training set using masked language modeling. The total number of optimization steps is

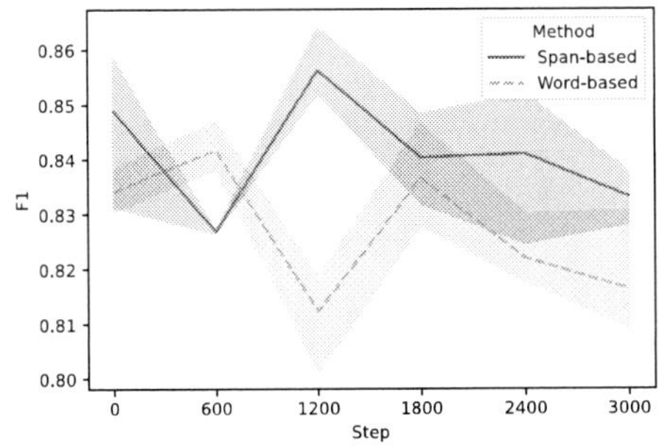

Figure 2: F_1 scores evaluated on the development set when task-adaptive pre-trained checkpoints are used. Step 0 means the vanilla RoBERTa-large is used.

3,000 ($\approx$ 100 epochs), and we save checkpoints every 600 steps. During the task-adaptive pre-training stage, we observe both the training and development losses keep decreasing, however, the resulting task-adaptive pre-trained checkpoints seem to be very unstable and do not guarantee improved effectiveness (Figure 2). Note that Gururangan et al. (2020) reported improved effectiveness via task-adaptive pre-training RoBERTa-base, whereas we use RoBERTa-large. We conjecture the observed instability may be attributed to the optimization difficulties discussed by Mosbach et al. (2021), when continue training large size models on small data.

Errors due to over-segmentation One problem we observe is that many domain-specific terminologies are split into multiple sub-tokens and then taken as input to the encoder. Taking the sentence in Figure 1 as an example, since the term 'COSMOS' is not in the vocabulary associated with the RoBERTa pre-trained models, it is split into four

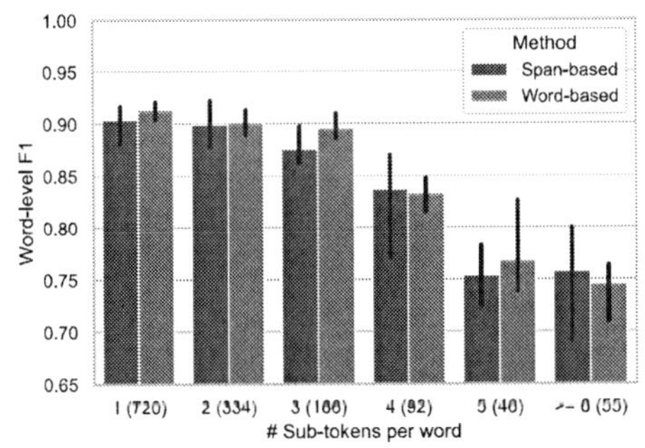

Figure 3: Word-level F_1 scores calculated on words that belong to entity names. Number in brackets are the number of corresponding words.

	Development	Validation	Testing
Orig	0.8490	0.8267	0.8034
Innermost	**0.8533**	0.8293	0.8033
Outermost	0.8491	**0.8298**	**0.8065**

Table 3: The results of applying simple post-processing on outputs from span-based methods. We post-process outputs from span-based model using RoBERTa-large. Bold indicates highest number in the column.

sub-tokens: 'C', 'OS', 'M', and 'OS'.

We calculate the fragmentation ratio—the total number of sub-tokens divided by the total number of words—on the training set of DEAL. The result, 1.380, is much higher than the ones calculated on clinical notes (1.233) and legal documents (1.118) as reported by Dai et al. (2022). This problem becomes more severe when we only consider words that are part of entity names. Less than half of these words (49.8%) can be directly found from the RoBERTa vocabulary, and 25.5% of words are split into three or more sub-tokens.

We measure the impact of over-segmentation by calculating word-level F_1 score on tokens that are part of entity names and grouping words by the number of sub-tokens they are split into. Figure 3 shows that both word-based and span-based methods suffer from over-segmentation, especially when words are split into three or more sub-tokens.

Errors due to nested predictions Span-based methods were originally designed to tackle nested NER (Byrne, 2007; Ringland et al., 2019; Wang et al., 2020), where two entity names may nest each other. For example, the span-based method may predict both 'COSMOS Shared Memory system' and 'COSMOS Shared Memory system at DAMTP' as *ComputingFacility* entities. However, the annotations of DEAL shared task do not allow nested structure. We find that span-based method benefit from post-processing via resolving these nested predictions. Results in Table 3 show that simple post-processing—keeping only entity names that are not contained by any other names (Innermost) or only entity mentions that do not contain any other names (Outermost)—can bring moderate improvements.

6 Conclusions

We reported our experiments on extracting mentions of 31 different types of entities from astrophysics scientific literature. Two different sets of methods based on words and spans were compared. Results show that span-based method using RoBERTa-large pre-trained models outperforms the widely used word-based sequence tagging method.

Potential research directions include building better span representations with the help of external knowledge base; enhancing pre-trained models with domain-specific vocabulary; and, combing the strengths of word-based and span-based models.

Acknowledgements This work is supported by The Commonwealth Scientific and Industrial Research Organisation (CSIRO) Precision Health Future Science Platform (FSP). Experiments were undertaken with the assistance of resources and services from the National Computational Infrastructure (NCI), which is supported by the Australian Government.

References

Isabelle Augenstein, Mrinal Das, Sebastian Riedel, Lakshmi Vikraman, and Andrew McCallum. 2017. SemEval 2017 Task 10: ScienceIE - Extracting Keyphrases and Relations from Scientific Publications. In *SemEval@ACL*.

Marco Basaldella, Fangyu Liu, Ehsan Shareghi, and Nigel Collier. 2020. COMETA: A Corpus for Medical Entity Linking in the Social Media. In *EMNLP*.

Kate Byrne. 2007. Nested named entity recognition in historical archive text. In *ICSC*.

Bernardo Consoli, Joaquim Santos, Diogo Gomes, Fabio Cordeiro, Renata Vieira, and Viviane Moreira. 2020. Embeddings for Named Entity Recognition in Geoscience Portuguese Literature. In *LREC*.

Peter Corbett and John Boyle. 2018. Chemlistem: chemical named entity recognition using recurrent neural networks. *J. Cheminformatics*, 10.

Xiang Dai. 2021. *Recognising Biomedical Names: Challenges and Solutions*. Ph.D. thesis, University of Sydney.

Xiang Dai, Ilias Chalkidis, Sune Darkner, and Desmond Elliott. 2022. Revisiting Transformer-based Models for Long Document Classification. *arXiv*, 2204.06683.

Xiang Dai, Sarvnaz Karimi, Ben Hachey, and Cecile Paris. 2019. Using Similarity Measures to Select Pretraining Data for NER. In *NAACL*.

Jacob Devlin, Ming-Wei Chang, Kenton Lee, and Kristina Toutanova. 2019. BERT: Pre-training of deep bidirectional transformers for language understanding. In *NAACL*.

Annemarie Friedrich, Heike Adel, Federico Tomazic, Johannes Hingerl, Renou Benteau, Anika Maruscyk, and Lukas Lange. 2020. The SOFC-Exp Corpus and Neural Approaches to Information Extraction in the Materials Science Domain. In *ACL*.

Felix Grezes, Sergi Blanco-Cuaresma, Alberto Accomazzi, Michael J Kurtz, Golnaz Shapurian, Edwin Henneken, Carolyn S Grant, Donna M Thompson, Roman Chyla, and Stephen McDonald. 2021. Building astroBERT, a language model for Astronomy Astrophysics. *arXiv*, 2112.00590.

Suchin Gururangan, Ana Marasović, Swabha Swayamdipta, Kyle Lo, Iz Beltagy, Doug Downey, and Noah A Smith. 2020. Don't Stop Pretraining: Adapt Language Models to Domains and Tasks. In *ACL*.

Ben Hachey, Beatrice Alex, and Markus Becker. 2005. Investigating the Effects of Selective Sampling on the Annotation Task. In *CoNLL*.

Jeremy Howard and Sebastian Ruder. 2018. Universal Language Model Fine-tuning for Text Classification. In *ACL*.

Rezarta Islamaj Doğan, Robert Leaman, and Zhiyong Lu. 2014. NCBI disease corpus: A resource for disease name recognition and concept normalization. *JBI*, 47.

Sarthak Jain, Madeleine van Zuylen, Hannaneh Hajishirzi, and Iz Beltagy. 2020. SciREX: A Challenge Dataset for Document-Level Information Extraction. In *ACL*.

Sarvnaz Karimi, Alejandro Metke-Jimenez, Madonna Kemp, and Chen Wang. 2015. CADEC: A corpus of adverse drug event annotations. *JBI*, 55.

Yinhan Liu, Myle Ott, Naman Goyal, Jingfei Du, Mandar Joshi, Danqi Chen, Omer Levy, Mike Lewis, Luke Zettlemoyer, and Veselin Stoyanov. 2019. RoBERTa: A Robustly Optimized BERT Pretraining Approach. *arXiv*, 1907.11692.

Lefteris Loukas, Manos Fergadiotis, Ilias Chalkidis, Eirini Spyropoulou, Prodromos Malakasiotis, Ion Androutsopoulos, and Georgios Paliouras. 2022. FiNER: Financial Numeric Entity Recognition for XBRL Tagging. In *ACL*.

Yi Luan, Luheng He, Mari Ostendorf, and Hannaneh Hajishirzi. 2018. Multi-Task Identification of Entities, Relations, and Coreference for Scientific Knowledge Graph Construction. In *EMNLP*.

Brian W Matthews. 1975. Comparison of the predicted and observed secondary structure of T4 phage lysozyme. *BBA*, 405.

Marius Mosbach, Maksym Andriushchenko, and Dietrich Klakow. 2021. On the Stability of Fine-tuning BERT: Misconceptions, Explanations, and Strong Baselines. In *ICLR*.

Tara Murphy, Tara McIntosh, and James R. Curran. 2006. Named Entity Recognition for Astronomy Literature. In *ALTA*.

Nicky Ringland, Xiang Dai, Ben Hachey, Sarvnaz Karimi, Cecile Paris, and James R Curran. 2019. NNE: A Dataset for Nested Named Entity Recognition in English Newswire. In *ACL*.

Maciej Rybinski, Xiang Dai, Sonit Singh, Sarvnaz Karimi, and Anthony Nguyen. 2021. Extracting Family History Information From Electronic Health Records: Natural Language Processing Analysis. *JMIR Med Inform*, 9.

Rico Sennrich, Barry Haddow, and Alexandra Birch. 2016. Neural Machine Translation of Rare Words with Subword Units. In *ACL*.

Ashish Vaswani, Noam Shazeer, Niki Parmar, Jakob Uszkoreit, Llion Jones, Aidan N Gomez, Łukasz Kaiser, and Illia Polosukhin. 2017. Attention is all you need. In *NeurIPS*.

Jue Wang, Lidan Shou, Ke Chen, and Gang Chen. 2020. Pyramid: A Layered Model for Nested Named Entity Recognition. In *ACL*.

Domain Specific Augmentations as Low Cost Teachers for Large Students

Po-Wei Huang
National University of Singapore
huangpowei@comp.nus.edu.sg

Abstract

Current neural network solutions in scientific document processing employ models pretrained on domain-specific corpi, which are usually limited in model size, as pretraining can be costly and limited by training resources. We introduce a framework that uses data augmentation from such domain-specific pretrained models to transfer domain-specific knowledge to larger general pretrained models and improve performance on downstream tasks. Our method improves the performance of Named Entity Recognition in the astrophysical domain by more than 20% compared to domain-specific pretrained models finetuned to the target dataset.

1 Introduction

Scientific Document Processing (SDP) is an emerging field in Natural Language Processing (NLP) that proves to have more obstacles than everyday text due to the extensive scientific jargon and long text spans. Recent work in SDP on transformer architectures (Vaswani et al., 2017) has placed emphasis on constructing pretrained models in scientific corpi, such as BioBERT (Lee et al., 2019), SciBERT (Beltagy et al., 2019), and astroBERT (Grezes et al., 2021). However, such models are usually trained on the base size of its corresponding architectures, limiting the potential inference performances due to the smaller number of trainable parameters compared to the large-size models usually used in state-of-the-art (SOTA) performance for benchmarks in everyday text. *Are we able to achieve similar or better results with finetuning models larger in size whilst transferring knowledge from such pretrained scientific models to increase robustness?*

In this paper, we propose a training method inspired by the Unsupervised Data Augmentation (Xie et al., 2020a) and the Noisy Student (Xie et al., 2020b) framework. We first augment the training data with model that is trained on a corpus that is more closely aligned with the context domain of the target dataset. We then train a larger model on both the original training data and the augmented training data, combining the computational availability of the larger model with the domain-specific trained knowledge of the smaller domain-pretrained model.

We describe the shared task DEAL (Grezes et al., 2022) and its dataset in Section 2 and briefly review the previous work we used in Section 3. We detail our model architecture and methodology in Section 4, and go through our experimental setup and results in Section 5. Finally, we go through an in depth discussion of our results in Section 6 and conclude our findings in Section 7.

2 Task Description and Dataset

Named Entity Recognition (NER) refers to the identification and recognition of entities from a string of text. Although this task is well explored in everyday text in benchmarks such as CoNLL-2003 (Tjong Kim Sang and De Meulder, 2003) and WNUT2017 (Derczynski et al., 2017), the focus of scientific text is not prominently showcased in such work. Even in benchmarks that focus on scientific document processing (SDP), the corpi in question often lie in the domain of biology and chemistry, such as the NCBI-Disease (Doğan et al., 2014) and BioCreative V CDR (Li et al., 2016) corpi, with a lack of evaluation and state-of-the-art models in the astrophysics domain.

The shared task DEAL (Detecting Entities in the Astrophysics Literature; Grezes et al. 2022) is a sequence labeling task that aims to increase the accuracy in Named Entity Recognition in the domain of astrophysics. Given the overlapping usage of historical names and acronyms in different types of astrophysical entities, it may be difficult to extract named entities in astrophysics purely by carefully constructed systematic rules. For exam-

Proceedings of the 1st Workshop on Information Extraction from Scientific Publications, pages 84–90
Nov 20, 2022.

ple, `Maxwell` may refer to either the physician James Clerk Maxwell, a crater on the far side of the moon, or a series of equations. DEAL aims not only to discern such entities, but also to discern between such different types of entities.

The training dataset consists of 1,753 samples of text fragments from the text and acknowledgments of astrophysics papers provided by the NASA Astrophysical Data System (NASA ADS; Kurtz et al. 1993). For evaluation purposes, the labeled development dataset consists of 20 samples, while the unlabeled validation and test dataset consists of 1,366 and 2,505 samples, respectively. We evaluate the performances based on the `seqeval` (Nakayama, 2018) F1 score at the entity level and Matthew's correlation coefficient (Matthews, 1975) at the token level in the validation and test dataset.

3 Literature Review

We briefly review some previous work that are utilized in our proposed system.

3.1 Pretrained Transformer Models

With the introduction of BERT (Devlin et al., 2019), the usage of pretraining as a self-supervised technique to optimize model weights in a particular text domain for transformer architectures has been widely used in scientific document processing and other domain-specific language tasks such as biomedical text (Lee et al., 2019) and clinical notes (Alsentzer et al., 2019). We now discuss key transformer models we use in our work.

- RoBERTa (Liu et al., 2019), which is more optimally pretrained on a larger corpus compared to BERT, and has a larger vocabulary.
- SciBERT (Beltagy et al., 2019), which is pretrained on a scientific corpus with a mixture of biology and computer science papers. SciBERT's vocabulary is also constructed separately, consisting of more scientific jargon than BERT, with a token overlap of 42%.
- SpaceTransformers (Berquand et al., 2021), a series of models including SpaceRoBERTa and SpaceSciBERT, which are further trained on astronomical text based on the base model of RoBERTa and the uncased version SciB ERT on its scientific vocabulary, respectively. SpaceTransformers do not construct a new vocabulary and instead reuse the vocabularies constructed in the original models.

3.2 Adapter Architecture

Adapters (Houlsby et al., 2019) are introduced as a parameter-efficient alternative to finetune transformer models (Vaswani et al., 2017) for downstream tasks. Unlike finetuning, which modifies the top layer of the transformer, adapters inject layers of parameters into the architecture itself, training only on these injected parameters while freezing the parameters of the original network. Adapter training consumes much less computational cost when compared to direct finetuning, making it a more cost-efficient architecture to adopt while training large sized models.

3.3 Data Augmentation and Semi-Supervised Methods

Data augmentation is a commonly used technique in semi-supervised training in conjunction with unlabeled data to increase the robustness of the model. Xie et al. (2020a) noted that such augmentations should have both diversity and validity compared to the original data. They proposed using backtranslation (Sennrich et al., 2016; Edunov et al., 2018) as an augmentation method to produces paraphrases of the original text that can be utilized for sequence classification tasks.

In the same paper, the authors introduced a semi-supervised learning technique named Unsupervised Data Augmentation (UDA; Xie et al. 2020a) which compares unlabeled data with its augmented version by introducing a consistency loss term, reasoning that a robust enough model should yield similar predictions. For sequence labeling tasks, Lowell et al. (2021) proposed to augment the data by randomly masking parts of the test and filling in the masked tokens with BERT (Devlin et al., 2019), similar to a cloze test, as known as the MaskLM task. Furthermore, Lowell et al. (2021) also showed that even without the inclusion of unlabeled data, adding a consistency loss term by comparing training data and its augmented version can also increase the robustness of the inference model.

Another semi-supervised learning framework, the Noisy Student, proposed by (Xie et al., 2020b), utilizes self-training and pseudo-labeling to iteratively train a series of student-teacher models that increase in performance level. A normal teacher model is first trained on labeled images. The teacher model is then used to generate pseudo labels for the unlabeled data. The labeled and now pseudo-labeled data would then be used to train an equal-or-larger student model with noise injected via data augmentation and model dropout. The process can then be iterated using the student model as the new teacher model and training a new student model.

4 Architecture and Methodology

We propose a system that uses data augmentation as a low-cost method of teacher-student training to transfer domain-specific knowledge to a larger adapter-based model.

4.1 Preprocessing

The DEAL training dataset contains samples that far exceed the size of the token number of 512 that transformer models such as BERT (Devlin et al., 2019) and RoBERTa (Liu et al., 2019) are pretrained on. Although transformer architectures for long text such as Big Bird (Zaheer et al., 2020) can be used train the entire text in less than quadratic time, we reason that the recognition of named entities may not require the contextual information of text in sentences in which the named entity itself does not reside. We instead partition the sample text into multiple input cases, separating the text by sentence via regex.

We first identify end-of-sentence characters, namely periods, question marks, and exclamation marks. We then partition the text unless the end-of-sentence character is followed by another punctuation or whitespace followed by punctuation, in which case we partition after the punctuation. Using the `nltk` library (Bird et al., 2009), we avoid tokenizing common abbreviations such as "Mr." and "Dr.", as well as other abbreviations found in the training data and scientific text in general such as "fig.", "tab.", "et al.", etc. Due to capitalization being important in the identification of named entities, we retain capitalization after tokenization.

The training dataset is partitioned into 25596 samples after our preprocessing, with an average of 22.39 words and a standard deviation of 15.64 words. Furthermore, the number of named entities in a sample has an average of 1.6, and a standard deviation of 2.6, with 41159 named entities in the training dataset in total.

4.2 Augmentation

For our data augmentation step, we borrowed the consistency loss term from UDA (Xie et al., 2020a) on a supervised basis and augment our text by

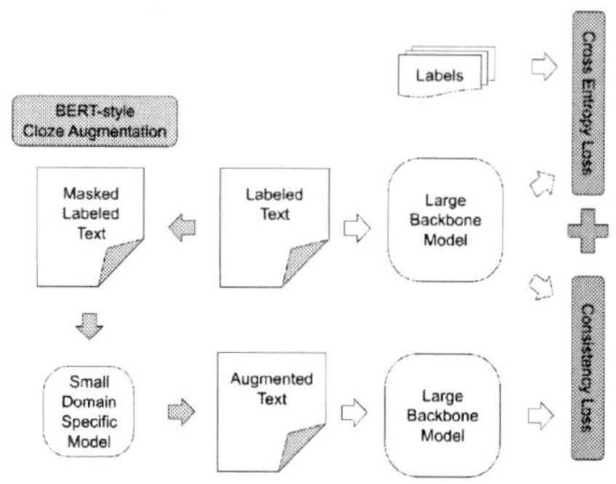

Figure 1: Our Proposed Architecture for Low Cost Domain Specific Teachers

BERT based MaskLM as suggested by Lowell et al. (2021). We take this a step further and view the MaskLM data augmentation technique as a low-cost teacher model that we can use to further train a larger student model while finetuning the training dataset. Replacing the simple BERT for data augmentation domain-specific pretrained models such as SciBERT (Beltagy et al., 2019), we aim to transfer the domain-specific knowledge of such models to the main backbone model. We randomly mask 30% of the total tokens as suggested by Lowell et al. (2021), and, following Devlin et al. (2019), replacing 80% of such tokens with the `[MASK]` token, 10% of such tokens with a random token, and keep 10% unchanged. However, as our task requires the augmented text to have the same amount of words as the original, since our labels are provided on a word-level basis, we revert the tokens to the original if the replaced token causes a reduction or increase of words in the augmented sentence.

4.3 Backbone Model Architecture

Instead of training smaller student models to perform knowledge distillation, we take inspiration from the Noisy Student framework (Xie et al., 2020b) and train a student model larger than the teacher model to act as our backbone model for training. Due to its various SOTA performances in GLUE (Wang et al., 2018), we select DeBERTaV3-large (He et al., 2021a,b). as our backbone model.

As opposed to finetuning the backbone model directly, we use the adapter (Houlsby et al., 2019) version of the model to decrease computational costs, while obtaining similar results to finetuning the full model itself.

Original:	This research made use of NASA's Astrophysics Data System Bibliographic Services; the SIMBAD data base (Wenger et al. 2000) and VizieR catalogue access tool (Ochsenbein, Bauer Marcout 2000), both operated at CDS, Strasbourg, France; and the Jean-Marie Mariotti Center Aspro2 service 1 .
Augmented:	**The project** made use of NASA's Astrophysics Data System Bibliographic **database**; the SIMBAD data base (Wenger et al. 2000) and VizieR **data** access tool (**Sch,ouin, and** Marcout 2000), which operated at **CNR**, Strasbourg, France; and the Jean-Marie Mariotti Center **Asprox** service 1 .

* Bold text indicates augmented text.
† ulined text indicates named entities.

Table 1: Sample Augmentations by CosmicRoBERTa

4.4 Loss Function Engineering

Incorporating the augmented data created from the MaskLM task, we add an additional consistency loss between the original data and the augmented data during training, as shown in Figure 1.

We now write the full loss term that we use for training. Let $\mathcal{X} = \{(x_b, y_b) : b \in 1, 2, \cdots, b\}$ be a batch of B labeled data samples with x_b being the input sample and y_b being the ground-truth label. We denote $\hat{y}(x)$ as the predicted class distribution of sample x made by the model. Further, we also denote $H(q, p)$ the standard cross-entropy loss of predicted distribution p and target distribution q, and $D(q||p)$ as the Kullback–Leibler divergence (Kullback and Leibler, 1951) between distributions p and q. Denoting the augmentation via MaskLM as $\mathcal{A}(\cdot)$, we get the loss term that we use for training:

$$\mathcal{L} = \frac{1}{B}\sum_{i=1}^{B} H(y_b, \hat{y}(x_b)) + D(\hat{y}(\mathcal{A}(x_b))||\hat{y}(x_b)) \tag{1}$$

For validation and testing purposes, we compute the loss term based on the cross entropy loss alone.

5 Experiments

We describe the experimental setup and the results in this section.

5.1 Experimental Setup

We implement our model using PyTorch (Paszke et al., 2019) and Lightning[1], importing pretrained model weights from Huggingface (Vaswani et al., 2017). We set the learning rate of 3×10^{-4} on the AdamW optimizer (Loshchilov and Hutter, 2019). Training was conducted on a single core 12GB NVIDIA K80 kernel.

5.2 Results

We present an abridged comparison of our results and established baselines provided in the DEAL task in Table 2. Our best model on the DEAL *testing dataset* uses Pfeiffer et al. (2020)'s adapter architecture of the DeBERTaV3-large model as the backbone model and uses CosmicRoBERTa[2], a further pretrained version of SpaceRoBERTa (Berquand et al., 2021), as the augmentation teacher model. Our model has a +20 improvement on the F1 score, while having a +8 improvement on the MCC score, indicating an increase in performance both on the token-level and the entity-level recognition of entities.

6 Analysis

We now present a more detailed analysis of the performance of different variants of our model and some considerations between experimental setups.

6.1 Large Parameter Efficient Models

Our first idea to increase performance is simple: Use a larger model to boost performance, as the increased number of hyperparameters to tune and the larger architecture indicates a larger capacity to generalize to the training dataset. In order to train a large sized model on limited training resources to increase accuracy, we adopt the usage of adapter architecture due to the reduction of tunable parameters by two orders without affecting training convergence (Houlsby et al., 2019), which also reduces memory usage as less gradient computations need to be computed and stored. According to the

[1] https://github.com/Lightning-AI/lightning

[2] https://huggingface.co/icelab/cosmicroberta

	F1(entity)	MCC(word)
Random	0.0166	0.1089
BERT (Devlin et al., 2019)	0.4738	0.7405
SciBERT (Beltagy et al., 2019)	0.5595	0.8016
astroBERT (Grezes et al., 2021)	0.5781	0.8104
(*Ours*) DeBERTaV3$_{\text{adapter}}$ (He et al., 2021a,b; Houlsby et al., 2019)		
+ SciBERT (Beltagy et al., 2019)	0.7751	0.8898
+ CosmicRoBERTa (Berquand et al., 2021)	*0.7799*	*0.8928*

Table 2: Evaluation Results on Testing Dataset

	F1(entity)	MCC(word)	Accuracy(entity)
astroBERT	0.5781	0.8104	0.9389
DeBERTaV3$_{\text{adapter}}$ (He et al., 2021a,b; Houlsby et al., 2019)	0.7896	0.8987	0.9667
+ SciBERT$_{\text{cased}}$ (Beltagy et al., 2019)	**0.7988**	**0.9063**	**0.9692**
+ RoBERTa (Liu et al., 2019)	0.7970	0.9057	0.9690
+ CosmicRoBERTa (Berquand et al., 2021)	0.7972	0.9050	0.9687
+ SpaceSciBERT$_{\text{uncased}}$ (Berquand et al., 2021)	0.7859	0.9030	0.9680

Table 3: Augmentation Model Comparison on Validation Dataset

empirical results of Rücklé et al. (2021), the use of adapters speeds up training approximately 1.35 times. With such settings, we are able to construct the baseline model directly by using DeBERTV3-large in an adapter setting, achieving a +21 improvement on the entity-level F1 metric and a +8 improvement on the word-level MCC metric without further augmentations. (See Tab. 3)

6.2 Augmentation as Teacher Models

Using the results of direct finetuning of the DeBERTaV3 model as our baseline, we explore the effects of using different pretrained "teacher models" to augment training data. We present the training results in Table 3, evaluated in the validation dataset.

We find that augmentation via SciBERT seems to provide the best performance on the validation dataset, while augmentation via CosmicRoBERTa provides the best performance on the test dataset.

As we are using the MaskLM task to augment sentences, the model would only fill the masked tokens with tokens in its vocabulary, which would rely on both the vocabulary itself and the model's ability to fill in the correct token. While CosmicRoBERTa is pretrained on an astronomical corpus, the vocabulary itself is based on RoBERTa, thus producing a more valid augmentation, but not diverse enough. On the other hand, SciBERT has a self-constructed vocabulary, thus such an augmentation would produce a more diverse augmentation, or at least an augmentation containing more scientifically oriented text, but not valid enough. On the other hand, while SpaceSciBERT seems to fit the above two criteria of diversity and validity, the model itself is uncased, hence the produced augmented words are uncased, leading to a poor augmentation, the model would underfit on the augmented data and overfit on the training data, leading to poorer performance during inference.

For further work, we expect the usage of astroBERT as an augmentation teacher model to be more beneficial than previous attempts, as the model is both pretrained on astrophysical text, and contains a vocabulary with more jargon, achieving both diversity and validity in augmentation.

7 Conclusion

In this paper, we show that we are able to surpass models pretrained on domain-specific knowledge by utilizing general corpus pretrained adapter models of larger sizes. Furthermore, such a method can by used in conjunction to the aforementioned domain-specific pretrained models via data augmentation to transfer such knowledge to the backbone model. Further work may explore other methods of augmentation to act as teacher models or combining multiple augmentations in training.

References

Emily Alsentzer, John Murphy, William Boag, Wei-Hung Weng, Di Jindi, Tristan Naumann, and Matthew McDermott. 2019. Publicly available clinical BERT embeddings. In Proceedings of the 2nd Clinical Natural Language Processing Workshop, pages 72–78, Minneapolis, Minnesota, USA. Association for Computational Linguistics.

Iz Beltagy, Kyle Lo, and Arman Cohan. 2019. SciBERT: A pretrained language model for scientific text. In Proceedings of the 2019 Conference on Empirical Methods in Natural Language Processing and the 9th International Joint Conference on Natural Language Processing (EMNLP-IJCNLP), pages 3615–3620, Hong Kong, China. Association for Computational Linguistics.

Audrey Berquand, Paul Darm, and Annalisa Riccardi. 2021. SpaceTransformers: Language modeling for space systems. IEEE Access, 9:133111–133122.

Steven Bird, Ewan Klein, and Edward Loper. 2009. Natural language processing with Python: analyzing text with the natural language toolkit. " O'Reilly Media, Inc.".

Leon Derczynski, Eric Nichols, Marieke van Erp, and Nut Limsopatham. 2017. Results of the WNUT2017 shared task on novel and emerging entity recognition. In Proceedings of the 3rd Workshop on Noisy User-generated Text, pages 140–147, Copenhagen, Denmark. Association for Computational Linguistics.

Jacob Devlin, Ming-Wei Chang, Kenton Lee, and Kristina Toutanova. 2019. BERT: Pre-training of deep bidirectional transformers for language understanding. In Proceedings of the 2019 Conference of the North American Chapter of the Association for Computational Linguistics: Human Language Technologies, Volume 1 (Long and Short Papers), pages 4171–4186, Minneapolis, Minnesota. Association for Computational Linguistics.

Rezarta Islamaj Doğan, Robert Leaman, and Zhiyong Lu. 2014. NCBI disease corpus: A resource for disease name recognition and concept normalization. volume 47, pages 1–10.

Sergey Edunov, Myle Ott, Michael Auli, and David Grangier. 2018. Understanding back-translation at scale. In Proceedings of the 2018 Conference on Empirical Methods in Natural Language Processing, pages 489–500, Brussels, Belgium. Association for Computational Linguistics.

Felix Grezes, Thomas Allen, Tirthankar Ghosal, and Sergi Blanco-Cuaresma. 2022. Overview of the first shared task on detecting entities in the astrophysics literature (deal). In Proceedings of the 1st Workshop on Information Extraction from Scientific Publications, Taipei, Taiwan. Association for Computational Linguistics.

Felix Grezes, Sergi Blanco-Cuaresma, Alberto Accomazzi, Michael J. Kurtz, Golnaz Shapurian, Edwin Henneken, Carolyn S. Grant, Donna M. Thompson, Roman Chyla, Stephen McDonald, Timothy W. Hostetler, Matthew R. Templeton, Kelly E. Lockhart, Nemanja Martinovic, Shinyi Chen, Chris Tanner, and Pavlos Protopapas. 2021. Building astroBERT, a language model for astronomy & astrophysics.

Pengcheng He, Jianfeng Gao, and Weizhu Chen. 2021a. DeBERTaV3: Improving DeBERTa using ELECTRA-style pre-training with gradient-disentangled embedding sharing.

Pengcheng He, Xiaodong Liu, Jianfeng Gao, and Weizhu Chen. 2021b. DeBERTa: Decoding-enhanced BERT with disentangled attention. In International Conference on Learning Representations.

Neil Houlsby, Andrei Giurgiu, Stanislaw Jastrzebski, Bruna Morrone, Quentin De Laroussilhe, Andrea Gesmundo, Mona Attariyan, and Sylvain Gelly. 2019. Parameter-efficient transfer learning for NLP. In Proceedings of the 36th International Conference on Machine Learning, volume 97 of Proceedings of Machine Learning Research, pages 2790–2799. PMLR.

S. Kullback and R. A. Leibler. 1951. On Information and Sufficiency. The Annals of Mathematical Statistics, 22(1):79 – 86.

M. J. Kurtz, T. Karakashian, C. S. Grant, G. Eichhorn, S. S. Murray, J. M. Watson, P. G. Ossorio, and J. L. Stoner. 1993. Intelligent Text Retrieval in the NASA Astrophysics Data System. In Astronomical Data Analysis Software and Systems II, volume 52 of Astronomical Society of the Pacific Conference Series, page 132.

Jinhyuk Lee, Wonjin Yoon, Sungdong Kim, Donghyeon Kim, Sunkyu Kim, Chan Ho So, and Jaewoo Kang. 2019. BioBERT: a pre-trained biomedical language representation model for biomedical text mining. Bioinformatics, 36(4):1234–1240.

Jiao Li, Yueping Sun, Robin J. Johnson, Daniela Sciaky, Chih-Hsuan Wei, Robert Leaman, Allan Peter Davis, Carolyn J. Mattingly, Thomas C. Wiegers, and Zhiyong Lu. 2016. BioCreative V CDR task corpus: a resource for chemical disease relation extraction. Database, 2016.

Yinhan Liu, Myle Ott, Naman Goyal, Jingfei Du, Mandar Joshi, Danqi Chen, Omer Levy, Mike Lewis, Luke Zettlemoyer, and Veselin Stoyanov. 2019. RoBERTa: A robustly optimized BERT pretraining approach.

Ilya Loshchilov and Frank Hutter. 2019. Decoupled weight decay regularization. In International Conference on Learning Representations.

David Lowell, Brian Howard, Zachary C. Lipton, and Byron Wallace. 2021. Unsupervised data augmentation with naive augmentation and without unlabeled data. In Proceedings of the 2021 Conference on Empirical Methods in Natural Language Processing, pages 4992–5001, Online and Punta Cana, Dominican Republic. Association for Computational Linguistics.

B.W. Matthews. 1975. Comparison of the predicted and observed secondary structure of t4 phage lysozyme. Biochimica et Biophysica Acta (BBA) - Protein Structure, 405(2):442–451.

Hiroki Nakayama. 2018. seqeval: A python framework for sequence labeling evaluation. Software available from https://github.com/chakki-works/seqeval.

Adam Paszke, Sam Gross, Francisco Massa, Adam Lerer, James Bradbury, Gregory Chanan, Trevor Killeen, Zeming Lin, Natalia Gimelshein, Luca Antiga, Alban Desmaison, Andreas Kopf, Edward Yang, Zachary DeVito, Martin Raison, Alykhan Tejani, Sasank Chilamkurthy, Benoit Steiner, Lu Fang, Junjie Bai, and Soumith Chintala. 2019. Pytorch: An imperative style, high-performance deep learning library. In Advances in Neural Information Processing Systems 32, pages 8024–8035. Curran Associates, Inc.

Jonas Pfeiffer, Andreas Rücklé, Clifton Poth, Aishwarya Kamath, Ivan Vulić, Sebastian Ruder, Kyunghyun Cho, and Iryna Gurevych. 2020. AdapterHub: A framework for adapting transformers. In Proceedings of the 2020 Conference on Empirical Methods in Natural Language Processing: System Demonstrations, pages 46–54, Online. Association for Computational Linguistics.

Andreas Rücklé, Gregor Geigle, Max Glockner, Tilman Beck, Jonas Pfeiffer, Nils Reimers, and Iryna Gurevych. 2021. AdapterDrop: On the efficiency of adapters in transformers. In Proceedings of the 2021 Conference on Empirical Methods in Natural Language Processing, pages 7930–7946, Online and Punta Cana, Dominican Republic. Association for Computational Linguistics.

Rico Sennrich, Barry Haddow, and Alexandra Birch. 2016. Improving neural machine translation models with monolingual data. In Proceedings of the 54th Annual Meeting of the Association for Computational Linguistics (Volume 1: Long Papers), pages 86–96, Berlin, Germany. Association for Computational Linguistics.

Erik F. Tjong Kim Sang and Fien De Meulder. 2003. Introduction to the CoNLL-2003 shared task: Language-independent named entity recognition. In Proceedings of the Seventh Conference on Natural Language Learning at HLT-NAACL 2003, pages 142–147.

Ashish Vaswani, Noam Shazeer, Niki Parmar, Jakob Uszkoreit, Llion Jones, Aidan N Gomez, Ł ukasz Kaiser, and Illia Polosukhin. 2017. Attention is all you need. In Advances in Neural Information Processing Systems, volume 30. Curran Associates, Inc.

Alex Wang, Amanpreet Singh, Julian Michael, Felix Hill, Omer Levy, and Samuel Bowman. 2018. GLUE: A multi-task benchmark and analysis platform for natural language understanding. In Proceedings of the 2018 EMNLP Workshop BlackboxNLP: Analyzing and Interpreting Neural Networks for NLP, pages 353–355, Brussels, Belgium. Association for Computational Linguistics.

Qizhe Xie, Zihang Dai, Eduard Hovy, Thang Luong, and Quoc Le. 2020a. Unsupervised data augmentation for consistency training. In Advances in Neural Information Processing Systems, volume 33, pages 6256–6268. Curran Associates, Inc.

Qizhe Xie, Minh-Thang Luong, Eduard Hovy, and Quoc V. Le. 2020b. Self-training with noisy student improves imagenet classification. In Proceedings of the IEEE/CVF Conference on Computer Vision and Pattern Recognition (CVPR).

Manzil Zaheer, Guru Guruganesh, Kumar Avinava Dubey, Joshua Ainslie, Chris Alberti, Santiago Ontanon, Philip Pham, Anirudh Ravula, Qifan Wang, Li Yang, and Amr Ahmed. 2020. Big bird: Transformers for longer sequences. In Advances in Neural Information Processing Systems, volume 33, pages 17283–17297. Curran Associates, Inc.

Moving beyond word lists: towards abstractive topic labels for human-like topics of scientific documents

Domenic Rosati
scite.ai / Brooklyn, NY

Abstract

Topic models represent groups of documents as a list of words (the topic labels). This work asks whether an alternative approach to topic labeling can be developed that is closer to a natural language description of a topic than a word list. To this end, we present an approach to generating human-like topic labels using abstractive multi-document summarization (MDS). We investigate our approach with an exploratory case study. We model topics in citation sentences in order to understand what further research needs to be done to fully operationalize MDS for topic labeling. Our case study shows that in addition to more human-like topics there are additional advantages to evaluation by using clustering and summarization measures instead of topic model measures. However, we find that there are several developments needed before we can design a well-powered study to evaluate MDS for topic modeling fully. Namely, improving cluster cohesion, improving the factuality and faithfulness of MDS, and increasing the number of documents that might be supported by MDS. We present a number of ideas on how these can be tackled and conclude with some thoughts on how topic modeling can also be used to improve MDS in general.

1 Introduction

Topic modeling, a common approach for extracting themes from scientific documents, is currently facing many challenges: methodological validity (Shadrova, 2021), validity of automated evaluation (Doogan and Buntine, 2021; Hoyle et al., 2021), and utility of classical approaches (Sia et al., 2020; Zhang et al., 2022). We propose an additional challenge: *are lists of words the best we can do for topic labels?*

Topic models have tended to represent a topic as a list of words. Traditional topic labels are supposed to be "a set of terms, when viewed together, enable human recognition of an identifiable category" (Hoyle et al., 2021). However, a set of terms do not align with our intuitive understandings of what a topic is: a common theme or concept explicated as a word, phrase, or natural language description (Shadrova, 2021). In this paper, we present an exploratory case study using multi-document summaries (MDS) as labels for clusters of citations in order to understand current limitations and future work needed for using abstractive topic labels for human-like topics of scientific documents. To our knowledge, it is the first work that proposes to use MDS for topic labeling on top of topic clusters constructed with contextualized embeddings.

In addition to word lists not aligning with natural understanding of what a topic is, Shadrova (2021) has presented an extensive criticism of why traditional topic models based on lexical overlap measures lead to problematic topic models. Namely that they they *fail to understand word sense and capture context*. Recent approaches have relaxed these restrictions when constructing topic clusters (Bianchi et al., 2021; Grootendorst, 2022) by using contextualized word embeddings. However topic labels in those models are still constructed as word lists drawn from documents such as through TF-IDF.

Some work has anticipated this challenge by developing topic representations with phrases (Popa and Rebedea, 2021) and summaries (Basave et al., 2014; Gourru et al., 2018; Wan and Wang, 2016). But those works tend to be extractive, drawing the phrase or summary from a single document in the cluster[1]. In the extractive setting, *there may be no existing and fluent phrase or sentence that is capable of describing all documents in the cluster* or there may be multiple and even conflicting subtopics in the cluster that require a longer abstractive representation for producing a factual summary.

[1] see Alokaili et al. (2020); Popa and Rebedea (2021) for recent abstractive works.

Proceedings of the 1st Workshop on Information Extraction from Scientific Publications, pages 91–99
Nov 20, 2022.

2 Proposed Method

2.1 Topic modeling as clustering and MDS

In order to address the issues presented above, we propose using abstractive MDS as an approach to topic labeling. Topic modeling can be reframed as a set of two tasks: (1) finding meaningful clusters for documents (Sia et al., 2020; Zhang et al., 2022) and (2) performing MDS on those individual clusters to find meaningful topic labels. In this framework, LDA (Blei et al., 2003) uses document-word distributions to construct clusters and word lists drawn from those clusters as a form of MDS. Since we are looking at abstractive MDS that moves beyond word lists, we propose that the *topic representation be a sentence or paragraph* but there is no reason why an abstractive MDS can't be trained to generate phrases or even word lists (see Alokaili et al. (2020)) since word lists may still be appropriate in some situations.

In order to accomplish this, one can first use an approach for document clustering that uses contextualized word embeddings to avoid the issues mentioned above. By separating the clustering step from the representation step, we can use separate measures of cluster coherence to evaluate the quality of document clusters before we proceed to topic representation. We can also use evaluations of resulting topic representations later as an additional step to inspect the quality of our topic clusters.

After obtaining document clusters, MDS models such as (Lu et al., 2020) can be used to produce natural language summaries that synthesize common themes from documents. Recent work on MDS within the scientific and biomedical domain (DeYoung et al., 2021; Lu et al., 2020; Shen et al., 2022) show good results in producing both single sentence (extreme) summaries as well as long form summaries over many scientific documents.

2.2 Evaluation

Topic model evaluation is challenging (see Chang et al. (2009); Hoyle et al. (2021); Doogan and Buntine (2021)). Traditional metrics like coherence (NPMI), perplexity, and diversity scores are studied in the context of topic word lists and validated with correlation to human ratings of the utility or coherence of those topic word lists. Since we suggest developing abstractive topic representations, we want a way to compare various forms of both abstractive and extractive topic representations presented by the model. Since we are treating representation as a summarization task and this task includes measures that work across extractive and abstractive settings, we suggest that we start with standard summarization metrics such as overlap metrics like Rogue (as used in Cui and Hu (2021) or semantic metrics such as BERTScore (Zhang et al., 2022) (as used in Alokaili et al. (2020)).

Model	Source
multi-lexsum-long	Shen et al. (2022)
multi-lexsum-tiny	Shen et al. (2022)
ms2	DeYoung et al. (2021)
multixscience	Lu et al. (2020)
topic lists	Bianchi et al. (2021)

Table 1: Generative models used for abstractive MDS topic representations.

3 Case study: how has a scientific document been cited?

To evaluate our proposed method, we chose topic modeling over scientific documents as a setting. While several methods exist for determining citation intent function (Basuki and Tsuchiya, 2022; Nicholson et al., 2021) and the relationship between two papers (Luu et al., 2021), there is very little work on topic models over citations (for some representative work on "citation summary" see Elkiss et al. (2008); Wang et al. (2021); Zou et al. (2021)). Topic representations of citations are interesting for characterizing trends in how a paper has been cited or helping researchers identify relevant citations to read among potentially thousands of other citations. In this work, we treat topic labels as a "citation intent" label and use the proposed approach to understand the utility of MDS for topic modeling in this setting.

4 Experimental Setup

We apply the method described in section 2 in order to identify clusters of citations and provide labels for those clusters without any supervision. Specifically, we present a case study of what this looks like on a single paper to illustrate the potential of our approach and try to assess future work needed in order to make MDS a good solution for topic labeling in general and citation summarization in particular.

For this study, we used scite.ai (Nicholson et al., 2021) to extract in-text passages which contained citations (citation statements) to the paper (Lau

Model	R-1	BERTScore
multi-lexsum-long	38	85
multi-lexsum-tiny	3	81
ms2	3	81
multixscience	15	80
topic lists	1	76

Table 2: Rouge-1 (R-1) and BERTScore (F1) results for each models topic representations measured against.

et al., 2014), a well known paper that introduces the NPMI metric in topic modeling. This resulted in 183 citation statements which is the corpus we will use for topic modeling.

In order to identify meaningful groups of clusters we use contextualized topic models (CTM) (Bianchi et al., 2021) since this method uses contextualized word embeddings (we used SPECTER for constructing embeddings (Cohan et al., 2020)). We selected CTM since we still get word lists as topic labels which we used for evaluation. In order to select the number of topics hyperparameter, we trained CTM several times steadily increasing the number of topics from 3 to 50 and selected the best model according to coherence (NPMI) resulting in a 10 topic model (see Appendix A for more details) over 183 citation statements.

The models selected for generating abstractive MDS are outlined in Table 1. All MDS models used are based on the longformer architecture (Beltagy et al., 2020) and used beam search (5 beams) with greedy decoding.

5 Results

Table 2 shows the Rogue-1 (R-1) and BERTScore (average F1 across topics) for each of the models selected for generating topic representations using MDS as well as the topic lists generated by CTM. It is important to underscore that R-1 and BERTScore are not validated against human studies for topic representations and this is simply a small case study on what an approach might look like. In spite of this, our results paint an initial picture of how these methods perform, especially when compared to model outputs (see Appendix B for samples). Topic word lists have the worst R-1 and BERTScore. The MDS models do a little bit better with multi-lexsum-long having the best overall score. multixscience also does well with regards to R-1. Since multixscience and multi-lexsum-long are long form summaries, it appears that R-1 is potentially biased towards longer summaries and may not be a good measure across representations, in particular it may be uninformative for evaluating the performance of topic lists. ms2 and multi-lexsum-tiny are smaller and have better BERTScore then multixscience indicating they might provide more semantically similar representations. We are also not sure whether BERTScore suffers from the same bias towards longer or more sentence-like inputs.

We randomly sampled 3 topics to explore their representations. As an example, table 3 shows representations using the multi-lexsum-tiny model (full details are available in Appendix B. In representations for topic 0 (Table 5), we see there is a general agreement across models that the citing documents are discussing measurement. We can see that the topic representations appear to be split between measuring interpretability (multixscience, multi-lexsum-long) and those discussing the correlation between measures (ms2, multi-lexsum-long) or even potentially an additional topic of describing measures used (multi-lexsum-tiny). Conflicting summaries are not surprising given issues in MDS with regards to summarizing diverse and potentially conflicting documents (DeYoung et al., 2021). Table 5 shows a diversity of topic labels that might be appropriate under different scenarios of applying topic models. Labels like the ones in Table 3 might be useful for labels that are easy and fast to read while longer summaries in multixscience and multi-lexsum-long might be useful for users who want to engage deeper.

6 Discussion

In order to ensure downstream topic labels are coherent, document clusters must represent meaningful and well separated clusters. Grootendorst (2022); Sia et al. (2020); Zhang et al. (2022) have shown that traditional clustering methods might provide good candidates for moving beyond topic models like LDA that suffer from lack of contextualized natural language understanding due to their use of word co-occurence statistics for constructing topic clusters. However in order to fully replace traditional methods we would like to see: (1) the demonstration of effective mixed-membership approaches in abstractive topic modeling to recover the ability for documents to belong to multiple topic clusters, (2) the demonstration of cluster evaluation measures that correlate well with how hu-

Topic 0
NPMI and Topic Coherence are measures used to measure the semantic coherence of topics.
Topic 4
Topic model quality and interpretability are two different metrics used to measure the semantic interpretability of a topic.
Topic 2
Evaluation metrics: Log predictive probability (LPP) and topic interpretability

Table 3: Topic representations produced by multi-lexsum-tiny. Compared to word lists they are much more readable and closer to everyday notions of topics.

mans might group documents and possibly (3) the development of fully learnable architectures where clustering might be learned with feedback from topic representation quality.

DeYoung et al. (2021) has shown that MDS struggles with factual consistency. We see an opportunity for topic clustering as a step before performing MDS as a potential method for improving factual consistency since a contradicting source document that would normally be in the document set might be separated out with initial topic clustering. Furthermore, initial topic clustering might provide a way for developing more granular multi-aspect summarization techniques by clustering documents by aspect. Either way, we are weary of the known issues with factuality in MDS (DeYoung et al. (2021)) especially in the scientific domain where factual consistency is critical. To develop our approach along these lines, we suggest continuing to extend evaluation of factuality and faithfulness to the MDS setting (as identified in (DeYoung et al., 2021)).

In order to make this approach work for a wide variety of application and analysis scenarios, controllable summarization (such as Keskar et al. (2019)) should be investigated so that users can control for length of summaries (such as question, phrase, sentence, or paragraph) or style of summary (such as in the style of a paper title, abstract, citation, or literature review). Additional controls such as the ones suggested in Shadrova (2021) like granularity of topic label can also be developed in a controllable summarization framework in such a way as to make topic representations better fit for user's needs.

Finally while methods like longformer (Beltagy et al., 2020) enable the use of transformers with multiple documents as input, more research needs to be done to enable a method like the one we proposed on large sets of documents. In the scientific domain, where we might want to model hundreds or even thousands of full-text articles belonging to a single cluster, the approaches presented would be intractable without further development of long-attention transformer models.

One advantage of our approach is that since we are breaking topic models out into clustering and MDS as separate steps we can rely on a established work for evaluation of document clusters and summaries to assess models performance. While we'd need to validate the application of these metrics in end-to-end topic modeling scenarios, if text clustering and summarization metrics do correlate with human judgements of topic cluster and representation quality then we can avoid using topic modeling metrics which have come into question repeatedly Chang et al. (2009); Hoyle et al. (2021); Doogan and Buntine (2021)). However, we will not know this until we design robust human studies to validate the approach we have proposed above.

7 Conclusion

In this paper, we presented a reframing of topic modeling as document clustering with MDS applied to produce topic representations that might (1) align more intuitively with what humans understand as topics and (2) overcome some of the issues with topic models using bag of word assumptions such as inability to capture context. An initial case study on using this approach for unsupervised discovery of citation intents was explored. We found that while cohesive alternatives to topic representations can be produced using MDS in a variety of styles (short and long summaries), there are still many obstacles that need to be overcome before we can fully evaluate whether this approach could provide a viable alternative to traditional topic modeling and representation. Namely, improving cluster cohesion, improving the factuality and faithfulness of MDS, and increasing the number of documents that might be supported by MDS. While there might be an advantage in utilizing well validated approaches for evaluating clustering and summarization as measures of our approach, future studies will need to validate those with human studies. It is our hope that further work in this area can use our discussion as a roadmap towards what needs to be done if we want to move past word lists as topic representations.

References

Areej Alokaili, Nikolaos Aletras, and Mark Stevenson. 2020. Automatic Generation of Topic Labels. *Proceedings of the 43rd International ACM SIGIR Conference on Research and Development in Information Retrieval.*

Amparo Elizabeth Cano Basave, Yulan He, and Ruifeng Xu. 2014. Automatic Labelling of Topic Models Learned from Twitter by Summarisation. *Proceedings of the 52nd Annual Meeting of the Association for Computational Linguistics (Volume 2: Short Papers).*

Setio Basuki and Masatoshi Tsuchiya. 2022. SDCF: semi-automatically structured dataset of citation functions. *Scientometrics*, 127(8):4569–4608.

Iz Beltagy, Matthew E. Peters, and Arman Cohan. 2020. Longformer: The long-document transformer.

Federico Bianchi, Silvia Terragni, and Dirk Hovy. 2021. Pre-training is a Hot Topic: Contextualized Document Embeddings Improve Topic Coherence. In *Proceedings of the 59th Annual Meeting of the Association for Computational Linguistics and the 11th International Joint Conference on Natural Language Processing (Volume 2: Short Papers)*, pages 759–766, Online. Association for Computational Linguistics.

David M. Blei, Andrew Y. Ng, and Michael I. Jordan. 2003. Latent dirichlet allocation. *The Journal of Machine Learning Research*, 3(null):993–1022.

Jonathan Chang, Sean Gerrish, Chong Wang, Jordan Boyd-graber, and David Blei. 2009. Reading Tea Leaves: How Humans Interpret Topic Models. In *Advances in Neural Information Processing Systems*, volume 22. Curran Associates, Inc.

Arman Cohan, Sergey Feldman, Iz Beltagy, Doug Downey, and Daniel Weld. 2020. SPECTER: Document-level representation learning using citation-informed transformers. In *Proceedings of the 58th Annual Meeting of the Association for Computational Linguistics*, pages 2270–2282, Online. Association for Computational Linguistics.

Peng Cui and Le Hu. 2021. Topic-Guided Abstractive Multi-Document Summarization. *Findings of the Association for Computational Linguistics: EMNLP 2021.*

Jay DeYoung, Iz Beltagy, Madeleine van Zuylen, Bailey Kuehl, and Lucy Wang. 2021. MS^2: Multi-Document Summarization of Medical Studies. In *Proceedings of the 2021 Conference on Empirical Methods in Natural Language Processing*, pages 7494–7513, Online and Punta Cana, Dominican Republic. Association for Computational Linguistics.

Caitlin Doogan and Wray Buntine. 2021. Topic Model or Topic Twaddle? Re-evaluating Semantic Interpretability Measures. *Proceedings of the 2021 Conference of the North American Chapter of the Association for Computational Linguistics: Human Langua.*

Aaron Elkiss, Siwei Shen, Anthony Fader, Güneş Erkan, David States, and Dragomir Radev. 2008. Blind men and elephants: What do citation summaries tell us about a research article? *Journal of the American Society for Information Science and Technology*, 59(1):51–62. _eprint: https://onlinelibrary.wiley.com/doi/pdf/10.1002/asi.20707.

Antoine Gourru, Julien Velcin, Mathieu Roche, Christophe Gravier, and Pascal Poncelet. 2018. United we stand: Using multiple strategies for topic labeling. In *NLDB: Natural Language Processing and Information Systems*, volume LNCS, pages 352–363, Paris, France. Issue: 10859.

Maarten Grootendorst. 2022. BERTopic: Neural topic modeling with a class-based TF-IDF procedure. ArXiv:2203.05794 [cs].

Alexander Hoyle, Pranav Goel, Denis Peskov, Andrew Hian-Cheong, Jordan Boyd-Graber, and Philip Resnik. 2021. Is Automated Topic Model Evaluation Broken?: The Incoherence of Coherence. ArXiv:2107.02173 [cs].

Nitish Shirish Keskar, Bryan McCann, Lav R. Varshney, Caiming Xiong, and Richard Socher. 2019. CTRL: A Conditional Transformer Language Model for Controllable Generation.

Jey Han Lau, David Newman, and Timothy Baldwin. 2014. Machine Reading Tea Leaves: Automatically Evaluating Topic Coherence and Topic Model Quality. In *Proceedings of the 14th Conference of the European Chapter of the Association for Computational Linguistics*, pages 530–539, Gothenburg, Sweden. Association for Computational Linguistics.

Yao Lu, Yue Dong, and Laurent Charlin. 2020. Multi-XScience: A Large-scale Dataset for Extreme Multi-document Summarization of Scientific Articles. ArXiv:2010.14235 [cs].

Kelvin Luu, Xinyi Wu, Rik Koncel-Kedziorski, Kyle Lo, Isabel Cachola, and Noah A. Smith. 2021. Explaining Relationships Between Scientific Documents. In *Proceedings of the 59th Annual Meeting of the Association for Computational Linguistics and the 11th International Joint Conference on Natural Language Processing (Volume 1: Long Papers)*, pages 2130–2144, Online. Association for Computational Linguistics.

Josh M. Nicholson, Milo Mordaunt, Patrice Lopez, Ashish Uppala, Domenic Rosati, Neves P. Rodrigues, Peter Grabitz, and Sean C. Rife. 2021. scite: A smart citation index that displays the context of citations and classifies their intent using deep learning. *Quantitative Science Studies*, 2(3):882–898.

Cristian Popa and Traian Rebedea. 2021. BART-TL: Weakly-Supervised Topic Label Generation. In *Proceedings of the 16th Conference of the European Chapter of the Association for Computational Linguistics: Main Volume*, pages 1418–1425, Online. Association for Computational Linguistics.

Anna Shadrova. 2021. Topic models do not model topics: epistemological remarks and steps towards best practices. *Journal of Data Mining &Amp; Digital Humanities*, 2021.

Zejiang Shen, Kyle Lo, Lauren Yu, Nathan Dahlberg, Margo Schlanger, and Doug Downey. 2022. Multi-LexSum: Real-World Summaries of Civil Rights Lawsuits at Multiple Granularities.

Suzanna Sia, Ayush Dalmia, and Sabrina J. Mielke. 2020. Tired of Topic Models? Clusters of Pretrained Word Embeddings Make for Fast and Good Topics too! In *Proceedings of the 2020 Conference on Empirical Methods in Natural Language Processing (EMNLP)*, pages 1728–1736, Online. Association for Computational Linguistics.

Xiaojun Wan and Tianming Wang. 2016. Automatic Labeling of Topic Models Using Text Summaries. *Proceedings of the 54th Annual Meeting of the Association for Computational Linguistics (Volume 1: Long Papers)*.

Mingyang Wang, Dongtian Leng, Jinjin Ren, and Peng Yu. 2021. Generating a Citation Summary Based on Cited Sentences and the Implied Citation Emotions. *IEEE Access*, 9:18042–18051. Conference Name: IEEE Access.

Zihan Zhang, Meng Fang, Ling Chen, and M. Namazi-Rad. 2022. Is Neural Topic Modelling Better than Clustering? An Empirical Study on Clustering with Contextual Embeddings for Topics. *undefined*.

Lixue Zou, Xiwen Liu, Wray Buntine, and Yanli Liu. 2021. Citation context-based topic models: discovering cited and citing topics from full text. *Library Hi Tech*, 39(4):1063–1083. Publisher: Emerald Publishing Limited.

A Topic Model Selection

Table 4 describes the evaluation of all the CTM (Bianchi et al., 2021) models we trained by coherence (NPMI), diversity, and topic number. We trained the model on a dataset of 183 citation statements which are in-text passages from publications citing (Lau et al., 2014) retrieved from scite.ai (Nicholson et al., 2021). This dataset was also used as the reference corpus for evaluating NPMI in this initial case study. We acknowledge that when building robust topic models a standard reference corpus should be used so results can be comparable in future works.

coherence (NPMI)	diversity	topics
-0.25	0.97	10
-0.27	0.97	20
-0.32	0.96	25
-0.32	0.97	15
-0.35	1.00	5
-0.38	1.00	3
-0.38	0.97	50

Table 4: Selecting CTM topic model by evaluating CTM coherence (NPMI) and diversity on different topic numbers parameters.

B Topic Representations

Three randomly sampled topics are presented here so readers can inspect the quality of the topic labels as well as the original topic labels produced by CTM.

Model: topic lists
measure perplexity npmi probability paper correlation high log_p ranking correspond
Model: ms2
In conclusion, NPMI has a positive correlation with the human evaluation of topic coherence.
Model: multixscience
NPMI has been shown to correlate better with human evaluation of topic coherence than PMI cite cite cite. The NPMI measure was first introduced by Lau et. al cite and has been used extensively in the literature since cite. It is used to evaluate the coherence of the top @math words of a topic and to measure the difficulty of associating an individual topic with a single semantic concept, and consequently, evaluating topic models by their interpretability. It has also been used as a measure of the performance of automatic topic evaluation methods, and has shown to be more correlated with human performance than other traditional topic measures such as perplexity cite, co-occurrence cite cite, and held-out likelihood cite. In this paper, we focus on NPM I since it has been found to have a higher correlation with the human evaluation than other topic measures, such as PMI, and will be used as the evaluation measure in this paper. We refer the reader to cite cite for more details.
Model: multi-lexsum-tiny
NPMI and Topic Coherence are measures used to measure the semantic coherence of topics.
Model: multi-lexsum-long
For simplicity, we will refer to this measure as NPMI since it has been shown to have a higher correlation with the human evaluation of topic coherence than PMI (Lau et al, 2014). For more on this topic, see our related article. Introduction to Topic Coherence. In the literature, human-annotated topic models are usually measured using the Coherence and Normalized Pointwise Mutual Information (NPMI), which consider the probability that both terms in a particular term pair, where frequent terms will be downweighted with respect to those that occur less frequently, such as education from this example. However, in this paper, the authors adapted it to measure the difficulty of associating an individual topic with a single semantic concept, and consequently, evaluating topic models by their interpretability. The authors of this paper also used the predictive Probability and Predictive Probability to see the performance of the learning methods. The results of this study were shown to be significantly improved compared with the counterparts without PPMI, especially in terms of perplexity and topic-coherence and with low proportion of the training words. The performance measure was estimated using 2 measures to evaluate the methods: Log predictive probability (LPP) which considers the generalization of a model and Normalization pointwise mutual information (NPI) which evaluates the coherence in the most significant words (top words) of a topic. The coherence score was estimated through the point-wars mutual information. The Coherence Score was calculated using the standard linear predictive probability method and was estimated to correlate well with human judging.

Table 5: Outputs for topic #0

Model: topic lists
automate measure mutual correlate röderal coherence draw recent pointwise topic
Model: ms2
The meta- analysis showed that topic coherence was positively correlated with the interpretability of the topic models. In contrast, the meta-analyses did not find a significant association between topic co-occurrence and interpretability.
Model: multixscience
Topic coherence is a measure of the interpretability of a topic model. It is based on the coherence of the words assigned to a topic and has been studied extensively in the context of topic modeling. Various measures have been proposed to measure topic coherence, such as the pointwise mutual information (PMI) between the topic words and the co-occurrence frequency of these words in the reference corpus, as well as the number of topics in the model. The PMI-based methods have been widely used in the evaluation of topic models (see for example cite cite and the references therein). However, these methods do not take into account the internal representation of the topic models. To the best of our knowledge, there is no prior work that evaluates the topic interpretability by measuring the PMI. However, there has been a large body of work on evaluating topic models by measuring their interpretability, including methods based on model perplexity, coherence, predictiveness cite, NPMI, topic diversity, and distributional semantics
Model: multi-lexsum-tiny
Topic model quality and interpretability are two different metrics used to measure the semantic interpretability of a topic.
Model: multi-lexsum-long
More specifically, Chang et al showed that models that fare better in predictive perplexity often have less interpretable topics, suggesting that evaluation should consider the internal representation of topic models and aim to quantify their interpretability. The idea soon gave rise to a new family of methods (Newman et al, 2010). Auto-Auto-NPMI that evaluate the semantic interpretability by measuring the number of chosen topics. These methods assume that topic coherence correlates with the coherence of the words assigned to that topic and thus quantify topic model quality. The resulting output does not explicitly provide an interpretation to human users, but remains a list of words with associated topic probabilities, which humans must interpret (as rated by human annotators) despite the observation that evaluation methods such as perplexity are often not correlated with human judgements of topic quality. According to the most recent work in topic design evaluation, indirect approach with word intrusion, and direct approach with observed coherence are two major approaches to measure the human interpretability in ML algorithms. The direct approach is to choose the model with the lowest perplexity on unseen data, which may generate topics that are hardly interpretable, and the direct approach uses the automated evaluation measure OC-Auto NPMI in Grieser et al. that evaluates the co-occurrence frequencies of terms within a reference corpus. Both methods have been developed to provide empirical evidence for the number chosen topics, because they are based on topic diversity; it is the percentage of unique words in the top 25 words of all topics, without mention of obstruction 5/10/20 topic words. The second method is to use coherence, which is to compute topic diversity by measuring topic diversity. The third method uses coherence to offer empirical evidence.

Table 6: Outputs for topic #4

Model: topic lists
compute word mutual coherence draw interpretability similarity assess pointwise human
Model: ms2
Meta-analyses of topic coherence showed that the coherence of topics was in line with human evaluation of the interpretability of the topics.
Model: multixscience
Topic coherence is a quantitative measure of the interpretability of individual topics. It is the average pointwise mutual information of two words drawn randomly from the same document cite. The coherence between top words within a topic is estimated using the PMI between topic words cite cite cite. Various formulations have been proposed to compute topic coherence, including those based on the NPMI cite cite, PMI and its variations cite, the Normalised PMI cite, and the Point-wise Mutual Information (PMI) cite. Topic coherence scores judged by human annotators cite cite are used as a measure of topic interpretability. The most popular evaluation metrics are LPP cite, which measures the generalization of a topic model on unseen data, and NPMI cite, that measures the coherence of the topics. However, LPP is not the best measure for evaluating topic coherency.
Model: multi-lexsum-tiny
Evaluation metrics: Log predictive probability (LPP) and topic interpretability
Model: multi-lexsum-long
Evaluation metrics: Log predictive probability (LPP) and Normalized pointwise mutual information (NPMI) are used. While LPP measures the generalization of a model on unseen data, NPMI examines the coherence and interpretability of the learned topics. For each topic t, Experiments show topic coherence (TC), which is in line with human evaluation of topic interpretability, and Experiments ShowTopic Coherence Experiments (TC) computed with the Coherence between a topic's most representative words (e.g., top 10 words) is inline with human eval of topic interpretationability. As the reference corpus for computing word occurrences, we use the English Wikipedia. As various formulations have been proposed to compute TC, we refer readers to Röder et al. (2015) for more concrete ways to see how the topic models interact with each other. To quantitatively measure the interpretability or the semantic quality of individual topics, we used the observed coherence measure from (Lau et al., 2014), which was adopted from psychology theory and showed better topic interpretation compared with other measures [1, 2]. In addition to the above measures, we looked for the observed relationship between the topic and human interpretation of topic models. The observed correlation between the top N words within a topic and its coherence between the bottom 10 words was inline with the human evaluation in evaluations 2-5 8. It is a preferred method for such tasks (Aletras and Stevenson, 2013;Newman and al, 2010a) as it is unaffected by variability in the range for each dataset.

Table 7: Outputs for topic #2

Astro-mT5: Entity Extraction from Astrophysics Literature using mT5 Language Model

Madhusudan Ghosh *, Payel Santra *, Sk Asif Iqbal, Partha Basuchowdhuri
Indian Association for the Cultivation of Science, Kolkata
{madhusuda.iacs, payel.iacs, skasifiqbal31}@gmail.com,
partha.basuchowdhuri@iacs.res.in

Abstract

Scientific research requires reading and extracting relevant information from existing scientific literature in an effective way. To gain insights over a collection of such scientific documents, extraction of entities and recognizing their types is considered to be one of the important tasks. Numerous studies have been conducted in this area of research. In our study, we introduce a framework for entity recognition and identification of NASA astrophysics dataset, which was published as a part of the DEAL SharedTask. We use a pre-trained multilingual model, based on a natural language processing framework for the given sequence labeling tasks. Experiments show that our model, **Astro-mT5** [1], outperforms the existing baseline in astrophysics related information extraction.

1 Introduction

Extracting information about entities and their relationships from unstructured text is an important area in natural language processing (NLP). Fast evolution of many scientific disciplines has led to a continuous influx of a large number of research papers into the publication repositories (e.g., Arxiv [2], Anthology [3] and Biorxiv [4]). Literature study is an important step in any scientific study. Till now, this has been limited to human effort i.e., the amount of previous literature that an individual is exposed to is limited to human capabilities. This may lead to a few fundamental problems, such as, the researcher's inability to find out relevant previous works and identify suitable baselines for performance comparison. It poses a significant problem due to the limitation of human abilities, unless a framework could be designed to obtain the literature corpus by using machine learning methods. To overcome this problem, Luan et al. (2018); Jain et al. (2020); Hou et al. (2021); Mondal et al. (2021) proposed an end-to-end information extraction (IE) system from AI-based scientific documents for preparing suitable knowledge graph (KG). Recently, fine-tuning of pre-trained language models (PLMs) have shown remarkable performance on IE task such as named entity recognition (NER), and relation extraction (RE) from unstructured text in NLP (Baldini Soares et al., 2019). Self-supervised pre-training allows these PLMs to learn highly accurate linguistic, semantic, and factual information from a significant quantity of unlabeled data (Wang et al., 2022).

While tremendous progress has been made in the field of AI, the area of astrophysics has been rarely explored as an area of application by AI researchers. The current search engine of NASA Astrophysics Data System (ADS) shows poor performance on information retrieval (IR) tasks due to the absence of suitable KG (Grezes et al., 2021). Grezes et al. (2021) have recently developed astroBERT, a language model pre-trained on astrophysics literature, in order to apply it to downstream tasks of NLP in the astrophysics domain.

The first edition of the shared task, named Detecting Entities from Astrophysics Literature (DEAL) took place in 2022, for building a system that is capable of extracting fine-grained entities of different *categories* such as CelestialObjectRegion, CelestialRegion, Instrument (Grezes et al., 2022).

We participated in DEAL SharedTask 2022 and proposed a neural architecture based model to identify the required entities from a collection of astrophysics articles. Our proposed model namely, Entity Extraction from Astrophysics Literature using mT5 Language Model (**Astro-mT5**), seeks to devise a transfer learning strategy by fine-tuning the mT5 (Xue et al., 2020) model. Furthermore, we apply conditional random field (CRF) decoder to

* Equal Contribution to this work

[1] Our source code is available at https://github.com/MLlab4CS/Astro-mT5.git

[2] http://arxiv.org

[3] http://anthology.org

[4] http://www.biorxiv.org

Proceedings of the 1st Workshop on Information Extraction from Scientific Publications, pages 100–104
Nov 20, 2022. ©2022 Association for Computational Linguistics

implement the entity extraction task. Experimental results show that the proposed framework achieves state-of-the-art (SOTA) performance on this task.

2 Related Works

Recently, researchers have explored many directions for applying information extraction from the unstructured text of scientific articles written in english. Adding token-level classifiers or CRFs above the sentence encoders is a popular strategy for NER task (Chiu and Nichols, 2015; Strubell et al., 2017; Ma and Hovy, 2016). Pennington et al. (2014) empirically showed that using pre-trained word embeddings such as GloVe along with CNN-based (Ma and Hovy, 2016) and LSTM-based models (Lample et al., 2016) produced better results on the NER task. Recent releases of transformer based PLMs such as BERT (Devlin et al., 2019), SciBERT (Beltagy et al., 2019), T5 (Raffel et al., 2019), RoBERTa (Liu et al., 2019), BigBIRD (Zaheer et al., 2020), ALBERT (Lan et al., 2019), RemBERT (Chung et al., 2020), and Longformer (Beltagy et al., 2020) showed a significant performance improvement in many downstream tasks in NLP such as NER and RE. Additionally, Akbik et al. (2018) developed an easy-to-use interface namely FLAIR, that allows users to fine-tune any word embedding and any PLMs to produce improved results on the NER task. There has been a recent surge in proposing multilingual pre-trained language models such as mBERT (Devlin et al., 2018), mBART (Liu et al., 2020), XLM-R (Conneau et al., 2019), mT5 for achieving SOTA results in many downstream IE tasks in NLP.

3 System Description

Given a sentence from the astrophysics documents, we follow a sequence labeling approach for the fine-grained entity extraction task. Formally, given a sentence (word sequence) $s = (\mathrm{w}_1, \mathrm{w}_2 ... \mathrm{w}_n)$, the objective is to learn a function f_θ (parameterized by θ) that maps an observed sequence of embedded vectors to a sequence of labels $f_\theta : (\mathbf{w_1}, \ldots, \mathbf{w_n}) \rightarrow (y_1, \ldots, y_n)$, where each $\mathbf{w_i} \in \mathbb{R}^d$ is an embedded vector of the token w_i, and each $y_i \in \{\mathrm{B}, \mathrm{I}, \mathrm{O}\}$ stands for a label, which indicates if it is the beginning, continuation or the end of a text span (in the context of our work - predicted entity category). Given a set of examples of such $\mathcal{D} = \{(s, y)\}$ sequence pairs, the parameters θ of a sequence classification models are learned by op-

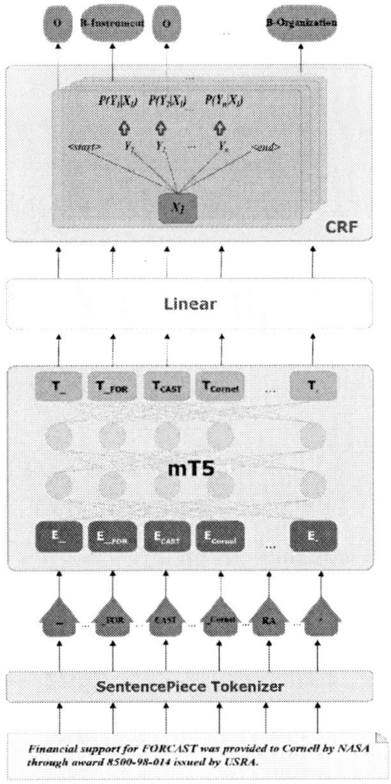

Figure 1: The overall architecture of our proposed model **Astro-mT5**

timizing the cross-entropy loss. In our work we use FLAIR [5], a neural framework, proposed by Akbik et al. (2018). In this framework, we employ **mT5** as a base pre-trained language model, which gets fine-tuned on our downstream entity extraction sequence labeling task. Say, the internal output representation produced at the fine-tuning stage is $\mathbf{x_i} \in \mathbb{R}^{d_1}$. Then, we pass it to the CRF decoder layer and get the probability sequence over the possible sequence labels $\mathbf{y}$ by using the Eqns. 1 and 2.

$$P(\mathbf{y_{0:n}}|\mathbf{x_{0:n}}) \propto \prod_{i=1}^{n} \phi_i(\mathbf{y_{i-1}}, \mathbf{y_i}, \mathbf{x_i}) \quad (1)$$

where,

$$\phi_i(\mathbf{y_{i-1}}, \mathbf{y_i}, \mathbf{x_i}) = exp(\mathbf{W}_{\mathbf{y_{i-1}}, \mathbf{y_i}} \mathbf{x_i} + \mathbf{b}_{\mathbf{y_{i-1}}, \mathbf{y_i}}) \quad (2)$$

Here, W, $\mathbf{b} \in \mathbb{R}^{d_2}$ are the required parameters, which are trained during end-to-end training of our model.

[5]https://github.com/flairNLP/flair

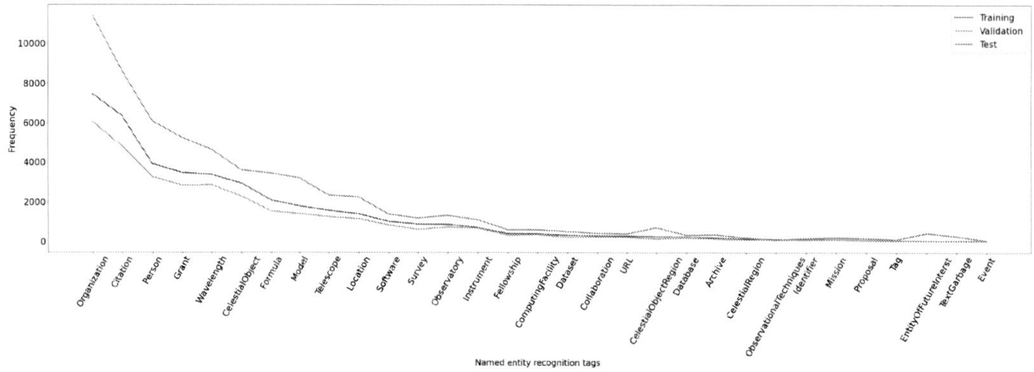

Figure 2: Frequency of each NER tag in the training, testing, and validation dataset.

The overall architecture diagram of our proposed model, **Astro-mT5**, has been shown in Fig. 1.

4 Experimental Setup

4.1 Data Description

Throughout our experiments, we have used the astrophysics dataset released for the DEAL Shared-Task. The dataset mainly consists of the full texts and the acknowledgement sections of a collection of astrophysics articles. The total number of entity categories used for the sequence classification task is 32 and the frequency of the categories (NER tags) has been depicted in Fig. 2. The dataset statistics has been shown in Table 1. A sample snippet of the dataset has been presented in Table 2.

Dataset	# of Samples
Training Data	1753
Validation Data	1366
Test Data	2505

Table 1: DEAL Dataset statistics

DEAL Dataset
The question of whether the Sun^{CelestialObject} acts (magnetically) as other SLS^{EntityofFutureInterest} is difficult to answer. If all such stars are indeed magnetically similar, it implies that stars have a consistent magnetic variability over stretches only 0.01 million years into the past (Wu et al. 2018^{Citation}).

Table 2: A sample snippet of the tagged astrophysics data.

4.2 Implementation Details

We submitted three experimental results in different settings against the released test data. We apply the stratified train-test split[6] strategy with a splitting ratio of 80:10:10 on the released training dataset to train and tune our model accordingly. We fine-tune different transformer based language models and apply separate subtoken pooling strategy at the penultimate layer of the used language model. For our first submission, namely DEAL_1, we use `xlm-roberta-large` [7] language model by applying subtoken pooling operation namely 'first and last' on the internal transformer embeddings. For our second and third submissions, namely DEAL_2 and DEAL_3 (**Astro-mT5**), we fine-tune `mt5-large` [8] language model with different pooling strategies such as 'first' and also 'first and last' on the transformer embeddings. In all the experiments, we utilize the FLAIR framework and train all the neural models for 100 epochs with the batch size of 4 using AdamW (Loshchilov and Hutter, 2019) optimizer with a very small initial learning rate of $5e^{-5}$ and a stopping criterion as mentioned in Conneau et al. (2020). We use Google Colab PRO plus to carry out all the experiments.

Models	F1-Score	MCC
Random	0.0166	0.1089
BERT	0.4738	0.7405
SciBERT	0.5595	0.8016
astroBERT	0.5781	0.8104
DEAL_1	0.8168	0.9053
DEAL_2	0.8261	0.9085
Astro-mT5	**0.8364**	**0.9129**

Table 3: Validation results

[6] https://scikit-learn.org/stable/modules/generated/sklearn.model_selection.train_test_split.html

[7] https://huggingface.co/xlm-roberta-large

[8] https://huggingface.co/google/mt5-large

Models	F1-Score	MCC
DEAL_1	0.7881	0.8874
DEAL_2	0.7977	0.8933
Astro-mT5	**0.8056**	**0.8954**

Table 4: Test results

4.3 Results

In our experiments, we adopt F1-Score and Matthews correlation coefficient (MCC score) as the required evaluation metrics for the given entity extraction task. We compare our results produced on the validation dataset with the previous baselines released by the DEAL SharedTask team. From Table 3, we can see that our model, **Astro-mT5**, outperforms all the baselines in terms of both F1-Score and MCC score on the validation dataset. Table 4[9] shows that our model also achieves SOTA results in terms of F1-Score against the test dataset released by the SharedTask team.

5 Conclusion

This study discusses a transformer-based deep neural architecture to identify named entities from an astrophysics literature dataset provided by the DEAL SharedTask team. Our model, **Astro-mT5**, has achieved F1-score of 80.58% and MCC of 89.54% on the test data, which remarkably outperforms previously reported models and all other competing models submitted in the DEAL SharedTask. Our future work will include more research on fine-grained NER and boundary detection in context of astrophysics to support a wide range of practical applications. We can plan to enhance our framework by introducing fine-grained NER in place of coarse-grained NER to handle a named entity with various types. We can also investigate data-driven factored modeling approaches to handle the class imbalancing problem.

References

Alan Akbik, Duncan Blythe, and Roland Vollgraf. 2018. Contextual string embeddings for sequence labeling. In *Proceedings of the 27th International Conference on Computational Linguistics*, pages 1638–1649, Santa Fe, New Mexico, USA. Association for Computational Linguistics.

Livio Baldini Soares, Nicholas FitzGerald, Jeffrey Ling, and Tom Kwiatkowski. 2019. Matching the blanks: Distributional similarity for relation learning. In *Proceedings of the 57th Annual Meeting of the Association for Computational Linguistics*, pages 2895–2905, Florence, Italy. Association for Computational Linguistics.

Iz Beltagy, Kyle Lo, and Arman Cohan. 2019. SciBERT: A pretrained language model for scientific text. In *Proceedings of the 2019 Conference on Empirical Methods in Natural Language Processing and the 9th International Joint Conference on Natural Language Processing (EMNLP-IJCNLP)*, pages 3615–3620, Hong Kong, China. Association for Computational Linguistics.

Iz Beltagy, Matthew E Peters, and Arman Cohan. 2020. Longformer: The long-document transformer. *arXiv preprint arXiv:2004.05150*.

Jason P. C. Chiu and Eric Nichols. 2015. Named entity recognition with bidirectional lstm-cnns. *CoRR*, abs/1511.08308.

Hyung Won Chung, Thibault Fevry, Henry Tsai, Melvin Johnson, and Sebastian Ruder. 2020. Rethinking embedding coupling in pre-trained language models. *arXiv preprint arXiv:2010.12821*.

Alexis Conneau, Kartikay Khandelwal, Naman Goyal, Vishrav Chaudhary, Guillaume Wenzek, Francisco Guzmán, Edouard Grave, Myle Ott, Luke Zettlemoyer, and Veselin Stoyanov. 2019. Unsupervised cross-lingual representation learning at scale. *arXiv preprint arXiv:1911.02116*.

Alexis Conneau, Kartikay Khandelwal, Naman Goyal, Vishrav Chaudhary, Guillaume Wenzek, Francisco Guzmán, Edouard Grave, Myle Ott, Luke Zettlemoyer, and Veselin Stoyanov. 2020. Unsupervised cross-lingual representation learning at scale. In *Proceedings of the 58th Annual Meeting of the Association for Computational Linguistics*, pages 8440–8451, Online. Association for Computational Linguistics.

Jacob Devlin, Ming-Wei Chang, Kenton Lee, and Kristina Toutanova. 2018. Bert: Pre-training of deep bidirectional transformers for language understanding. *arXiv preprint arXiv:1810.04805*.

Jacob Devlin, Ming-Wei Chang, Kenton Lee, and Kristina Toutanova. 2019. BERT: Pre-training of deep bidirectional transformers for language understanding. In *Proceedings of the 2019 Conference of the North American Chapter of the Association for Computational Linguistics: Human Language Technologies, Volume 1 (Long and Short Papers)*, pages 4171–4186, Minneapolis, Minnesota. Association for Computational Linguistics.

Felix Grezes, Thomas Allen, Tirthankar Ghosal, and Sergi Blanco-Cuaresma. 2022. Overview of the first shared task on detecting entities in the astrophysics literature (deal). In *Proceedings of the 1st Workshop*

[9]It is notable that we cannot compare our results with astroBERT model on the test dataset due to unavailability of requried source code.

on Information Extraction from Scientific Publications, Taipei, Taiwan. Association for Computational Linguistics.

Felix Grezes, Sergi Blanco-Cuaresma, Alberto Accomazzi, Michael J Kurtz, Golnaz Shapurian, Edwin Henneken, Carolyn S Grant, Donna M Thompson, Roman Chyla, Stephen McDonald, et al. 2021. Building astrobert, a language model for astronomy & astrophysics. *arXiv preprint arXiv:2112.00590*.

Yufang Hou, Charles Jochim, Martin Gleize, Francesca Bonin, and Debasis Ganguly. 2021. TDMSci: A specialized corpus for scientific literature entity tagging of tasks datasets and metrics. In *Proceedings of the 16th Conference of the European Chapter of the Association for Computational Linguistics: Main Volume*, pages 707–714, Online. Association for Computational Linguistics.

Sarthak Jain, Madeleine van Zuylen, Hannaneh Hajishirzi, and Iz Beltagy. 2020. SciREX: A challenge dataset for document-level information extraction. In *Proceedings of the 58th Annual Meeting of the Association for Computational Linguistics*, pages 7506–7516, Online. Association for Computational Linguistics.

Guillaume Lample, Miguel Ballesteros, Sandeep Subramanian, Kazuya Kawakami, and Chris Dyer. 2016. Neural architectures for named entity recognition. In *Proceedings of the 2016 Conference of the North American Chapter of the Association for Computational Linguistics: Human Language Technologies*, pages 260–270, San Diego, California. Association for Computational Linguistics.

Zhenzhong Lan, Mingda Chen, Sebastian Goodman, Kevin Gimpel, Piyush Sharma, and Radu Soricut. 2019. Albert: A lite bert for self-supervised learning of language representations. *arXiv preprint arXiv:1909.11942*.

Yinhan Liu, Jiatao Gu, Naman Goyal, Xian Li, Sergey Edunov, Marjan Ghazvininejad, Mike Lewis, and Luke Zettlemoyer. 2020. Multilingual denoising pretraining for neural machine translation. *Transactions of the Association for Computational Linguistics*, 8:726–742.

Yinhan Liu, Myle Ott, Naman Goyal, Jingfei Du, Mandar Joshi, Danqi Chen, Omer Levy, Mike Lewis, Luke Zettlemoyer, and Veselin Stoyanov. 2019. Roberta: A robustly optimized bert pretraining approach. *arXiv preprint arXiv:1907.11692*.

Ilya Loshchilov and Frank Hutter. 2019. Decoupled weight decay regularization. In *International Conference on Learning Representations*.

Yi Luan, Luheng He, Mari Ostendorf, and Hannaneh Hajishirzi. 2018. Multi-task identification of entities, relations, and coreference for scientific knowledge graph construction. In *Proceedings of the 2018 Conference on Empirical Methods in Natural Language Processing*, pages 3219–3232, Brussels, Belgium. Association for Computational Linguistics.

Xuezhe Ma and Eduard Hovy. 2016. End-to-end sequence labeling via bi-directional lstm-cnns-crf. *arXiv preprint arXiv:1603.01354*.

Ishani Mondal, Yufang Hou, and Charles Jochim. 2021. End-to-end construction of NLP knowledge graph. In *Findings of the Association for Computational Linguistics: ACL-IJCNLP 2021*, pages 1885–1895, Online. Association for Computational Linguistics.

Jeffrey Pennington, Richard Socher, and Christopher Manning. 2014. GloVe: Global vectors for word representation. In *Proceedings of the 2014 Conference on Empirical Methods in Natural Language Processing (EMNLP)*, pages 1532–1543, Doha, Qatar. Association for Computational Linguistics.

Colin Raffel, Noam Shazeer, Adam Roberts, Katherine Lee, Sharan Narang, Michael Matena, Yanqi Zhou, Wei Li, and Peter J. Liu. 2019. Exploring the limits of transfer learning with a unified text-to-text transformer. *CoRR*, abs/1910.10683.

Emma Strubell, Patrick Verga, David Belanger, and Andrew McCallum. 2017. Fast and accurate entity recognition with iterated dilated convolutions. In *Proceedings of the 2017 Conference on Empirical Methods in Natural Language Processing*, pages 2670–2680, Copenhagen, Denmark. Association for Computational Linguistics.

Liwen Wang, Rumei Li, Yang Yan, Yuanmeng Yan, Sirui Wang, Wei Wu, and Weiran Xu. 2022. Instructionner: A multi-task instruction-based generative framework for few-shot ner. *arXiv preprint arXiv:2203.03903*.

Linting Xue, Noah Constant, Adam Roberts, Mihir Kale, Rami Al-Rfou, Aditya Siddhant, Aditya Barua, and Colin Raffel. 2020. mt5: A massively multilingual pre-trained text-to-text transformer. *arXiv preprint arXiv:2010.11934*.

Manzil Zaheer, Guru Guruganesh, Kumar Avinava Dubey, Joshua Ainslie, Chris Alberti, Santiago Ontanon, Philip Pham, Anirudh Ravula, Qifan Wang, Li Yang, et al. 2020. Big bird: Transformers for longer sequences. *Advances in Neural Information Processing Systems*, 33:17283–17297.

NLPSharedTasks: A Corpus of Shared Task Overview Papers in Natural Language Processing Domains

Anna Martin[1], **Ted Pedersen**[2], **and Jennifer D'Souza**[3]
[1]University of Minnesota, Minneapolis, MN 55455*
mart5877@umn.edu
[2]University of Minnesota, Duluth, MN 55812
tpederse@d.umn.edu
[3]TIB Leibniz Information Centre for Science and Technology, Hannover, Germany
jennifer.dsouza@dtib.eu

Abstract

As the rate of scientific output continues to grow, it is increasingly important to be able to develop systems to improve interfaces between researchers and scholarly papers. Training models to extract scientific information from the full texts of scholarly documents is important for improving how we structure and access scientific information. However, there are few annotated corpora that provide full paper texts. This paper presents the NLPSharedTasks corpus, a new resource of 254 full text Shared Task Overview papers in NLP domains with annotated task descriptions. We calculated strict and relaxed inter-annotator agreement scores, achieving Cohen's kappa coefficients of 0.44 and 0.95, respectively. Lastly, we performed a sentence classification task over the dataset, in order to generate a neural baseline for future research and to provide an example of how to preprocess unbalanced datasets of full scientific texts. We achieved an F1 score of 0.75 using SciBERT, fine-tuned and tested on a rebalanced version of the dataset.

1 Introduction

Scholarly Document Processing (SDP) research is concerned with developing methods for improving the retrieval and organization of information from academic papers. This interest is partly driven by the rapid growth rate of scientific publications, which Larsen and von Ins (2010) estimate to be between 2.7 and 13.5 percent between 1997 and 2006. Some disciplines are expanding even more rapidly. Dhawan et al. (2020) examined the global output of machine learning research between 2009 and 2018 and estimated a growth rate of roughly 28 percent per year, while Li et al. (2020) suggest an average annual growth rate of 152.9 percent in the deep learning domain between 2013 and 2019.

Because of the rapid expansion of scientific literature, it is beneficial to use natural language processing (NLP) and information extraction (IE) techniques to structure scientific and bibliometric data into machine-actionable forms. One method is to automatically identify scientific and bibliometric entites and relations from scholarly literature and organize them into knowledge graphs, which can be used to improve access to scholarly documents by enhancing Digital Libraries (Ammar et al., 2018, Auer et al., 2020).

One scientific entity type relevant to NLP and Machine Learning domains is TASK. Machine Learning and NLP tasks can be useful to extract, as they are a unit of information relevant to understanding research trends and constructing leaderboards (Hou et al., 2019). We are particularly interested in the utility of augmenting scholarly digital library resources with automatically extracted task descriptions such that a reader could quickly understand the NLP task described in the paper at hand. We find that NLP shared task workshop overview papers are a rich resource for training a model to extract such task descriptions.

Our contribution towards information extraction (IE) from scientific articles is a new gold-standard corpus of task description annotations from Shared Task Overview papers. This corpus provides an interesting IE situation for two reasons. First, the full texts are provided for each paper in the corpus rather than individual sentences or paragraphs. Second, the annotation goal was to extract a single span of text from each paper rather than any number of qualifying phrases. The benefit of this kind of annotation strategy is that it provides test data that is close to the "real world" data that downstream applications might encounter, such as a digital library tool tasked with extracting the task descriptions from NLP papers. This IE scenario is also difficult, since extracting a single span from full paper texts results in an extremely

*The work presented in this paper was performed while the first author was affiliated with the University of Minnesota, Duluth.

Proceedings of the 1st Workshop on Information Extraction from Scientific Publications, pages 105–120
Nov 20, 2022.

unbalanced dataset. For this reason, we describe in detail the data preparation and preprocessing steps we performed for the sentence classification task we ran over the NLPSharedTasks corpus. The original NLPSharedTasks corpus, preprocessed dataset, and experimental code is available at `https://github.com/anmartin94/martin-masters-thesis-2022`.

2 Related Work

Numerous corpora for scientific information extraction have been hand-annotated by experts in computational linguistics and NLP domains. Many of these corpora provide parts of scientific papers, such as paragraphs (Augenstein et al., 2017), abstracts (Gábor et al., 2018, Gábor et al., 2016, QasemiZadeh and Schumann, 2016, Luan et al., 2018), and sentences (Hou et al., 2021).

The SemEval-2021 Task 11 (NLP Contribution Graph) (D'Souza et al., 2021) provided the corpus that serves as the main source of inspiration for our annotation project. The NLPContributionGraph corpus comprises 442 scholarly papers in NLP domains, with 12 different types of information annotated at three levels of granularity (D'Souza and Auer, 2020). It is similar to our work in that full paper texts and sentence-level annotations are provided, but the annotation scheme allowed for multiple spans to be extracted for each entity type, rather than a single sequence from each paper. Additionally, the NLPContributionGraph annotation scheme includes a TASKS information unit, which was applied to 277 triples found across approximately 69 sentences in eight papers.

The differences between the NLPContributionGraph and NLPSharedTask annotation schemes relate to the different intended downstream tasks. The information extracted by D'Souza et al., 2021 is designed to populate a research knowledge graph with a variety of types of scientific information, while the information extracted in NLPSharedTasks is intended to convey to a human reader the task described in the Shared Task Overview paper.

3 Corpus Selection

The resource we drew from was the annual research workshop SemEval and similar initiatives. These venues host shared tasks that approach a wide variety of semantic problems and provide a rich resource for understanding the state of the art in semantic analysis. We assembled our task description corpus by searching the ACL Anthology for shared task description papers, including all SemEval task description papers from the year 2001 to 2021, all CoNLL[1] shared tasks 2000-2020, and selected shared tasks from a variety of other conferences and workshops (see Table 1). The dataset was developed in two stages. The first stage selected only Shared Task Overview papers associated with the SemEval workshop from 2001 to 2020, yielding 165 papers. During the second stage we added 89 papers to the dataset. These papers were found by searching the ACL Anthology for Shared Task Overview papers published at non-SemEval workshops hosted by the venues described in Table 1. Additionally, this second batch of papers contained the newly published set of papers from SemEval 2021. The final dataset contains a total of 254 shared task description papers between the years 2000 and 2021 and encompasses twenty natural language processing research topics that we identified (see Figure 1).

Venue	Frequency
SemEval Workshop	176 (69%)
CoNLL Conference	21 (8%)
ACL Conference	18 (7%)
EMNLP Conference	12 (5%)
NAACL Conference	8 (3%)
EACL Conference	7 (3%)
IJCNLP Conference (2017)	5 (2%)
BioNLP Workshop (2011)	3 (1%)
AACL Conference	2 (<1%)
*SEM Workshop	2 (<1%)
Total	254

Table 1: The conferences and workshops that hosted the Shared Tasks in our corpus and the number of papers from each venue.

4 Annotation Methodology

The aim of this annotation project was to develop a gold standard corpus of shared task overview papers with annotations of shared task descriptions. We define "shared task description" as a span of text containing information on an NLP or computational linguistics task to be performed by participating systems. This information must describe in brief what is to be done to accomplish the task, and may also contain details on the dataset the task is performed over.

[1] `https://www.conll.org/`

Set #	Strict Score	Relaxed Score
Set 1	.3830	.6401
Set 2	.4374	.9488

Table 2: This table presents the inter-annotator agreement scores measured with Cohen's kappa coefficient. Strict scores were calculated by comparing the exact spans of text. The relaxed scores were calculated by including the full sentence(s) containing the span. The difference between rows 2 and 3 is due to guideline revisions. The annotators often chose sequences that overlapped but were not exactly the same, resulting in the difference between columns 2 and 3.

The first annotator extracted a task description sequence[2] from every paper in the corpus, generated a set of guidelines for the second annotator to follow, and created two representative sets of twenty papers each. Intra-annotator agreement was determined using Cohen's kappa coefficient. A strict score and a relaxed score were calculated for each dataset, where the strict score compared the exact sequence spans and the relaxed score counted overlapping annotations as matches. After the first subset was annotated by the second annotator, the guidelines were refined by the first annotator to address ambiguities before releasing the second set to annotator 2.

4.1 Guidelines

The final version of annotation guidelines performs two functions: it defines Task Description and describes various subtypes and task-description scenarios including "full task description", "partial task description", and "multiple subtasks description"; and it provides two sets of rules, one explaining how the task description sequence boundaries should be determined, and another detailing how ambiguous annotation situations might be resolved. See Appendix A.6 for more information on the annotation process.

5 Annotation Results

We calculated the inter-annotator agreement between annotator 1 and annotator 2 using Cohen's kappa coefficient (Cohen, 1960). The strict Cohen's kappa coefficient for the first subset was 0.383, and the relaxed Cohen's kappa coefficient was 0.6401, indicating fair to substantial agreement (Viera et al., 2005). After we made revisions and clarifications to the annotation guidelines, we annotated the second subset, and achieved a strict score of 0.4373 and a relaxed score of 0.9488, indicating moderate to almost perfect agreement. The difference between the strict and relaxed scores indicates that, though the annotators often spans from the same sentence context, mutually choosing equivalent sequences is somewhat difficult. For example, from the following sentence

> The 2020 iteration of our task is similar to CoNLL-SIGMORPHON 2017 (Cotterell et al., 2017) and 2018 (Cotterell et al., 2018) in that participants are required to design a model that learns to generate inflected forms from a lemma and a set of morphosyntactic features that derive the desired target form.
> -*SIGMORPHON 2020 Shared Task 0: Typologically Diverse Morphological Inflection*, Vylomova et al. (2020),

annotator 1 extracted "design a model that learns to generate inflected forms from a lemma and a set of morphosyntactic features that derive the desired target form", and annotator 2 extracted "*participants are required to* design a model that learns to generate inflected forms from a lemma and a set of morphosyntactic features that derive the desired target form".

6 Corpus Statistics

One benefit of annotating shared task overview papers published over a long period of time is that this resource could potentially be used to study NLP research progress and trends. For this reason, we provide some basic statistics on the content of the papers included (see Section 6.1). We also provide data on the extracted task descriptions in Section 6.2, as such information may be useful to others for building task description extraction systems.

6.1 Characteristics of Shared Task Overview Papers

The 254 shared task overview papers collected for this dataset encompass a wide variety of research topics. We identified 20 distinct topics (see Figure 1), and found that the frequency of publications

[2]on occasion, the first annotator extracted two sequences if the texts were extremely similar. Following is such an example: "Given a set of documents and a set of target entities, the task consisted of building a timeline for each entity, by detecting, anchoring in time and ordering the events involving that entity" and "Given a set of documents and a set of target entities, the task consists of building a timeline related to each entity, i.e., detecting, anchoring in time, and ordering the events in which the target entity is involved".

	mean ± std	max	min
word count	29±21.8	126	3
sentences in span	1.17±.48	4	1

Table 3: Mean word count and sentences per task description

included in our corpus increases between the year 2000 and 2021 (see Figure 2). Another interesting characteristic of these shared tasks is that not all tasks are novel; it is fairly common for tasks to be re-run for several years. This allows participants to improve benchmarks by building on previous work, and allows task organizers to add to the complexity of the task. Approximately 65 papers in the corpus describe rerun tasks.

6.2 Task Description Characteristics

One of the most consistent patterns observed is that task descriptions tend to appear under the same limited set of section headers (Figure 3). While they are most commonly found in the abstract, they also frequently appear in introduction sections. Unsurprisingly, sections with titles such as "Task Description" or "Task Overview" often contain task descriptions suitable for our project. Rarely, papers may not contain a good task description until the conclusion or discussion section. Furthermore, there were thirteen papers that did not contain a task description in the body, but had a title that was sufficient. Consequently, the first quadrant of full paper texts contain a higher concentration of task descriptions, as seen in Figure 4. This pattern persists within sections as well; more than half of the task descriptions were found in the first half of the containing section (see Figure 5).

A complicating aspect of this corpus in terms of information extraction and text classification is the varying lengths of task descriptions. This low-homogeneity can make it more difficult to train traditional classifiers, but is important because it provides a more "real-world" environment. The extracted sequences span between 1 and 4 sentences, and contain between 3 and 126 tokens (Table 3).

7 Dataset Preparation

Scholarly papers are often stored as PDFs, which are not very machine-actionable[3]. For this reason the full text for each paper had to be extracted and stored in a different format. We processed paper PDFs into XML encoded files using GROBID (Lopez, 2009), then extracted the text data into plain text files. GROBID is not always completely accurate, so we manually compared each text file with the original PDF. Two papers had to be manually typed because the PDF files could not be processed by GROBID. For the majority of papers with tables, the table output from GROBID had to be manually removed.

To prepare our corpus for a sentence classification task, we randomly divided the 254 papers into a training set of 228 papers and a test set of 26 papers. The resulting training set contains 259 positive samples and 41,493 negative samples, and test set contains 34 positive and 4725 negative samples. This is an extremely unbalanced dataset, where less than 1% (0.63%) of the total sentences are positive samples. The reason for this is the annotation goal was to extract a single candidate per paper. However, extra steps must be taken to change the balance enough so that machine classifiers are able to learn how to identify task descriptions.

7.1 Leveraging Paper Context and Hierarchical Structure

Scholarly papers tend to have a predictable structure. Task description overview papers usually start with an abstract and introduction, which tend to be followed by task description and dataset preparation sections, before describing the system solutions and reporting results. There are patterns within sections as well; for example, sections that contain a task description often contain the sequence near the beginning of the section. For this reason, we added positional data as features to the dataset following the example of (Liu et al., 2021).

We added a section header feature to the dataset by iterating through the plain text files and capturing the header for each section. Each sentence's position was quantified with four values: the sentence index relative to its section; the sentence index relative to the full paper; the quadrant of the sentence's section; and the quadrant of the paper that the sentence is found in.

We ran experiments with and without the header feature and positional features and ultimately found that the additional features did not improve model performance (see Table 6 to compare results).

In addition to extracting positional information

[3]Some journals and archives such as arXiv (https://arxiv.org/) provide LaTeX source code for papers in addition to PDFs.

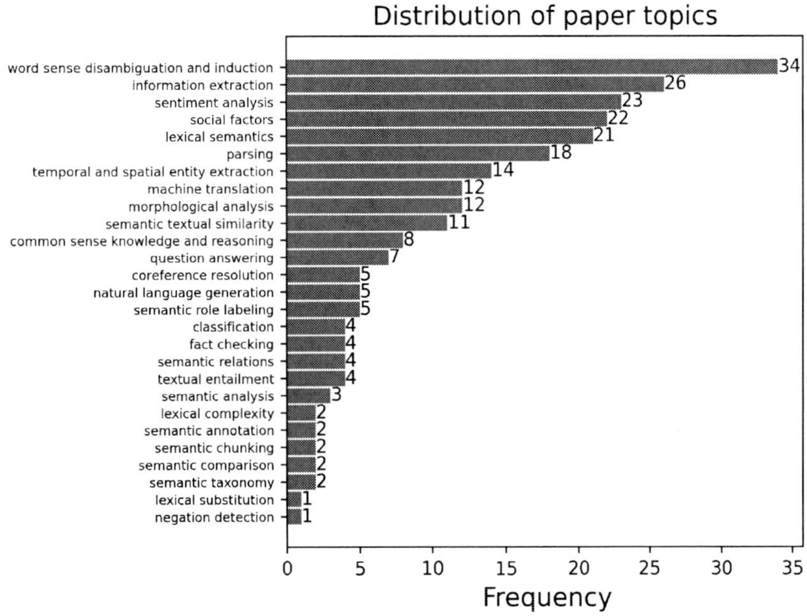

Figure 1: The distribution of paper topics. There were situations where a Shared Task encompassed more than one topic. In this situation, we chose the more specific topic. For example, note that the topic **classification** appears to only contain five papers. There are more classification tasks found in the corpus, but they were assigned other desciptors such as **sentiment analysis** and **social factors**.

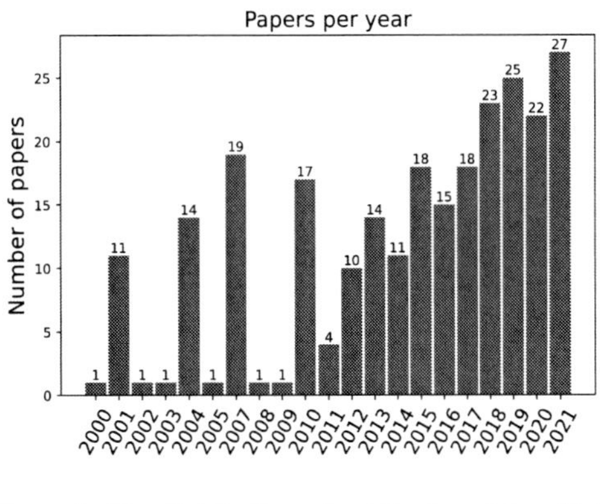

Figure 2: The distribution of publication dates. Note that the years 2000, 2002, 2003, 2005, 2008, and 2009 appear to be outliers. This is because most of the corpus (69.3%) was taken from the SemEval workshops, which were not held in those years.

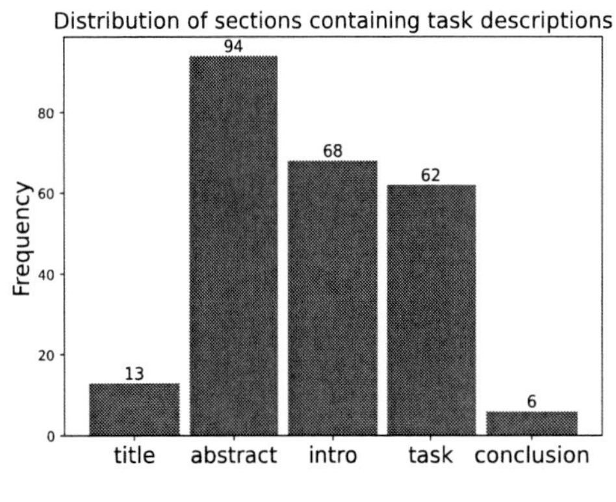

Figure 3: Distribution of sections containing task descriptions

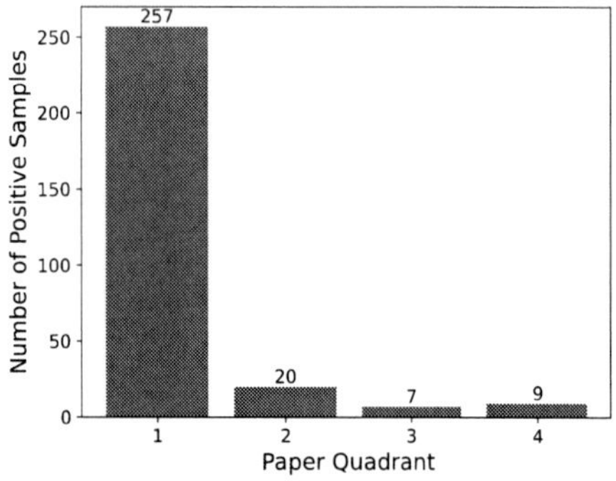

Figure 4: Distribution of task descriptions across paper quadrants

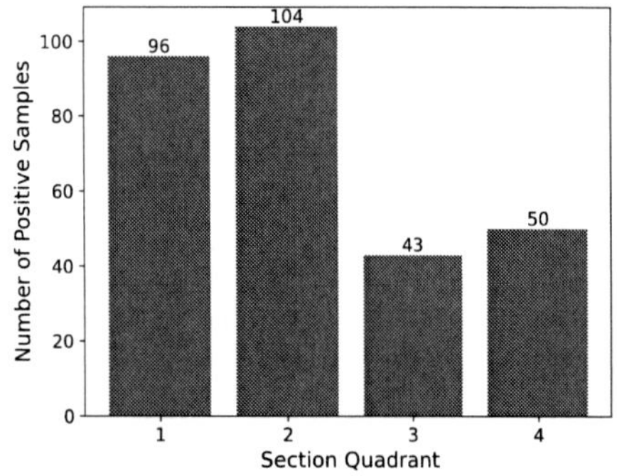

Figure 5: Distribution of task descriptions across section quadrants

for each sentence as features, we also removed any section for each publication that did not provide a task description. A paper with the task description in the introduction, for example, would only have its introduction included in our dataset. This improved the balance between positive and negative samples by increased the proportion of task descriptions to non-task descriptions. It also addressed the following problem: because the goal was to extract a single sequence from each paper, some papers have negative samples that would actually qualify as task descriptions if a better candidate had not been found. Reducing each paper to a single section eliminated some of those perplexing sentences. The resulting training set contains 259 positive samples and 2,304 negative samples, and the resulting test set contains 34 positive samples and 293 negative samples. After reducing the dataset, 11.28% of the total data is positive, which is more manageable than the previous 0.64%.

One problem with manually removing samples from the dataset based on which sections contain task descriptions is that the reduced test set is less "real world". In a non-experimental setting, the machine reader should be able to extract a task description from a whole paper, since it does not know ahead of time which section contains the task description. To address this issue, we tested our model on three versions of the test set. The first was manually reduced the same way as the training set. The second had sections automatically removed by fine-tuning a BERT model on section headers seen in the training set. This model was then applied to the test set to classify section headers as either likely or unlikely to contain a task description. This is a more fair test set because one could apply this classifier to any unseen papers to filter out paper sections. The third set is the full test set without any data removed.

8 Sentence Classification Experiments

Despite the fact that task descriptions are defined as sequences that can be longer or shorter than a single sentence, we designed a sentence classification task because we achieved much higher inter-annotator agreement scores when we compared the chosen sentences spanned by the sequences rather than the exact sequences (see Section 5). We fine-tuned the cased and uncased base versions of BERT (Devlin et al., 2019) and SciBERT (Beltagy et al., 2019) on every hyperparameter combination in Table 4.

hyperparameter	settings
epochs	2, 3, 4
batch size	16, 32
learning rate	2e-5, 3e-5, 5e-5

Table 4: The hyperparameter options are based on the fine-tuning recommendations made by Devlin et al. (2019).

8.1 Training Loop

Each hyperparameter and BERT model combination was fine-tuned on two versions of the training dataset, ten times each. The first version of the dataset contained the contextual features described in Section 7.1, and the second version contained only the text data. In between runs, the data was shuffled and a new validation set containing 10% of the training data was selected. The precision, recall, and F1 score was recorded for each training run. Then the mean scores and standard deviation were calculated for each classifier-encoding pair.

8.2 Baseline

We calculated a baseline based on common vocabulary and positional patterns. We analyzed common word patterns in the training set by tokenizing each sample, removing English stop words, and looking at the 10, 15, 20, 25, and 30 most frequent words in the positive and negative samples from the training set. The most common words for the positive and negative samples are identical, but the density of common words per sentence differs. The density of common words is greater in task description sentences: see Table 5 for the mean common word density per sentence for task descriptions and non-task descriptions. In calculating the baseline, we used a threshold density value of > 0.03 as one of the criteria for classifying a sentence as a task description, with the common word list containing 20 words.

We also experimented with the use of positional information seen in Figures 4 and 5 in calculating our baseline. We found that restricting positive classifications to the first halves of each paper section yielded the highest baseline scores. However, setting a threshold for the total paper quadrants lowered the scores.

The highest baseline scores were calculated by classifying sentences as task descriptions when the density of common words was greater than 0.03 and the sentence was found in the first half of its section. The F1, precision, and recall baseline scores are .4000, .2687, and .7826, respectively.

	Common word density	
N	Task	Non-task
10	0.0518	0.0281
15	0.0647	0.0314
20	0.0762	0.0349
25	0.0848	0.0435

Table 5: The mean density of N most common words among task description sentences and non-task description sentences. Density is calculated by dividing the number of common words in the sentence by the total number of words in the sentence.

8.3 BERT Training Results

The precision, recall, and F1 scores for the best model and hyperparameter combination are shown in Table 6. Scores are reported for both the dataset with additional contextual features and the dataset containing sentences alone.

The highest performing model scored better on the dataset comprising sentence data only without additional features. The cased scibert model earned an average F1 score of 0.72 on the simple dataset and an average F1 score of 0.69 on the dataset containing contextual features. However, the other three models all returned higher mean scores when trained on the dataset containing contextual features. The mean F1 score across all four models trained on the contextual dataset is 0.7, while the mean score across all four models trained on the simple dataset is 0.68. Notice also that the standard deviations are somewhat high, indicating a not insignificant spread around the mean. From this data it is unclear whether one variant of the dataset is better than the other.

8.4 Test Results

Tests were run using the cased SciBERT model fine-tuned on the simple dataset over four epochs with a batch size of 32 and a learning rate of 5e-05 (the model with the highest training results). Three versions of the test dataset were used in order to determine how well our system would perform given data of varying levels of preprocessing. The three versions of the test data are:

1. The dataset manually reduced in the same way that the training data is reduced. Only sections that contain a task description are included;

model	epochs	batch size	learning rate	metric	score
Training results using data annotated with positional features					
bert-cased	4	16	2e-05	Precision	0.69 ± 0.1
				Recall	0.73 ± 0.1
				F1	0.71 ± 0.09
scibert_uncased	3	16	3e-05	Precision	0.69 ± 0.03
				Recall	0.73 ± 0.12
				F1	0.71 ± 0.06
Training results using text data only					
bert-uncased	3	32	5e-05	Precision	0.63 ± 0.08
				Recall	0.7 ± 0.1
				F1	0.66 ± 0.08
scibert_cased	4	32	5e-05	Precision	0.73 ± 0.11
				Recall	0.71 ± 0.07
				F1	$\mathbf{0.72 \pm 0.08}$
Baseline					
baseline	-	-	-	Precision	0.27
				Recall	0.78
				F1	0.40

Table 6: Mean training results and standard deviations for BERT and SciBERT classifiers across ten runs. Only the results for the best hyperparameter and model combinations are reported here.

	Test set		Predicted Labels +	Predicted Labels -	Sum
True Labels	Manually reduced test set	+	24 (7.34%)	10 (3.06%)	34 (10.40%)
		-	6 (1.83%)	287 (87.77%)	293 (89.60%)
		Sum	30 (9.17%)	297 (90.83%)	Total=327
	Automatically reduced test set	+	21 (1.76%)	8 (0.67%)	29 (2.43%)
		-	63 (5.27%)	1104 (92.31%)	1167 (97.58%)
		Sum	84 (7.03%)	1112 (92.98%)	Total=1196
	Full test set	+	25 (0.53%)	9 (0.19%)	34 (0.72%)
		-	128 (2.69%)	4597 (96.60%)	4725 (99.29%)
		Sum	153 (3.22%)	4606 (96.79%)	Total=4759

Table 7: The confusion matrices for the test results on the manually reduced, automatically reduced, and full (non-reduced) test sets. The sums of the positive and negative labels are displayed for the predicted labels and the true labels, as well as the total number of samples in the respective test set. Occasionally the percentages don't sum to 100%; this occurs due to rounding.

test dataset	precision | recall | F1
manually reduced	0.80 | 0.71 | 0.75
automatically reduced	0.25 | 0.72 | 0.37
full test set	0.16 | 0.74 | 0.27

Table 8: Test results for each version of the test dataset

2. The dataset automatically reduced by learning which section headers are likely to appear over a section containing a task description. Only sections that have a high probability of containing a task description are included;

3. The full dataset without any sections removed from any papers.

Figure 7 shows the resulting confusion matrices for each version of the test dataset. The scores reflect the variation in proportion of positive to negative samples; the most balanced dataset is associated with the highest F1 score (0.75) and the least balanced is associated with the lowest (0.27).

Surprisingly, the F1 score for the manually reduced dataset (0.75) is higher than the mean training result (0.72). This is surprising because the hyperparameter settings were chosen based only on the training data; the test data was unseen during the process of hyperparameter selection. However, 0.75 is within one standard deviation of the mean training result (standard deviation = ± 0.08). The dataset used to train the model used to classify the test set was bigger than the dataset used during training experiments because 10% of it did not need to be set aside for validation. It is possible that, due to the relatively small amount of positive samples, that increasing the training data by a small amount could be enough to improve results on during testing.

8.5 Error Analysis

Many of the errors made by our system reflect the situations that were difficult or ambiguous for the human annotators. Papers with subtasks, joint tasks, and multiple tracks were particularly hard. There were two papers with subtasks in the test set for which the system failed to classify any sentences as task descriptions; one paper that describes multiple tracks for which the system wrongly chose multiple sentences (one for each track); and a paper describing four joint tasks for which the system found all but one of the four task descriptions[4].

There were six instances where, when faced with more than one good task description candidate, the system either chose both or chose the wrong one. One interesting pattern is that the false positives are often adjacent to true positives extracted by the system. While these false positives may be lacking in detail on their own, some of them work quite well as auxiliary sentences to the true positives.

Our system struggled in two cases to recognize short task description phrases embedded in broader, more generic statements. This indicates that taking a span-based approach to Task Description extraction could be more effective than sentence classification. See Appendix B for more examples.

9 Conclusion

Our primary contribution is the creation of a new Scholarly Document Processing corpus that provides full paper texts rather than short, curated contexts, and a method for reducing and rebalancing the dataset for an information extraction task. Corpora such as NLPSharedTasks can be used in scholarly information extraction systems to automatically identify and display fine grained scientific information to users of digital libraries. Our most significant finding is the importance of the data preparation and preprocessing decisions. These choices about how to build and filter the datasets had a much greater impact on the results than the hyperparameter settings.

A future annotation project could be conducted that is generally based on our rules but is more lenient in terms of the sentences to be extracted. Instead of focusing on conciseness, this project would prioritize obtaining as much information as is required to produce a more thorough account of the shared task. This resource might subsequently be utilized as the basis for an extractive task summary effort. A span-based information extraction task could be designed over our corpus to extract the original annotated sequences rather than full sentences. Sentence classification could be used as a preprocessing step to narrow down the search space.

[4]The guidelines instructed the annotators to only extract subtask descriptions if they appeared in consecutive sentences, did not allow annotators to extract track descriptions, and permitted annotators to choose multiple task descriptions for joint task papers even if the spans were discontiguous.

References

Waleed Ammar, Dirk Groeneveld, Chandra Bhagavatula, Iz Beltagy, Miles Crawford, Doug Downey, Jason Dunkelberger, Ahmed Elgohary, Sergey Feldman, Vu Ha, Rodney Kinney, Sebastian Kohlmeier, Kyle Lo, Tyler Murray, Hsu-Han Ooi, Matthew Peters, Joanna Power, Sam Skjonsberg, Lucy Wang, Chris Wilhelm, Zheng Yuan, Madeleine van Zuylen, and Oren Etzioni. 2018. Construction of the literature graph in semantic scholar. In *Proceedings of the 2018 Conference of the North American Chapter of the Association for Computational Linguistics: Human Language Technologies, Volume 3 (Industry Papers)*, pages 84–91, New Orleans - Louisiana. Association for Computational Linguistics.

S. Auer, A. Oelen, Muhammad Haris, M. Stocker, Jennifer D'Souza, K. Farfar, Lars Vogt, Manuel Prinz, Vitalis Wiens, and M. Y. Jaradeh. 2020. Improving access to scientific literature with knowledge graphs. *Bibliothek Forschung und Praxis*, 44:516 – 529.

Isabelle Augenstein, Mrinal Das, Sebastian Riedel, Lakshmi Vikraman, and Andrew McCallum. 2017. SemEval 2017 task 10: ScienceIE - extracting keyphrases and relations from scientific publications. In *Proceedings of the 11th International Workshop on Semantic Evaluation (SemEval-2017)*, pages 546–555, Vancouver, Canada. Association for Computational Linguistics.

Iz Beltagy, Kyle Lo, and Arman Cohan. 2019. SciBERT: A pretrained language model for scientific text. In *Proceedings of the 2019 Conference on Empirical Methods in Natural Language Processing and the 9th International Joint Conference on Natural Language Processing (EMNLP-IJCNLP)*, pages 3615–3620, Hong Kong, China. Association for Computational Linguistics.

Emily M. Bender and Batya Friedman. 2018. Data statements for natural language processing: Toward mitigating system bias and enabling better science. *Transactions of the Association for Computational Linguistics*, 6:587–604.

Jacob Cohen. 1960. A coefficient of agreement for nominal scales. *Educational and Psychological Measurement*, 20:37 – 46.

Jacob Devlin, Ming-Wei Chang, Kenton Lee, and Kristina Toutanova. 2019. BERT: Pre-training of deep bidirectional transformers for language understanding. In *Proceedings of the 2019 Conference of the North American Chapter of the Association for Computational Linguistics: Human Language Technologies, Volume 1 (Long and Short Papers)*, pages 4171–4186, Minneapolis, Minnesota. Association for Computational Linguistics.

S. M. Dhawan, B. M. Gupta, and N. K. Singh. 2020. Global machine-learning research: a scientometric assessment of global literature during 2009-18. *World Digit. Libr.*, 13:105–120.

Jennifer D'Souza, Sören Auer, and Ted Pedersen. 2021. SemEval-2021 task 11: NLPContributionGraph - structuring scholarly NLP contributions for a research knowledge graph. In *Proceedings of the 15th International Workshop on Semantic Evaluation (SemEval-2021)*, pages 364–376, Online. Association for Computational Linguistics.

Jennifer D'Souza and S. Auer. 2020. Nlpcontributions: An annotation scheme for machine reading of scholarly contributions in natural language processing literature. *ArXiv*, abs/2006.12870.

Kata Gábor, Davide Buscaldi, Anne-Kathrin Schumann, Behrang QasemiZadeh, Haïfa Zargayouna, and Thierry Charnois. 2018. SemEval-2018 task 7: Semantic relation extraction and classification in scientific papers. In *Proceedings of The 12th International Workshop on Semantic Evaluation*, pages 679–688, New Orleans, Louisiana. Association for Computational Linguistics.

Kata Gábor, Haïfa Zargayouna, Davide Buscaldi, Isabelle Tellier, and Thierry Charnois. 2016. Semantic annotation of the ACL Anthology corpus for the automatic analysis of scientific literature. In *Proceedings of the Tenth International Conference on Language Resources and Evaluation (LREC'16)*, pages 3694–3701, Portorož, Slovenia. European Language Resources Association (ELRA).

Jacek Haneczok, Guillaume Jacquet, Jakub Piskorski, and Nicolas Stefanovitch. 2021. Fine-grained event classification in news-like text snippets - shared task 2, CASE 2021. In *Proceedings of the 4th Workshop on Challenges and Applications of Automated Extraction of Socio-political Events from Text (CASE 2021)*, pages 179–192, Online. Association for Computational Linguistics.

Yufang Hou, Charles Jochim, Martin Gleize, Francesca Bonin, and Debasis Ganguly. 2019. Identification of tasks, datasets, evaluation metrics, and numeric scores for scientific leaderboards construction. In *Proceedings of the 57th Annual Meeting of the Association for Computational Linguistics*, pages 5203–5213, Florence, Italy. Association for Computational Linguistics.

Yufang Hou, Charles Jochim, Martin Gleize, Francesca Bonin, and Debasis Ganguly. 2021. TDMSci: A specialized corpus for scientific literature entity tagging of tasks datasets and metrics. In *Proceedings of the 16th Conference of the European Chapter of the Association for Computational Linguistics: Main Volume*, pages 707–714, Online. Association for Computational Linguistics.

Peder Olesen Larsen and Markus von Ins. 2010. The rate of growth in scientific publication and the decline in coverage provided by science citation index. *Scientometrics*, 84:575 – 603.

Yang Li, Zeshui Xu, Xinxin Wang, and Xizhao Wang. 2020. A bibliometric analysis on deep learning during 2007–2019. *International Journal of Machine Learning and Cybernetics*, pages 1–20.

Haoyang Liu, M. Janina Sarol, and Halil Kilicoglu. 2021. UIUC_BioNLP at SemEval-2021 task 11: A cascade of neural models for structuring scholarly NLP contributions. In *Proceedings of the 15th International Workshop on Semantic Evaluation (SemEval-2021)*, pages 377–386, Online. Association for Computational Linguistics.

Patrice Lopez. 2009. Grobid: Combining automatic bibliographic data recognition and term extraction for scholarship publications. In *Research and Advanced Technology for Digital Libraries*, pages 473–474, Berlin, Heidelberg. Springer Berlin Heidelberg.

Yi Luan, Luheng He, Mari Ostendorf, and Hannaneh Hajishirzi. 2018. Multi-task identification of entities, relations, and coreference for scientific knowledge graph construction. In *Proceedings of the 2018 Conference on Empirical Methods in Natural Language Processing*, pages 3219–3232, Brussels, Belgium. Association for Computational Linguistics.

Behrang QasemiZadeh and Anne-Kathrin Schumann. 2016. The ACL RD-TEC 2.0: A language resource for evaluating term extraction and entity recognition methods. In *Proceedings of the Tenth International Conference on Language Resources and Evaluation (LREC'16)*, pages 1862–1868, Portorož, Slovenia. European Language Resources Association (ELRA).

Lucia Specia, Sujay Kumar Jauhar, and Rada Mihalcea. 2012. SemEval-2012 task 1: English lexical simplification. In **SEM 2012: The First Joint Conference on Lexical and Computational Semantics – Volume 1: Proceedings of the main conference and the shared task, and Volume 2: Proceedings of the Sixth International Workshop on Semantic Evaluation (SemEval 2012)*, pages 347–355, Montréal, Canada. Association for Computational Linguistics.

Erik F. Tjong Kim Sang and Sabine Buchholz. 2000. Introduction to the CoNLL-2000 shared task chunking. In *Fourth Conference on Computational Natural Language Learning and the Second Learning Language in Logic Workshop*.

Anthony J Viera, Joanne M Garrett, et al. 2005. Understanding interobserver agreement: the kappa statistic. *Fam med*, 37(5):360–363.

Ekaterina Vylomova, Jennifer White, Elizabeth Salesky, Sabrina J. Mielke, Shijie Wu, Edoardo Maria Ponti, Rowan Hall Maudslay, Ran Zmigrod, Josef Valvoda, Svetlana Toldova, Francis Tyers, Elena Klyachko, Ilya Yegorov, Natalia Krizhanovsky, Paula Czarnowska, Irene Nikkarinen, Andrew Krizhanovsky, Tiago Pimentel, Lucas Torroba Hennigen, Christo Kirov, Garrett Nicolai, Adina Williams, Antonios Anastasopoulos, Hilaria Cruz, Eleanor Chodroff, Ryan Cotterell, Miikka Silfverberg, and Mans Hulden. 2020. SIGMORPHON 2020 shared task 0: Typologically diverse morphological inflection. In *Proceedings of the 17th SIGMORPHON Workshop on Computational Research in Phonetics, Phonology, and Morphology*, pages 1–39, Online. Association for Computational Linguistics.

A Data Statement

Provided in this is the Data Statement for our corpus NLPSharedTasks, version 1, following Bender and Friedman (2018).

A.1 Curation Rationale

Our corpus contains the full texts of 254 Shared Task Overview papers published in the ACL Anthology between the year 2000 and 2021. The criteria for inclusion are:

- The paper was written by the organizers of a Shared Task
- The paper provides a description of the Shared Task, including details on the dataset the task is performed over, the task to be implemented by participating systems, and an overview of participating systems
- The Shared Task described in the paper was hosted by some research workshop in the domain of computational linguistics or natural language processing (NLP)

These criteria ensure that the papers included in the corpus are likely to contain a Shared Task Description. The ACL Anthology was chosen as the source because it provides a catalog that is easy to browse for qualifying candidates for inclusion. Furthermore, choosing a single anthology to draw from provided some consistency of paper style and organization. The starting year (2000) was chosen because the formatting of papers describing earlier initiatives was too dissimilar.

A.2 Language Variety

The papers included in NLPSharedTasks are in English as used in scientific communication in linguistics, computer science, and natural language processing domains.

A.3 Speaker Demographic

The demographics of the paper authors are unknown. The speakers are likely researchers and students of computational linguistics and natural language processing.

A.4 Annotator Demographic

The annotation was performed by two English-speaking annotators well versed in a broad range of NLP topics. Annotator 1 is a graduate student in computer science with a B.S. in computer science, and annotator 2 is a post doctoral researcher in data science with a PhD in computer science. Both annotators had shared task experience, annotator 1 as a participant and annotator 2 as an organizer of SemEval 2021: NLPContributionsGraph (D'Souza et al., 2021). Neither annotator was compensated.

A.5 Speech Situation

The papers included in NLPSharedTasks were written between 2000 and 2021 in research settings. The speech included in these papers is written and is assumed to be scripted and edited, as well as peer-reviewed. In the case of multiple authors, it is unknown whether interaction was either synchronous or asynchronous. The intended audience of the papers included in NLPSharedTasks is researchers and practitioners of computational linguistics and natural language processing.

A.6 Text Characteristics

The genre of the texts included in NLPSharedTasks can be described as written scientific communication in computational linguistics domains and other fields. As such, scientific vocabulary is used throughout that is specific to these domains and the documents are structured in a formal way. Texts are structured with sections under headers including *Title*, *Abstract*, *Introduction*, *Related Work*, *Task Description*, *Results*, and *Conclusion*, among others.

We define a task description as a span of text containing information on the task that must be performed by participating systems. The annotation goal was to extract sequences of text that efficiently describe the Shared Task such that a human reader can understand the task outside of the context of the full paper. Encountering a variety of ways of describing tasks, we developed three sub-definitions: *full task description*, *partial task description*, and *multiple subtasks description*, where a *full task description* contains information on the input data and a brief description of what the participating system must accomplish with the input data, a *partial task description* only describes the task to be performed by participating systems without mention of the data to be used, and a *multiple subtasks description* is a sequence of text that covers multiple subtasks in a single continuous sequence (such a task description is permitted even if the content spans multiple sentences). See Table 9.

Type	Example	Frequency
Full	"<TASK>Given a short context, a target word in English, and several substitutes for the target word that are deemed adequate for that context, the goal of the English Simplification task at SemEval-2012 is to rank these substitutes according to how "simple" they are, allowing ties</TASK>." From *SemEval-2012 Task 1: English Lexical Simplification*, (Specia et al., 2012).	127
Partial	"We describe the CoNLL-2000 shared task: <TASK> dividing text into syntactically related non-overlapping groups of words, so-called text chunking</TASK>." From *Introduction to the CoNLL-2000 Shared Task Chunking*, (Tjong Kim Sang and Buchholz, 2000).	104
Subtask	"The task is <TASK>divided into three subtasks: (a) classification of text snippets reporting sociopolitical events (25 classes) for which vast amount of training data exists, although exhibiting slightly different structure and style vis-a-vis test data, (b) enhancement to a generalized zero-shot learning problem (Chao et al., 2016), where 3 additional event types were introduced in advance, but without any training data ('unseen' classes), and (c) further extension, which introduced 2 additional event types</TASK>, announced shortly prior to the evaluation phase." From *Fine-grained Event Classification in News-like Text Snippets - Shared Task 2, CASE 2021*, (Haneczok et al., 2021).	13
NULL	N/A	12

Table 9: Number of full, partial, subtask, and null task descriptions in 254 shared task overview papers with examples. The full task description contains a description of the input ("Given a short context, target word in English, and several substitutes for the target word"), and a description of what participating systems must do ("rank these substitutes according to how "simple" they are, allowing ties"). In contrast, the partial task description only contains a description of what participating systems must do ("dividing text into syntactically related non-overlapping groups of words, so-called text chunking").

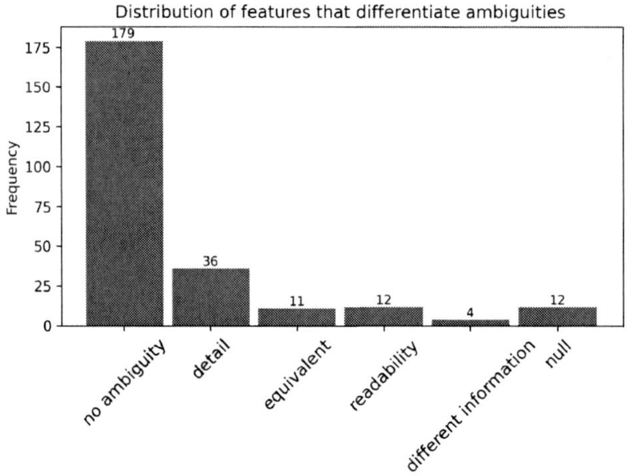

Figure 6: Distribution of features that help choose between two or more candidate task descriptions

Option 1	Option 2	Discussion
automatically assessing humor in edited news headlines	build systems for rating a humorous effect that is caused by small changes in text	We chose option 2 because it contains more **detail**.
quantify the degree of prototypicality of a target pair by measuring the relational similarity between it and pairs that are given as defining examples of a particular relation	rate word pairs by the degree to which they are prototypical members of a given relation class	This is a difficult example because initially option 1 seems better because it appears to have more detail. However, the second option has better **clarity**, and is more specific because of the phrase "word pairs" instead of "target pairs".
annotate instances of nouns, verbs, and adjectives using WordNet 3.1	label each instance with one or more senses, weighting each by their applicability	Both of these phrases provide **different pieces of information** about the task. Because these sentences are adjacent, the guidelines permit extracting the full sequence of text including both phrases and the text in between them.
given a set of documents and a set of target entities, the task consisted of building a timeline for each entity, by detecting, anchoring in time and ordering the events involving that entity	given a set of documents and a set of target entities, the task consists of building a timeline related to each entity, i.e. detecting, anchoring in time, and ordering the events in which the target entity is involved	Both phrases are equally good candidates and are **equivalent** in meaning. Either may be chosen.

Table 10: Examples of ambiguous annotation scenarios where it may be difficult to choose between two candidates

There are a number of situations that caused ambiguity during the annotation process. Certain kinds of sentences may appear at first glance to contain Task Descriptions, but actually served a different role. For example, task descriptions will often mention the research area, but a sequence that only describes the general research area is insufficient if it does not contain specific information on the task to be performed, as in the following example:

> "*Sensiting inflectionality*: Estonian task for SENSEVAL-2"
> **Discussion**: "Sensiting inflectionality" describes the research area, but is insufficient to describe the shared task to be performed.

One other pitfall we observed is the fact that sometimes paper authors use language when describing the aim, goal, or "task" of the task organizers or dataset annotators that makes it seem like they are describing the task to be performed by participating systems. A description of the organizers' aim or the dataset creation task would not be extracted as a task description according to our guidelines. For example:

> Aiming to *catalyze the development of models for predicting LE*, we organized the shared task described in this paper.
> **Discussion**: "catalyze the development of models for predicting LE" sounds like it could be a task description. The surrounding context shows us that it actually is describing the aim of the task organizers ("Aiming to... we organized the shared task").

Another source of ambiguity for the annotators is the presence of sub tasks, joint tasks, and multi-track or multi-language tasks. Developing a machine reader to determine how many subtasks are described in the paper and to extract a task description for each one from potentially disparate parts of the paper would not be trivial. For this reason, we do not annotate subtask descriptions unless they appear in consecutive sequences of text.

Another ambiguous situation is the scenario where there are two or more candidate task descriptions that are all decent choices. These ambiguities could be resolved by choosing the option that had either more **detail** or better **clarity**; choosing the sequence that works best out of context when the options contain complementary but **different information**; or choosing any candidate when the sequences are truly **equivalent**. The frequencies of each of these choices in the dataset can be seen in Figure 6, and examples of ambiguous cases can be seen in Table 10.

Lastly, sometimes a paper does not contain a sequence of text that sufficiently describes the task out of context. In any situation where a task description cannot be found, we use a portion of the title of the paper if the title contained a phrase describing the task. If no task description could be found in the body of the paper and the title did not sufficiently describe the task, then that paper would not receive an annotation. There were twelve such cases in the entire corpus.

A.7 Corpus Access

NLPSharedTasks corpus is available on GitHub and is licensed under a Creative Commons Attribution 4.0 International License.

B Error Analysis

Table 11 on the following page presents examples and analysis of errors made by our system on the test set.

Error Type	Sample In Context	Discussion
False Negative	Unsupervised Word Sense Induction and Discrimination (WSID, also known as corpus-based unsupervised systems) has followed this line of thinking, and tries to ***induce word senses directly from the corpus***.	This sentence may have been difficult for the system to classify because the actual task description span is relatively short compared to the overall sentence context.
False Negative	***Nine sub-tasks were included, covering problems in time expression identification, event expression identification and temporal relation identification***.	Papers with subtasks were difficult for the system. The system did not extract a single sentence from the paper containing this example.
Partial False Negative	***This task required participating systems to annotate instances of nouns, verb, and adjectives using Word-Net 3.1 (Fellbaum, 1998), which was selected due to its fine-grained senses. Participants could label each instance with one or more senses, weighting each by their applicability***.	Annotators were permitted to select sequences of text that spanned multiple sentences, if the additional text provided important details. Our system successfully classified the first sentence in this example as a task description, but missed the second sentence.
False Positive & False Negative	We present a counterfactual recognition (CR) task, the task of determining whether a given statement conveys counterfactual thinking or not, and further analyzing the causal relations indicated by counterfactual statements. In our counterfactual recognition task, we aim to ***model counterfactual semantics and reasoning in natural language.***	Some of the errors were also difficult cases for human annotators. In this example, the system selected the first sentence rather than the second. However, the annotator chose to prioritize readability over detail in this case.
Partial False Positive	This task seeks to evaluate the capability of systems for predicting dimensional sentiments of Chinese words and phrases. For a given word or phrase, participants were asked to ***provide a real-valued score from 1 to 9 for both the valence and arousal dimensions, respectively indicating the degree from most negative to most positive for valence, and from most calm to most excited for arousal***.	The system classified both of these sentences as task descriptions, although the annotator only chose a span from the second sentence.

Table 11: Examples of errors made by our system. The bolded and italicized spans of text are the original sequences identified by human annotators as task descriptions.

Parsing Electronic Theses and Dissertations Using Object Detection

Aman Ahuja Alan Devera Edward A. Fox
Department of Computer Science
Virginia Tech, Blacksburg, VA
{aahuja, alandeveral, fox}@vt.edu

Abstract

Electronic theses and dissertations (ETDs) contain valuable knowledge that can be useful for a wide range of purposes. To effectively utilize the knowledge contained in ETDs for downstream tasks such as search and retrieval, question-answering, and summarization, the data first needs to be parsed and stored in a format such as XML. However, since most of the ETDs available on the web are PDF documents, parsing them to make their data useful for downstream tasks is a challenge. In this work, we propose a dataset and a framework to help with parsing long scholarly documents such as ETDs. We take the Object Detection approach for document parsing. We first introduce a set of *objects* that are important elements of an ETD, along with a new dataset ETD-OD that consists of over 25K page images originating from 200 ETDs with bounding boxes around each of the objects. We also propose a framework that utilizes this dataset for converting ETDs to XML, which can further be used for ETD-related downstream tasks. Our code and pre-trained models are available at: `https://github.com/Opening-ETDs/ETD-OD`.

1 Introduction

Long scholarly documents like Electronic Theses and Dissertations (ETDs) contain a vast amount of information which can be of immense value to the scholarly community. Millions of ETDs are now publicly available on the web, and can serve as a rich source of scholarly information. However, relative to the large amount of information in such documents, a significant portion remains untapped.

Part of the problem is that these documents are often long and filled with highly specialized details. This makes it difficult for many users to understand the information contained in ETDs. In recent years, advances have been been made in NLP-based techniques such as question-answering and text summarization, which might be incorporated to make

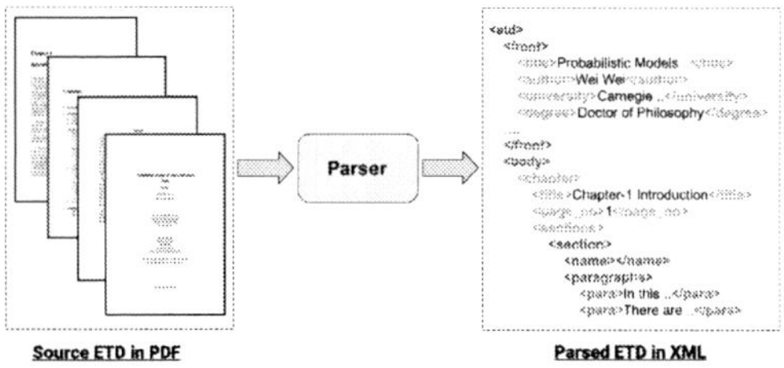

Figure 1: Illustration of the proposed framework. We take a source document in PDF as the input, and generate a parsed version in a structured format like XML.

ETDs more accessible. However, a majority of these documents exist as PDF files. While some tools can work with these files, the results we have observed have been poor; other tools require data in a structured format such as XML. This leads to the research question: *Is there a way to identify, parse, and extract the information from a PDF version of an ETD so that it is more accessible to a wider audience?*

Many research challenges arise when transforming ETDs from PDF to other formats. These scholarly documents do not have a standard layout. Different institutions have their own layouts and formats, making rule-based parsing methods difficult to apply. Moreover, the structure and organization of elements present in documents varies by domain and organization. For instance, documents from domains such as mathematics often contain equations, while documents from computer science frequently contain algorithms. Hence, there is a need to develop machine-learning based document-parsing methods that can generalize to documents with different layouts and across domains.

In recent years, with the advances in the field of computer vision, several methods have been proposed for extracting important elements from documents. Some of these approaches perform document layout analysis using object detection models (Girshick, 2015; Ren et al., 2015). However,

Proceedings of the 1st Workshop on Information Extraction from Scientific Publications, pages 121–130
Nov 20, 2022.

many of these works and the associated datasets are focused on a very narrow set of scholarly document elements. For instance, TableBank (Li et al., 2020a) only contains bounding boxes for tables, while ScanBank (Kahu et al., 2021) focuses on figures (and some tables). More recently, there has been research that primarily focuses on layout analysis of scholarly documents (Zhong et al., 2019; Li et al., 2020b). However, most existing work in the domain of scholarly document understanding focuses on research papers, which differ in many ways from longer documents like theses and dissertations. First, research papers tend to be shorter in length and have a narrower scope. As such, many elements such as *chapters*, *committee*, and *university* that are important in an ETD cannot be found in datasets derived from research papers. Moreover, research papers significantly differ from ETDs in their structure and format. For instance, many research papers are in double-column format, while ETDs typically have a single column, and have bigger font size and spacing. Consequently, existing methods for document understanding for research papers are not easily adapted to ETDs.

In this work, we propose ETD-OD, an object detection based framework to parse long PDF documents such as ETDs. Our approach works on the PDF version of an ETD by first identifying important elements such as figures, tables, captions, paragraphs, delimiters like chapter and section headers, and metadata such as title, author name, etc. This is done using object detection models such as Faster-RCNN (Ren et al., 2015) or YOLOv7 (Wang et al., 2022) on individual page images. For textual elements such as paragraphs and captions, the textual content is further extracted using PDF-based tools such as pymupdf, or optical character recognition (OCR). Finally, we put together all these elements in a structured XML format. We also introduce a new object detection dataset that contains over 25K page images originating from 200K ETDs, consisting of elements that commonly occur in ETDs, that can be important sources of information. An XML schema to support parsing with such objects is also introduced.

2 Related Work

2.1 Methods

Early works in the domain of document layout understanding used rule-based approaches (Lebourgeois et al., 1992; Ha et al., 1995). Other approaches, e.g., GROBID (Lopez and et al., 2008–2022) and CERMINE (Tkaczyk et al., 2015) designed for parsing scientific documents primarily focused on short documents such as research papers, and use an ensemble of sequence labeling methods for document parsing. With the advent of deep-learning based object detection methods such as Fast-RCNN (Girshick, 2015), Faster-RCNN (Ren et al., 2015), and YOLO (Redmon and Farhadi, 2018; Wang et al., 2022), document layout analysis based on object detection has been proposed. LayoutParser (Shen et al., 2021) uses object detection models that have been pre-trained on different object detection datasets to support layout understanding. However, since it primarily uses research-paper based datasets, it doesn't perform well on ETDs. Moreover, the number of object types it supports is very limited. More recently, layout-based language models (Xu et al., 2020, 2021; Huang et al., 2022) have been proposed. This line of work uses a multimodal architecture, i.e., a combination of visual and textual features, to pre-train the model on a large corpus of unlabeled data consisting of document images and their corresponding text. Although these models can then be fine-tuned on other downstream tasks such as object detection, they still require domain-specific annotated data for fine-tuning. Recently, to make the documents more accessible, services such as SciA11y (Wang et al., 2021) have been developed. However, their scope is limited to research papers, rather than long documents such as books and ETDs.

2.2 Datasets

With the growing interest in using object detection based methods for document layout analysis, several datasets have been introduced. Many of these datasets focus on specific object types. For instance, TableBank (Li et al., 2020a), ScanBank (Kahu et al., 2021), and MFD (Anitei et al., 2021) consist of tables, figures, and equations, respectively. Several datasets that consist of a diverse set of objects have also been introduced. HJDataset (Shen et al., 2020) consists of historical Japanese documents. PRImA (Antonacopoulos et al., 2009) consists of document images from magazines and research papers. PubLayNet (Zhong et al., 2019) is based on PDF articles from PubMed Central. The number of different objects, however, is limited in these datasets. DocBank (Li et al., 2020b) is a large dataset that consists of a diverse set of objects from research papers. But given the differences between research papers and long documents such as ETDs, models trained on DocBank do not generalize well on ETDs.

3 ETD Elements

Historically, ETDs do not conform to a universally accepted format, since different colleges and universities have their specific standards and requirements for ETDs. In this section we discuss the elements that are typically found in ETDs and would be important to extract for further analysis and downstream tasks. This list was curated after extensive discussions with digital librarians and researchers. We broadly categorize the different elements of ETDs into the following categories.

3.1 Metadata

The metadata consists of elements that contain unique identifiable information about an ETD, including information found on the front page. Key metadata elements are:

- **Title:** The main title of the document.
- **Author:** Name of the document author.
- **Date:** Date (or month/year) when the document was published, or of the final research defense.
- **University:** University/institution of the author.
- **Committee:** Committee that approved the document, e.g., the student's graduate committee.
- **Degree:** Degree (e.g., Master of Science, Doctor of Philosophy) being earned.

3.2 Abstract

The abstract is an important element of an ETD, as it contains a summary of the work, typically about a page long. Its elements include:

- **Abstract Heading:** Since some ETDs contain multiple abstracts, such as a technical abstract and general audience abstract, or an abstract in English as well as the original language, extracting the abstract heading makes it easier to segment, and could be helpful in categorizing the abstract by audience type.
- **Abstract Text:** The actual text of the abstract.

3.3 List of Contents

The list of contents (also referred to as table of contents) of an ETD determines where different components are located based on their page numbers. This helps with accurately mapping the chapters and sections, as well as figures and tables, since they are generally included in the list of contents. This subcategory includes the following elements:

- **List of Contents Heading:** This helps identify the specific type of list (e.g., list of chapters/sections, list of figures, list of tables).
- **List of Contents Text:** This is the actual list of entries for this type of content.

3.4 Main Content

Chapters are one of the most important components of an ETD, as they contain detailed information about the research described in the document. This subcategory consists of elements that can typically be found in the chapters of an ETD.

- **Chapter Title:** The title of the chapter.
- **Section:** Quite often, chapters themselves can be long. It may be desirable to have further delimiters such as sectional headers. Hence, we include the section names which can be used for further splitting of the document.
- **Paragraph:** The main textual content of the ETD.
- **Figure:** This includes figures, charts, and other visual illustrations included in the document.
- **Figure Caption:** The text caption that describes the figure.
- **Table:** The table element category.
- **Table Caption:** The text caption that describes the table.
- **Equation:** Mathematical equation/formula.
- **Equation Number:** Quite often, equations are numbered, which can be helpful in linking them to the list of equations that may be included in the document.
- **Algorithm:** Algorithm description, e.g., as pseudo-code.
- **Footnote:** We separate footnotes from regular paragraphs, as they typically provide auxiliary information which might be undesirable in many downstream tasks, such as summary generation.
- **Page Number:** Page numbers, which could be helpful in cross-referencing pages and the objects contained therein, to the list of contents.

3.5 Bibliography

We also include bibliographic elements in the list of objects. They are described below:

- **Reference Heading:** The header that indicates start of the references list.
- **Reference Text:** The actual list of references cited in the document.

In our dataset, we regard appendices as chapters, since they contain many elements that are found in the main chapters. They can however, be easily differentiated from main chapters based on the title.

4 Dataset

4.1 Dataset Source

The ETD-OD dataset consists of 25K page images from 200 theses and dissertations. These documents were downloaded from publicly accessible institutional repositories, and were randomly sampled with regards to degree, domain, and institution. Since object detection requires images as the input data, the documents were split into page images using the `pdf2image`[1] Python library. These images were then used for annotation.

4.2 Annotation

We use Roboflow[2] for annotating the page images in our dataset. The annotation was done by a group of 6 undergraduate students (Zhu et al., 2022), each of whom was a computer science student from junior year or above. Each data sample was further validated for correctness by two graduate students.

4.3 Dataset Statistics

Table 1 shows the detailed statistics for different object categories in our dataset. The dataset consists of ~25K page images and ~100K bounding boxes spanning across different object categories. Owing to the variation in the frequency of occurrence of various object categories in documents, some categories have many more samples as compared to others. Elements such as paragraphs can be found on most pages, and hence, it is the dominant category in our dataset. 80% of the images and their corresponding objects were used for training, while the remaining 20% were used as the validation set.

Category	# Instances
Title	439
Author	404
Date	338
University	309
Committee	282
Degree	279
Abstract Heading	169
Abstract Text	183
List of Contents Heading	512
List of Contents Text	1059
Chapter Title	2211
Section	9337
Paragraph	30359
Figure	6359
Figure Caption	5722
Table	2654
Table Caption	2213
Equation	5092
Equation Number	3051
Algorithm	96
Footnote	5722
Page Number	24543
Reference Heading	313
Reference Text	2088
Total Objects	99859
Total Images	25073

Table 1: Distribution of different object categories in our dataset. *Note: Some of the documents were accompanied with front matter (metadata) pages that are sometimes generated by the digital libraries. We include annotations for such documents as well, and hence, the number of metadata elements does not exactly match the number of documents.*

5 Proposed Framework

We now introduce the proposed framework for transforming long PDF documents into structured XML format. The architecture of our framework is illustrated in Figure 2. The different modules shown can broadly be divided into the following three categories.

5.1 Data and Preprocessing

Since our framework is primarily built for parsing long scholarly documents, it takes the PDF version of the document as input. The input file is converted to individual page images (.jpg format) using Python-based PDF libraries such as `pdf2image`. Next, the page images are individually fed to the Element Extraction module for further processing.

5.2 Element Extraction using Object Detection

This module forms the backbone of our system. It takes the individual page images as input, and uses an object detection model such as Faster-RCNN or YOLO for object detection. These models are first

[1] https://pypi.org/project/pdf2image/
[2] https://roboflow.com/

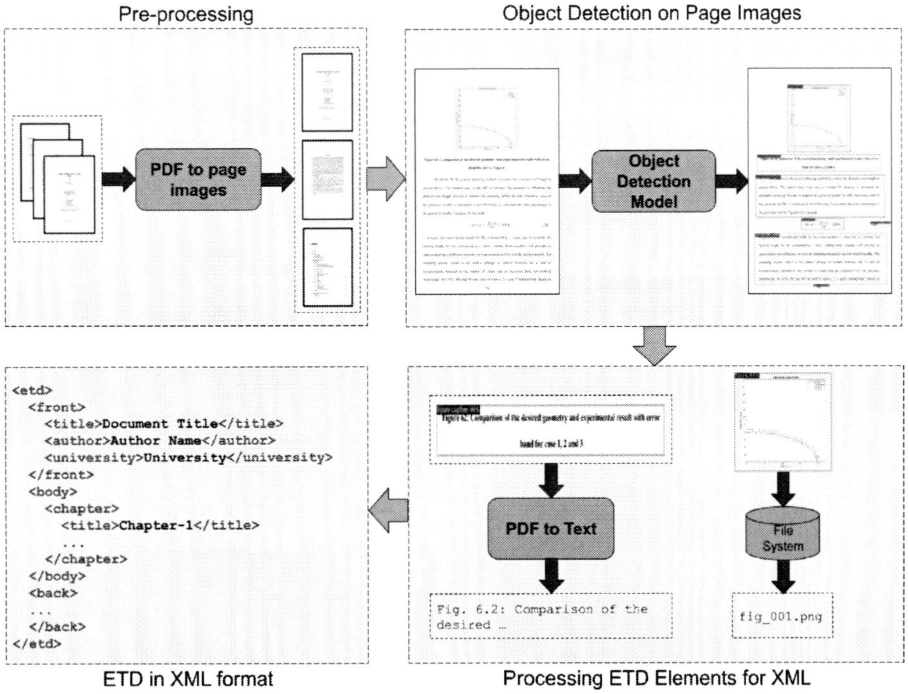

Figure 2: Architecture of the proposed PDF to XML parsing framework.

pre-trained on the dataset described in Section 4. The specific details about training object detection models are included in later sections of this paper. While using the object detection models as a part of this module, only inference is performed, and no updates are made to the model parameters. The output of object detection will be a list of elements, where each element contains information about the bounding boxes such as the coordinates, along with the category labels. This process is repeated for all of the pages in the document, and finally, a list of pages accompanied by their respective elements is populated.

In some instances, the object detected by the model is classified as one belonging to a different, yet similar category. In such cases, we use certain post-processing rules to correct the predictions. For example, *abstract heading* being mis-classified as chapter heading is one of the common errors, since both of these elements are often found in bigger font size at the beginning of a page. This can, however, be corrected by enforcing a constraint such as: a chapter heading in the first 10 pages with matching keyword "abstract" will be the abstract heading. We use a set of such rules for different object types to correct mis-classifications before the objects are sent to the XML module.

5.3 Structuring Objects into XML

After extracting all of the elements for all of the pages in the document, we generate the XML representation of the document. We regard the objects as broadly belonging to two types. The first type includes **image-based** objects such as figures, tables, algorithms, and equations, that need to be stored on the file system as an image. We regard tables as image-based objects even though they might contain text, since further extraction of information in structured format from tables is beyond the scope of this work. The second type of object includes **text-based** elements such as paragraphs, titles, etc., which need further processing to be converted to plain text. We regard all object categories excluding the image-based ones as textual elements.

For converting text-based objects to plain text, we use off-the-shelf tools and libraries. Some PDF documents are born-digital, where the text can be easily extracted using Python libraries such as `pymupdf`[3] based on page ID and bounding box coordinates. For scanned documents we use op-

[3] https://pymupdf.readthedocs.io/en/latest/

tical character recognition (OCR) tools such as `pytesseract`[4].

```
<etd>
  <front>
    <title>Document Title</title>
    <author>Author Name</author>
    <university>University</university>
    <degree>Degree Type</degree>
    <committee>Committee</committee>
    <date>Date or Month/Year</date>
    <abs_heading>Abstract</abs_heading>
    <abs_text>In this..</abs_text>
    <toc_heading>Table of..</toc_heading>
    <toc_text>1. Intro ...</toc_text>
  </front>
  <body>
    <chapter>
      <title>Chapter-1..</title>
      <page_no>1</page_no>
      <sections>
        <section>
          <name>1.1..</name>
          <paragraphs>
            <para>In this...</para>
            <para>Next, we...</para>
          </paragraphs>
          <figures>
            <figure>
              <path>fig_001.png</path>
              <caption>Fig.1...</caption>
            </figure>
          </figures>
          <tables>
            <table>
              <path>tab_001.png</path>
              <caption>Table.1.. </caption>
            </table>
          </tables>
          <equations>
            <equation>
              <path>eqn_001.png</path>
              <eq_no>1</eq_no>
            </equation>
          </equations>
          <algorithms>
            <algorithm>
              <path>alg_001.png</path>
            </algorithm>
          </algorithms>
          <footnotes>
            <footnote>...</footnote>
          </footnotes>
        </section>
      </sections>
    </chapter>
  </body>
  <back>
    <ref_heading>Ref..</ref_heading>
    <ref_text>..</ref_text>
  </back>
</etd>
```

Schema 1: XML Schema for Representing ETDs in Structured Format.

For image-based elements, we include the relative path of the image that is cropped based on the coordinates. Figures and tables are mapped to their respective captions based on proximity. For any figure/table element, the caption object closest to them based on Euclidean distance w.r.t. bounding box coordinates is assumed to be the caption. A similar method is followed to map equations with their equation numbers, with an added constraint that the y-coordinate of the center of the equation number should fall between min and max y-coordinates of the equation object. Finally, all the element values are put into the XML file under their corresponding tags. The detailed XML schema is shown in Schema 1.

[4]`https://pypi.org/project/pytesseract/`

6 Object Detection Training

We use the ETD-OD dataset introduced in this paper for training object detection models for our framework. The models currently supported are:

- **Faster-RCNN** (Ren et al., 2015): Faster-RCNN is an object detection model that has two stages. A region proposal network generates regions of interest, which are fed to another network for final detection. We use the version of Faster-RCNN that uses ResNeXt-101 (Xie et al., 2017) as the backbone model.
- **Faster-RCNN pre-trained on DocBank** (Li et al., 2020b): Faster-RCNN (with ResNeXt-101 backbone) pre-trained on DocBank (from the DocBank model zoo) is fine-tuned on ETD-OD. Although DocBank does not include all of the elements found in ETDs, we hypothesize that the scholarly nature of documents used in pre-training should help improve the performance over the vanilla version of the model.
- **YOLOv5** (Jocher et al., 2022): YOLO is a family of single stage object detection models that perform the processes of localization and detection using a single end-to-end network. This improves the speed without any significant drop in performance. These models have shown impressive performance on various datasets.
- **YOLOv7** (Wang et al., 2022): This is the most recent version of YOLO, which has been shown to outperform many object detection models.

Both of the Faster-RCNN models were trained on our dataset for 60K iterations with an inference score threshold of 0.7. The models were based on the implementation included in the open-source detectron2 (Wu et al., 2019) framework. For the DocBank-pretrained version of the model, we used the original set of weights and configurations open-sourced by the authors. Both of the versions of YOLO were based on the open-source implementations, and were trained for 150 epochs.

7 Experiments

In this section, we discuss the results obtained in the experimental analysis of our work.

7.1 Evaluation Metrics

For the quantitative evaluation of object detection models, the commonly used metrics are average precision (AP) and mean average precision (mAP). AP is defined as the area under the precision-recall curve for a specific class. mAP is the average of AP values for all object classes. Both of these metrics have different versions based on the overlap threshold (also referred to as *Intersection over Union or IoU*) used for comparing the predicted object against ground truth. For example, in *mAP@0.5*, all of the objects with an intersection of 50% or more with the ground truth will be regarded as correct predictions. Another commonly used version of mAP is *mAP@0.5-0.95*, which is the average mAP over different thresholds, from 0.5 to 0.95 with step 0.05.

7.2 Analysis of Various Object Detection Models trained on ETD-OD

Model	mAP@0.5	mAP@0.5-0.95
Faster-RCNN	39.1	19.6
Faster-RCNN*	76.2	44.0
YOLOv5	83.4	52.1
YOLOv7	<u>85.3</u>	<u>52.7</u>

Table 2: mAP comparison for object detection models on ETD-OD. Faster-RCNN* represents the model pre-trained on DocBank and fine-tuned on ETD-OD. Underlined values indicate best performing models.

Table 2 shows performance of different object detection models on the validation set of our dataset. The following observations can be made from the mAP values shown:

- **Pre-training on scholarly documents improves model performance:** The basic version of Faster-RCNN without any pre-training on scholarly documents has the lowest performance among all the models. The same model, after pre-training on DocBank, and then fine-tuned on the ETD dataset, gives much better performance. Since DocBank also consists of scholarly documents, albeit of different type, the pre-training process exposes the model to a diverse dataset, which eventually results in better generalization and predictive performance.
- **YOLO outperforms Faster-RCNN on ETD dataset:** YOLO models belong to the class of single stage detectors, which are designed with an emphasis on speed. YOLO typically performs worse than Faster-RCNN in scenarios where the objects are smaller or multiple objects are close to each other. However, in case of documents, most objects are typically of large size and have minimal overlap with each other due to white spaces and line breaks around objects (such as between a header and paragraph). Hence, it outperforms Faster-RCNN on the ETD dataset.

7.3 Analysis of Detection Performance on Different Object Categories

Category	AP@0.5	Category	AP@0.5
Title	92.5	Paragraph	97.4
Author	89.5	Figure	98.4
Date	68.3	Fig. Caption	95.4
University	91.1	Table	94.7
Committee	96.5	Tab. Caption	89.8
Degree	68.3	Equation	72.6
Abs. Heading	94.2	Eqn. Number	55.0
Abs. Text	86.7	Algorithm	66.6
LOC Heading	75.5	Footnote	98.9
LOC Text	99.3	Page Number	51.3
Chapter Title	88.8	Ref. Heading	80.7
Section	90.9	Ref. Text	99.3

Table 3: AP@0.5 values for different object categories for YOLOv7 (Abs. = Abstract, LOC = List of Contents).

In Table 3, we show the performance of the best performing model (YOLOv7) on various object categories in our dataset. The lower performance of certain categories can generally be attributed to two reasons:

- **Limited Number of Training Samples:** Elements such as degree, date, and algorithm have very few instances in our dataset. As such, the performance on these classes is lower.
- **Smaller Object Sizes:** Elements such as page number and equation number tend to be of smaller size as compared to other elements. Since object detection models tend to struggle with localization of smaller objects, performance of such classes is impacted.

7.4 Comparison against Other Layout Detection Datasets

To evaluate how the performance of similar models varies across different datasets from the document layout analysis domain on layout analysis of ETDs, we compare the per class AP values for object categories supported by the DocBank dataset.

Categories	DocBank only	ETD-OD only	DocBank ETD-OD
Abstract	2.29	0.0	67.42
Author	5.8	19.27	73.27
Caption	42.72	55.04 / 18.27	97.46 / 89.03
Date	0.0	0.0	76.28
Equation	8.13	62.28	76.19
Figure	72.44	78.21	95.01
Footer	69.38	85.03	97.64
List	NA	NA	NA
Paragraph	5.01	80.64	94.34
Reference	2.94	75.43	97.92
Section	19.88	66.99	77.63
Table	33.25	49.04	89.7
Title	1.1	11.3	73.85

Table 4: AP@0.5 values for categories supported by DocBank using Faster-RCNN trained on different datasets and evaluated on validation set of ETD-OD. For *Caption*, we list the Figure Caption / Table Caption values for models trained on ETD-OD.

These results are shown in Table 4. The **DocBank only** is the version of Faster-RCNN pre-trained on DocBank, that was evaluated on the ETD dataset without any fine-tuning. The **ETD only** model has been trained only on the ETD dataset without pre-training on any other scholarly dataset. The **DocBank ETD-OD** was pre-trained on DocBank and then fine-tuned on ETD-OD.

We can see that both of the models that were trained on the ETD dataset perform better than the model that was just trained on the DocBank dataset. This may be due to the fact that DocBank consists of images of research papers, which have different layouts as compared to long documents such as ETDs. On the other hand, since research papers do tend to have some similarities with ETDs, pre-training on DocBank followed by fine-tuning on ETD-OD gives the best results among all three.

7.5 Qualitative Analysis

In Fig. 3, we show example outputs generated by the best performing versions of Faster-RCNN (pre-trained on DocBank, fine-tuned on ETD-OD) and YOLO (v7) models. Faster-RCNN fails to detect many of the metadata elements, which is also reflected by its low mAP values. YOLOv7 is able to detect most of the elements on the page, with the exception of page number. We conclude that YOLOv7 is the best performing model on the ETD dataset.

8 Conclusion and Future Work

In this work, we presented a new dataset and a framework for parsing long scholarly documents such as ETDs from PDF to structured formats such as XML. We also presented a schema to represent ETDs in XML format, along with extensive experimental evaluation of multiple state-of-the-art models on the newly introduced ETD-OD dataset. In the future, we plan to extend this work to other types of documents, such as old archival documents which typically contain a great amount of noise, and make further improvements to the performance of minority categories.

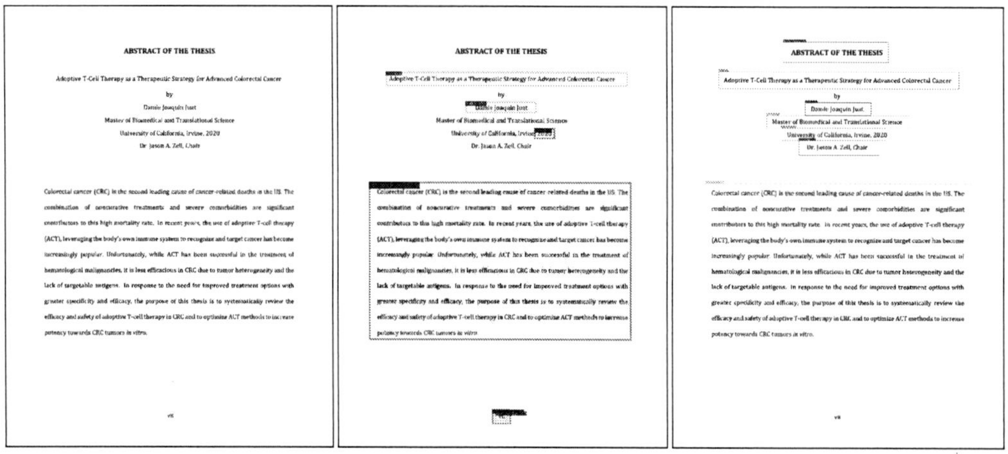

(a) Original Image (b) Faster-RCNN (DocBank, ETD-OD) (c) YOLOv7

Figure 3: Examples of outputs generated by the Faster-RCNN and YOLOv7 models.

Acknowledgements

This project was made possible in part by the Institute of Museum and Library Services [LG-37-19-0078-19], PI William A. Ingram. The authors are grateful to the University Libraries at Virginia Tech for their generous support of this research. We also thank Kecheng Zhu, Jiangyue Li, You Peng, Zach Gager, and Shelby Neal for their help in dataset curation.

References

Dan Anitei, Joan Andreu Sánchez, José Manuel Fuentes, Roberto Paredes, and José Miguel Benedí. 2021. ICDAR 2021 Competition on Mathematical Formula Detection. In *International Conference on Document Analysis and Recognition*, pages 783–795. Springer.

Apostolos Antonacopoulos, David Bridson, Christos Papadopoulos, and Stefan Pletschacher. 2009. A realistic dataset for performance evaluation of document layout analysis. In *2009 10th International Conference on Document Analysis and Recognition*, pages 296–300. IEEE.

Ross Girshick. 2015. Fast R-CNN. In *Proceedings of the IEEE International Conference on Computer Vision*, pages 1440–1448.

Jaekyu Ha, R.M. Haralick, and I.T. Phillips. 1995. Recursive X-Y cut using bounding boxes of connected components. In *Proceedings of 3rd International Conference on Document Analysis and Recognition*, volume 2, pages 952–955 vol.2.

Yupan Huang, Tengchao Lv, Lei Cui, Yutong Lu, and Furu Wei. 2022. LayoutLMv3: Pre-Training for Document AI with Unified Text and Image Masking. In *Proceedings of the 30th ACM International Conference on Multimedia*, MM '22, page 4083–4091, New York, NY, USA.

Glenn Jocher, Ayush Chaurasia, Alex Stoken, Jirka Borovec, NanoCode012, Yonghye Kwon, TaoXie, Kalen Michael, Jiacong Fang, Imyhxy, Lorna, Colin Wong, Zeng Yifu, Abhiram V, Diego Montes, Zhiqiang Wang, Cristi Fati, Jebastin Nadar, Laughing, UnglvKitDe, Tkianai, YxNONG, Piotr Skalski, Adam Hogan, Max Strobel, Mrinal Jain, Lorenzo Mammana, and Xylieong. 2022. ultralytics/yolov5: v6.2 - YOLOv5 Classification Models, Apple M1, Reproducibility, ClearML and Deci.ai integrations. https://zenodo.org/record/7002879.Y1nceezMIiw.

Sampanna Yashwant Kahu, William A. Ingram, Edward A. Fox, and Jian Wu. 2021. ScanBank: A Benchmark Dataset for Figure Extraction from Scanned Electronic Theses and Dissertations. In *2021 ACM/IEEE Joint Conference on Digital Libraries (JCDL)*, pages 180–191. IEEE Computer Society.

Frank Lebourgeois, Zbigniew Bublinski, and Hubert Emptoz. 1992. A fast and efficient method for extracting text paragraphs and graphics from unconstrained documents. In *11th IAPR International Conference on Pattern Recognition. Vol. II. Conference B: Pattern Recognition Methodology and Systems*, volume 1, pages 272–273. IEEE Computer Society.

Minghao Li, Lei Cui, Shaohan Huang, Furu Wei, Ming Zhou, and Zhoujun Li. 2020a. TableBank: Table Benchmark for Image-Based Table Detection and Recognition. In *Proceedings of the 12th Language Resources and Evaluation Conference*, pages 1918–1925.

Minghao Li, Yiheng Xu, Lei Cui, Shaohan Huang, Furu Wei, Zhoujun Li, and Ming Zhou. 2020b. DocBank: A Benchmark Dataset for Document Layout Analysis. In *Proceedings of the 28th International Conference on Computational Linguistics*, pages 949–960.

Patrice Lopez and et al. 2008–2022. GROBID. `https://github.com/kermitt2/grobid`.

Joseph Redmon and Ali Farhadi. 2018. YOLOv3: An incremental improvement. *arXiv preprint arXiv:1804.02767*.

Shaoqing Ren, Kaiming He, Ross Girshick, and Jian Sun. 2015. Faster R-CNN: Towards Real-Time Object Detection with Region Proposal Networks. In *Advances in Neural Information Processing Systems*, volume 28. Curran Associates, Inc.

Zejiang Shen, Kaixuan Zhang, and Melissa Dell. 2020. A large dataset of historical Japanese documents with complex layouts. In *Proceedings of the IEEE/CVF Conference on Computer Vision and Pattern Recognition Workshops*, pages 548–549.

Zejiang Shen, Ruochen Zhang, Melissa Dell, Benjamin Charles Germain Lee, Jacob Carlson, and Weining Li. 2021. LayoutParser: A unified toolkit for deep learning based document image analysis. In *International Conference on Document Analysis and Recognition*, pages 131–146. Springer.

Dominika Tkaczyk, Paweł Szostek, Mateusz Fedoryszak, Piotr Jan Dendek, and Łukasz Bolikowski. 2015. CERMINE: automatic extraction of structured metadata from scientific literature. *International Journal on Document Analysis and Recognition (IJDAR)*, 18(4):317–335.

Chien-Yao Wang, Alexey Bochkovskiy, and Hong-Yuan Mark Liao. 2022. YOLOv7: Trainable bag-of-freebies sets new state-of-the-art for real-time object detectors. *arXiv preprint arXiv:2207.02696*.

Lucy Lu Wang, Isabel Cachola, Jonathan Bragg, Evie Yu-Yen Cheng, Chelsea Haupt, Matt Latzke, Bailey Kuehl, Madeleine N van Zuylen, Linda Wagner, and Daniel Weld. 2021. SciA11y: Converting Scientific Papers to Accessible HTML. In *The 23rd International ACM SIGACCESS Conference on Computers and Accessibility*, pages 1–4.

Yuxin Wu, Alexander Kirillov, Francisco Massa, Wan-Yen Lo, and Ross Girshick. 2019. Detectron2. https://github.com/facebookresearch/detectron2.

Saining Xie, Ross Girshick, Piotr Dollár, Zhuowen Tu, and Kaiming He. 2017. Aggregated residual transformations for deep neural networks. In *Proceedings of the IEEE conference on computer vision and pattern recognition*, pages 1492–1500.

Yang Xu, Yiheng Xu, Tengchao Lv, Lei Cui, Furu Wei, Guoxin Wang, Yijuan Lu, Dinei Florencio, Cha Zhang, Wanxiang Che, et al. 2021. LayoutLMv2: Multi-modal Pre-training for Visually-rich Document Understanding. In *Proceedings of the 59th Annual Meeting of the Association for Computational Linguistics and the 11th International Joint Conference on Natural Language Processing (Volume 1: Long Papers)*, pages 2579–2591. DOI:10.18653/v1/2021.acl-long.201.

Yiheng Xu, Minghao Li, Lei Cui, Shaohan Huang, Furu Wei, and Ming Zhou. 2020. LayoutLM: Pre-training of Text and Layout for Document Image Understanding. In *Proceedings of the 26th ACM SIGKDD International Conference on Knowledge Discovery & Data Mining*, pages 1192–1200. https://www.kdd.org/kdd2020/accepted-papers/view/layoutlm-pre-training-of-text-and-layout-for-document-image-understanding.

Xu Zhong, Jianbin Tang, and Antonio Jimeno Yepes. 2019. PubLayNet: Largest dataset ever for document layout analysis. In *2019 International Conference on Document Analysis and Recognition (ICDAR)*, pages 1015–1022. IEEE. DOI:10.1109/ICDAR.2019.00166.

Kecheng Zhu, Zachary Gager, Shelby Neal, Jiangyue Li, and You Peng. 2022. Object Detection. Virginia Tech CS4624 team term project, http://hdl.handle.net/10919/109979.

TDAC, the First Time-Domain Astrophysics Corpus: Analysis and First Experiments on Named Entity Recognition

Atilla Kaan Alkan[*,†], **Cyril Grouin**[*], **Fabian Schüssler**[†], **Pierre Zweigenbaum**[*]
[*]Université Paris-Saclay, CNRS, Laboratoire interdisciplinaire des sciences du numérique, 91405, Orsay, France
[†]IRFU, CEA, Université Paris-Saclay, F-91191 Gif-sur-Yvette, France
{atilla.alkan, cyril.grouin, pierre.zweigenbaum}@lisn.upsaclay.fr
fabian.schussler@cea.fr

Abstract

The increased interest in time-domain astronomy over the last decades has resulted in a substantial increase in observation report publication leading to a saturation of how astrophysicists read, analyze and classify information. Due to the short life span of the detected astronomical events, information related to the characterization of new phenomena has to be communicated and analyzed very rapidly to allow other observatories to react and conduct their follow-up observations. This paper introduces TDAC: a Time-Domain Astrophysics Corpus. TDAC is the first corpus based on astrophysical observation reports. We also present the NLP experiments we made for named entity recognition based on annotations we made and annotations from the WIESP DEAL shared task.

1 Introduction

Time-domain astrophysics consists in observing and studying transient cosmic phenomena, *i.e.* unpredictable, short-lived, and the most violent phenomena occurring in the Universe, such as supernovae explosions or gamma-ray bursts (GRBs), which are highly energetic explosions lasting from milliseconds to a few hours or days only (Neronov, 2019). The short life span of these events requires a rapid sharing, analysis and synthesis of the information disseminated in observation reports. However, the increased interest in time-domain astronomy has led to a significant increase in observation reports, leading to a saturation of how astrophysicists analyze and classify information in observation reports. As the current manual reading and analyzing of available information is approaching saturation, new ways of handling information are necessary.

One of the most promising approaches is to build Natural Language Processing (NLP) methods that tackle the challenges of extracting and summarizing information on observation reports by detecting, for example, named entities. Named Entity Recognition (NER) can identify and extract information about an astrophysical object, such as the date of detection, its coordinates in the Universe, and numerous information, such as intensity and magnitude, to let astrophysicists know if they can trigger a follow-up observation. To train and evaluate an NER system, a corpus must first be created and annotated.

This paper presents TDAC: a Time-Domain Astrophysics Corpus for NLP, based on observation reports. To our knowledge, no existing resources and studies so far are based on time-domain astrophysics observation reports, and therefore there are no studies characterising the discourse used in astrophysics. Our objective is twofold: The first objective of our study, with the creation of this corpus, is to highlight differences between astrophysics corpora. What are their properties, and are they all the same? We provide some elements characterizing and revealing the specificity of the formulations used in astrophysics by conducting a corpus analysis (Section 4). Secondly, we started building an NER system for the domain. Section 5 presents our annotations and the first NER experiments we conducted on a sub-corpus of TDAC (75 documents). The annotated section of TDAC is the first annotated and publicly available[1] corpus based on observation reports for named entity recognition in time-domain astrophysics.

2 Research and Language Resources in Astrophysics

The vast majority of the limited research performed so far in NLP for astrophysics studies papers from the Astrophysics Data System (ADS[2]). The ADS is a database for researchers in astronomy with more than 15 million records covering publications in astronomy, astrophysics, and general physics.

[1]https://github.com/AtillaKaanAlkan/TDAC

[2]https://ui.adsabs.harvard.edu/

Proceedings of the 1st Workshop on Information Extraction from Scientific Publications, pages 131–139
Nov 20, 2022. ©2022 Association for Computational Linguistics

Abstracts and full text of astronomy paper publications are indexed and searchable through ADS, making it a rich exploitable platform for creating NLP resources.

2.1 The Astronomy Bootstrapping Corpus

The Astronomy Bootstrapping Corpus (ABC) (Becker et al., 2005; Hachey et al., 2005) is one of the unique existing annotated corpora for astrophysical Named Entity Recognition (NER). ABC consists of 209 abstracts of astronomical papers extracted from the ADS. The built corpus aimed to explore an active learning approach to reduce annotation costs for a NER task by defining four astrophysical named entities: `instrument_name`, `source_name`, `source_type` and `spectral_feature`, with respectively 136, 111, 499 and 321 instances. To our knowledge, the corpus is not available.

2.2 The Astro Corpus

Murphy et al. (2006) built a larger corpus than the ABC for named entities detection by downloading all the astronomical journal articles and conference papers (52 658 documents) from the astrophysics section (astro-ph) of arXiv. The annotated corpus consists of 7840 sentences (approximately 200 000 words) with an average of 26.1 tokens per sentence. There are 43 astrophysical named entities, including celestial objects, telescope names and categories related to astrophysical sources' properties. To our knowledge, this corpus is not available either.

2.3 The DEAL Shared Task Corpus

The Detecting Entities in the Astrophysics Literature (DEAL) shared task[3] consists of developping a system that identifies named entities in the astrophysics literature (Grezes et al., 2022). The organisers provided a baseline NER system using astroBERT (Grèzes et al., 2021), a deep contextual language model pre-trained on 395 499 publications (3 819 322 591 tokens, 16GB on disk) from the ADS database. The astroBERT model is not available yet, but preliminary results (F1-score of 0.902 on an NER task) are exposed in the above-cited paper. The DEAL corpus comprises full-text fragments and acknowledgements sections extracted from ADS papers for the shared task. The corpus was split into train, development and test sets, with 1753, 1366 and 2505 documents, respectively. During the shared task, only the labels for the training set were provided. We participated in the shared task and had access to the entire annotated collection[4] (train+development+test) at the end of the shared task. It is, therefore, the only annotated corpus we have for comparison with our TDAC corpus. We provide more detailed statistics on the DEAL corpus in the rest of the paper.

2.4 Other Studies

Information Retrieval and Recommendation System Kerzendorf (2019) downloaded astrophysics papers from the arXiv Bulk Data Access to build a corpus (201.997 articles). Their study aims to develop a robust text-based similarity tool to recommend articles given a reference input paper. Mukund et al. (2018) built and deployed another information retrieval and recommendation system, "Hey LIGO", an open access NLP-based web application for LIGO and VIRGO observatories (both aiming to detect gravitational waves). Documents used are extracted from the open source logbook data from both observatories. Therefore, to our knowledge, this is the only study not based on astrophysics papers. Data have been recorded since 2010, and the logbook consists of 83.911 entries, and an automatic check for new data entries is periodically done to update the models regularly.

Anaphora Resolution Kim and Webber (2006) used astrophysics articles from the Monthly Notices of the Royal Astronomical Society (MNRAS) to constitute a small corpus (it consists of more than a hundred articles) for anaphora resolution. To conclude this literature review, most NLP resources for astrophysics are mainly created and exploited using scientific papers. This paper presents TDAC, the first annotated corpus based on observation reports for named entity recognition in time-domain astrophysics.

3 Material for the TDAC Corpus

3.1 The resource platforms used

Reports are written and published on mainly three platforms by an extensive network of professional observers worldwide (astronomical observatories and satellites) and are accessible in open source to the entire research community. In this study, we

[3] `https://ui.adsabs.harvard.edu/WIESP/2022/SharedTasks`

[4] Data are accessible for participants only. We do not know how organisers will make the collection publicly available so far.

use these platforms to have a good coverage of the domain.

The Gamma-Ray Burst Coordinates Network The GCN[5] platform is dedicated mainly to the gamma-ray bursts astrophysicists community, where observers report their observations and analysis of GRBs in the form of "GCN Circulars" (Barthelmy et al., 1995).

The Astronomer's Telegram This system is a communication channel[6] that allows instantaneously sharing and reporting information to the astrophysicists' community in the form of astronomer's telegrams or "ATel" (Rutledge, 1998). Observers report discoveries regarding a large variety of astronomical sources with no restrictions on the type of discoveries (black holes, blazars, neutron stars etc.).

The Transient Name Server The TNS[7] is mainly a dedicated platform for the astronomers' community interested in confirmed supernovae candidates. Astrophysicists report their observations in the form of "AstroNotes" (Gal-Yam, 2021).

3.2 Collecting the raw corpus

An archive with the complete set of published GCN circulars in text files is available on the GCN website. Thus, to collect raw data and build up our corpus, we downloaded it. However, unlike GCN circulars, there is no direct way to bulk download all past ATel and AstroNotes. Therefore, we set up a Python script using the BeautifulSoup package to perform an automated extraction of the HTML code of all reports published from 1997 to 2021 and parsed the content into a text file. Figure 1 shows the evolution of reports published annually.

The increase in published reports is due to the number of observations monitored by various observers, particularly with the launch of the Swift telescope in 2004, leading to a significant increase in GCN circulars regarding GRB detection. However, we note a slight decrease in the number of ATel telegrams since 2015. A migration of publications to the TNS platform could be the reason for the decrease in the number of ATel published per year. Another explanation for this decrease could be that the types of objects processed in the telegrams have been less observed in recent years.

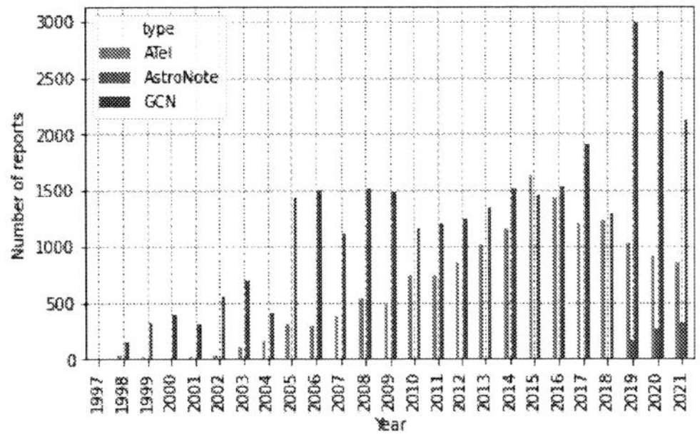

Figure 1: Number of published reports from 1997 to 2021 (GCN circulars in blue, ATel in red, AstroNotes in green)

4 Corpus Analysis

4.1 Statistics

As descibed in Table 1, within the TDAC corpus, AstroNotes are the least numerous, as the platform is more recent than GCN and ATel platforms. It explains the significant difference in the total number of tokens for each type of document. However, although AstroNotes are less numerous, they have the highest lexical diversity. GCN circulars and ATels seem to be quite similar in terms of vocabulary richness. We notice that the DEAL corpus has the least lexical diversity. Perhaps the documents in this corpus are all from the same theme, or all deal with the same types of astrophysical phenomena. Among observation reports, GCN circulars are the longest.

Corpus	# Doc	# Tokens	Lex.	Len.
ATel	15 108	3 250 292	0.068	260
GCN	31 964	7 283 252	0.065	319
AstroNotes	741	165 303	0.076	277
DEAL	5624	1815237	0.057	322

Table 1: Astrophysics corpus statistics comparison (number of focuments, number of tokens, lexical diversity, and average length)

4.2 Most Frequent Word N-grams

Before counting the most frequent unigrams and bigrams characterising the observation reports, we proceeded to some text preprocessing[8]. Results in

[5]https://gcn.gsfc.nasa.gov/gcn3_archive.html

[6]https://astronomerstelegram.org/

[7]https://www.wis-tns.org/astronotes/

[8]We removed stopwords, normalised all digits/numerical values, and lemmatised each word.

TDAC	Unigrams	Bigrams
ATel	num_val, *source, observation, atel, spectrum, flux, telescope, image, x-ray, transient*	*atel* link, *dec* num_val, *apj* num_val, *reference image*, num_val *mcrab, unfiltered magnitude, host galaxy, autodetection system, redshift* num_val
GCN	num_val, *grb, gcn, observation, report, burst, team, kev, swift*	*grb* num_val, *gcn* num_val, num_val gmt, num_val kev, *light curve, upper limit, fermi gbm, swift-xrt team, grb observation, photon index*
AstroNotes	*transient, atlas, survey, object, related, report, telescope, observation, classification, search, supernova, system, galaxy*	*related files*, num_val *mpc, grant* num_val, *near earth, transient name, iau transient,* num_val *arcsec, queens university, zwicky transient, follow-up observation*

Table 2: Most frequent unigrams and bigrams in the TDAC corpus

Table 2 show that more digits and numerical values (num_val token) exist in the GCNs and ATels compared to the AstroNotes. We note and identify different astronomical facilities and objects according to the report's type, such as *swift* and *fermi* telescopes in the GCNs, or even *atlas* and *zwicky transient* facility in the AstroNotes. We note different energy ranges and measurement units (*kev, mcrab, arcsec*), or different wavelengths (*x-ray*) depending on the type of report. Astrophysicists we are collaborating with confirmed our conclusion: in astrophysics, each community uses dedicated platforms according to the discoveries that interest them. Finally, the main thing we notice when analyzing the bigrams is the strong interconnection inside ATel and GCN circulars. Indeed, there are many explicit references between the observation reports (*gcn* num_val and *atel* link) regarding detected events. Since the information concerning an astrophysical event is disseminated across several linked documents, it is essential to gather all the documents and aggregate them by the event.

4.3 Syntactic Analysis

Campbell and Johnson (2001) showed the usefulness of the Pointwise Mutual Information (PMI) and the chi-square χ^2 distance to compare syntactic complexity between corpora. Thus, we decided to compute these two metrics to characterise the discourse used in astrophysics. We computed the positive PMI (see equation 1) on parts-of-speech (POS) bigrams between two corpora: our TDAC corpus composed of observation reports and the DEAL challenge corpus.

$$PMI(x, y) = \log_2\left(\frac{P(xy)}{P(x) * P(y)}\right) \quad (1)$$

The mutual information allows highlighting the proximity between two corpora. We also compared the frequency of occurrence of single POS and POS bigrams between corpora using the χ^2 metric (see equation 2).

$$\chi^2 = \sum\left(\frac{Observed - Expected}{Expected}\right)^2 \quad (2)$$

We used SciSpacy (Neumann et al., 2019) for POS tagging after conducting performance tests[9] of POS labelling, and obtaining better performance than NLTK, TreeTagger, Spacy and Genia tools.

4.3.1 Pointwise Mutual Information of POS

We divided each corpus into ten sections of the same size in order to ensure stability of results. We only considered the positive mutual information and then set the negative values to zero. Table 3 reports the average postitive PMI for POS bigrams.

These results seem to point to a less complicated syntactic structure in the DEAL corpus compared to the TDAC one. Indeed, the average PMI value of the DEAL corpus is slightly higher than the average PMI score of the TDAC corpus. When looking inside the TDAC corpus, we notice that compared to ATels et GCNs, the occurrence of POS bigrams

[9] To compare tagging performances, we manually annotated 20 documents from the TDAC corpus and compared performances on POS tagging of 5 different tools to determine the appropriate one for astrophysics texts.

Corpus	# token/section	Avg PMI
TDAC	1 500 000	0.469 (0.028)
- ATel	450 000	0.554 (0.050)
- GCN	960 000	0.524 (0.009)
- AstroNotes	21 000	0.961 (0.044)
DEAL	210 000	0.622 (0.026)

Table 3: Average Positive PMI for POS bigrams (standard deviation of mean in parentheses)

in AstroNotes seems more dependent than those in ATels and GCNs, as seen by the higher score in the positive PMI. The syntactic structure seems to be less complicated in AstroNotes.

4.3.2 Frequency Distributions of POS

We computed the chi-square metric to calculate the distances between each corpora. The chi-square distances for single and POS bigrams comparisons are reported in Table 4. POS and POS bigrams

Corpus	χ^2 POS	χ^2 POS bigram
ATel-GCN	1 075 610.83	1 234 413.99
ATel-AstroNotes	1 594 932.63	1 597 152.56
GCN-AstroNotes	4 017 655.62	4 012 353.21
TDAC-DEAL	3 986 047.13	4 053 795.68

Table 4: χ^2 distance comparison for single POS and POS bigram frequencies.

distributions are relatively different between the TDAC and DEAL corpus, which explains these large χ^2 values between the two corpora. Within the TDAC corpus, we can see a high distance between GCN circulars and the AstroNotes, whereas it is less marked between the ATel and AstroNotes. These first results regarding syntactic analysis show a diversity between the corpora used, but further analysis is needed to qualify these differences.

5 Named Entity Recognition

5.1 Astrophysical Named Entities

We used the same categories defined in the DEAL shared task. This annotation guide comprises 31 named entities and covers the entities of interest, such as astronomical facilities, celestial objects, coordinates, formulae or observational techniques contained in observation reports. Detailed tags list is presented in Table 8 in Appendix. Figure 2 shows the normalised distribution of annotated named entities on the TDAC and DEAL corpora for comparison purposes.

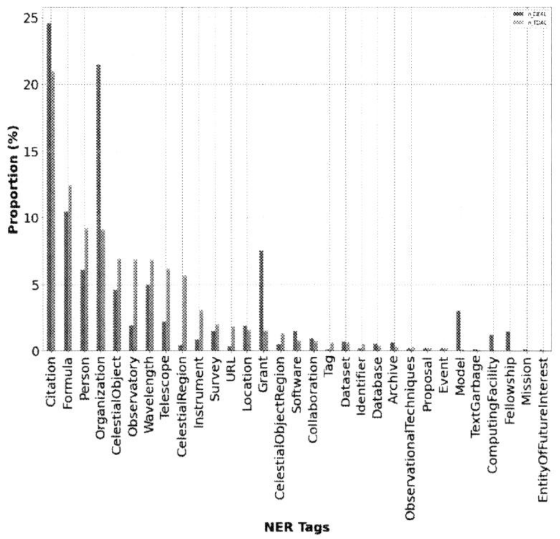

Figure 2: Normalised distribution of named entities in the TDAC (orange) and DEAL (blue) corpus.

Classes' distribution within the two corpora is not similar. Indeed, in the TDAC corpus, the most frequent categories *e.g.* `Formula`, `CelestialObject`, `Observatory`, or `CelestialRegion`. These are particular categories in the astrophysics domain. Most of these specific classes are less present in the DEAL corpus, in which we find mainly the classes of types: `Citation`, `Organization`, `Grant` or `Person`, which seems to be more generic named entity categories.

5.2 Annotation Procedure

The reports used to build the TDAC corpus for NER were randomly selected from the extracted observation reports and annotated in two stages. First, we used one of the models fine-tuned for the DEAL shared task to perform an automatic pre-annotation of 75 observation reports, followed by a manual correction stage by a PhD student with a background in astrophysics. The evaluation of the quality of the pre-annotation using the fine-tuned model corresponds to experiment 1 presented in the rest of this article (see Table 5). During the manual correction phase of the 75 documents, a double annotation was carried out on 30 documents (*i.e.* 7584 double annotated tokens) between the PhD student and a senior in NLP. The average time spent per document is about 4.5 minutes for the PhD student and 5.7 min for the NLP expert. This double annotation allowed us to calculate an inter-annotator agreement (IAA) using recall, precision, and F1 score; metrics considered adapted for computing IAA in several studies (Grouin et al., 2011). After a first double annotation of the 30 documents between the two annotators, we obtained an overall F1 score of 0.7839. After a second pass, we reached an F1 score of 0.8490, high enough for the PhD student to continue annotating the remaining documents alone.

5.3 Experiments

The Baseline Model We used one of the models fine-tuned as part of the DEAL shared task to perform an automatic pre-annotation of the TDAC corpus. It corresponds to the PyTorch HuggingFace's `scibert_scivocab_cased` version of SciBERT model (Beltagy et al., 2019). It has been fine-tuned on the DEAL corpus that we split into train and development sets. The training set consists of 1653 annotated documents (542 550 tokens), and the development set comprises 100 documents (30 582 tokens). For the shared task, the model has been tested on 1366 documents (447 366 tokens). Fine-tuning was performed on 11 epochs, with a learning rate $\alpha = 2.10^{-5}$ and a training batch size of 4. One epoch took approximately 170 seconds. More information is provided in the corresponding system description paper (Alkan et al., 2022).

Experiment 1: Testing directly on TDAC This first experiment evaluates the baseline model fine-tuned on the DEAL corpus directly to the TDAC corpus and analyzes whether performances stay maintained when applying to another type of corpus of the same specialised domain. Thus, we evaluate the model on the 75 annotated documents.

Experiment 2: Continue Model's Fine-Tuning using TDAC We will continue the model's fine-tuning on 9 additional epochs in this second experiment using the TDAC corpus. We split the TDAC corpus into training and test sets (approximately 80%-20%), *i.e.* 59 documents for training (18 ATels, 21 GCNs and 20 AstroNotes) which represents a total of 15 374 tokens and 16 documents for evaluation (7 ATels, 4 GCNs, and 4 AstroNotes) which represents a total of 3638 tokens. Since the corpus size is still small, one epoch lasts about 6 seconds when fine-tuning on TDAC.

Experiment 3: Fine-Tuning a New Model From Scratch on TDAC For this third experiment, we fine-tuned from scratch on TDAC the `scibert_scivocab_cased` with same hyper-parameters configuration than the baseline model, *i.e.* ($epoch = 20$, $\alpha = 2.10^{-5}$, $batch = 4$). We used the same training and test sets as experiment 2.

5.4 Results

For evaluation we used both the CoNLL-2000 shared task seqeval[10] F1-Score at the entity level and scikit-learn's Matthews correlation coefficient (MCC[11]) method at the token level.

Experiment 1 For comparison purposes, we also reminded the performances of the system trained and tested on the DEAL corpus as part of the shared task. The performances of the NER system on the TDAC corpus (75 documents) are given in Table 5.

Corpus	P	R	F1	MCC
DEAL	0.7752	0.8284	0.8009	0.9025
TDAC	0.4993	0.7043	0.5843	0.7760
– ATel	0.5809	0.7325	0.6480	0.8213
– GCN	0.5236	0.7230	0.6074	0.7653
– AstroNotes	0.3952	0.6421	0.4893	0.7474

Table 5: Performance of the baseline NER system fine-tuned on DEAL (as part of the shared task) and tested on our TDAC corpus (with details by type of document). Metrics used are Precision (P), Recall (R), F1-score and MCC.

Experiment 2 Table 6 shows the performance of the baseline NER system we fine-tuned on 9 additional epochs.

Corpus	P	R	F1	MCC
TDAC	0.720	0.796	0.756	0.855
– ATel	0.667	0.703	0.684	0.854
– GCN	0.745	0.822	0.781	0.842
– AstroNotes	0.874	0.891	0.882	0.943

Table 6: Performance of the baseline NER system after fine-tuning on 9 additional epochs using our TDAC corpus (with details by type of document). Metrics used are Precision (P), Recall (R), F1-score and MCC.

Experiment 3 Table 7 shows the performance of the NER system we built and fine-tuned from scratch on the TDAC corpus.

[10] `https://github.com/chakki-works/seqeval`

[11] `https://scikit-learn.org/stable/modules/generated/sklearn.metrics.matthews_corrcoef.html`

Corpus	P	R	F1	MCC
TDAC	0.693	0.777	0.733	0.814
– ATel	0.672	0.733	0.701	0.846
– GCN	0.728	0.793	0.759	0.796
– AstroNotes	0.684	0.792	0.734	0.877

Table 7: Performance of a NER system after fine-tuning from scratch on 20 epochs using our TDAC corpus (with details by type of document). Metrics used are Precision (P), Recall (R), F1-score and MCC.

6 Discussion and Outlook

Experiment 1 is not comparable to experiments 2 and 3 because the test sample size is not the same. However, it allows us to first appreciate the baseline model's robustness by testing it on our TDAC corpus. When tested on the TDAC corpus, we noticed a considerable drop in performance (a loss of 0.2166 on the F1 score globally). The results may appear low or moderate. This could be explained by a strict evaluation (identical label and border). With experiments 2 and 3, we notice relatively similar results. Overall, the model fine-tuned from scratch performs slightly worse than the baseline model for which we continued the fine-tuning over nine additional epochs. Experiment 3 shows that the system performs better on the ATels when fine-tuning from scratch. These preliminary results on this first small annotated corpus nevertheless show that the DEAL corpus is a good starting point for building an entity detection system and can be adapted to other types of documents in the astrophysical domain. However, it is necessary to analyze whether this behaviour is confirmed on a larger scale.

While the first annotations have been made by a PhD student with a background in astrophysics in order to make a proof-of-concept, we are now experiencing new annotations made by two senior experts, one in astrophysics, the other in NLP.

Joining the two corpora (DEAL+TDAC) would be complementary because of the distribution of classes in the two corpora (Figure 2). We observe that certain classes of entities are more present in the TDAC corpus than in DEAL (*e.g.* `Formula`, `CelestialObject`, `Observatory`, or `CelestialRegion`). The TDAC corpus thus makes it possible to fill the lack of specific classes and vice versa. Therefore, joining these two corpora would thus allow for building a more efficient system for a more significant number of classes.

7 Conclusion

In this paper, we presented the TDAC corpus, composed of astrophysics textual content from three sources (ATel, GCN circulars, and AstroNotes). Our corpus has been manually annoted in named entity, based on the annotation schema used in the DEAL corpus. We also presented the experiments we made in order to make it easier the manual annotation process, using a SciBERT-based model fine-tuned on the WIESP 2022 NLP Challenge. We observed that a model trained on the DEAL corpus is not sufficient since it obtained moderate results, while a quite light fine-tuning (9 additional epochs) on our TDAC corpus allows us to improve the performances of our NER system.

In the future, we plan to enrich the corpus with morpho-syntactic annotations and relations between named entities. We estimate this corpus would be a useful resource for NLP applications in astrophysics.

Once the information extraction system we are developing is considered reliable enough, we aim to deploy them in Astro-COLIBRI, a real-time platform that evaluates alerts sent by observers regarding transient sources (Reichherzer et al., 2021). The deployment of our NLP models in Astro-COLIBRI will allow both professional and amateur astronomers to access the most relevant information disseminated through GCN circulars, ATels and AstroNotes instantaneously.

References

Atilla Kaan Alkan, Cyril Grouin, Fabian Schüssler, and Pierre Zweigenbaum. 2022. A majority voting strategy of a scibert-based ensemble models for detecting entities in the astrophysics literature (shared task). In *Proceedings of the 1st Workshop on Information Extraction from Scientific Publications*, Taipei, Taiwan. Association for Computational Linguistics.

Scott Douglas Barthelmy, Paul S. Butterworth, Thomas L. Cline, Neil Gehrels, Gerald J. Fishman, Chryssa Kouveliotou, and Charles A. Meegan. 1995. BACODINE, the real-time BATSE gamma-ray burst coordinates distribution network. *Astrophysics and Space Science*, 231:235–238.

Markus Becker, Ben Hachey, Beatrice Alex, and Claire Grover. 2005. Optimising selective sampling for bootstrapping named entity recognition. In *In Proceedings of the ICML Workshop on Learning with Multiple Views*, pages 5–11.

Iz Beltagy, Kyle Lo, and Arman Cohan. 2019. Scibert:

A pretrained language model for scientific text. In *EMNLP*. Association for Computational Linguistics.

DA Campbell and S Johnson. 2001. Comparing syntactic complexity in medical and non-medical corpora. *Proceedings / AMIA ... Annual Symposium. AMIA Symposium*, pages 90–4.

A. Gal-Yam. 2021. The TNS alert system. *Bulletin of the AAS*, 53(1). Https://baas.aas.org/pub/2021n1i423p05.

Felix Grezes, Thomas Allen, Tirthankar Ghosal, and Sergi Blanco-Cuaresma. 2022. Overview of the first shared task on detecting entities in the astrophysics literature (deal). In *Proceedings of the 1st Workshop on Information Extraction from Scientific Publications*, Taipei, Taiwan. Association for Computational Linguistics.

Félix Grèzes, Sergi Blanco-Cuaresma, Alberto Accomazzi, Michael J. Kurtz, Golnaz Shapurian, Edwin A. Henneken, Carolyn S. Grant, Donna M. Thompson, Roman Chyla, Stephen McDonald, Timothy W. Hostetler, Matthew R. Templeton, Kelly E. Lockhart, Nemanja Martinovic, Shinyi Chen, Chris Tanner, and Pavlos Protopapas. 2021. Building astroBERT, a language model for astronomy & astrophysics. *CoRR*, abs/2112.00590.

Cyril Grouin, Sophie Rosset, Pierre Zweigenbaum, Karën Fort, Olivier Galibert, and Ludovic Quintard. 2011. Proposal for an extension of traditional named entities: From guidelines to evaluation, an overview. In *Proceedings of the 5th Linguistic Annotation Workshop*, pages 92–100, Portland, Oregon, USA. Association for Computational Linguistics.

Ben Hachey, Beatrice Alex, and Markus Becker. 2005. Investigating the effects of selective sampling on the annotation task. In *Proceedings of the Ninth Conference on Computational Natural Language Learning (CoNLL-2005)*, pages 144–151, Ann Arbor, Michigan. Association for Computational Linguistics.

W. E. Kerzendorf. 2019. Knowledge discovery through text-based similarity searches for astronomy literature. *Journal of Astrophysics and Astronomy*, 40:1–7.

Yunhyong Kim and Bonnie Webber. 2006. Implicit reference to citations: a study of astronomy. *ERPANET*.

Nikhil Mukund, Saurabh Thakur, Sheelu Abraham, A. K. Aniyan, Sanjit Mitra, Ninan Sajeeth Philip, Kaustubh Vaghmare, and D. P. Acharjya. 2018. An Information Retrieval and Recommendation System for Astronomical Observatories. *Astrophysical Journal Supplement*, 235(1):22.

Tara Murphy, Tara McIntosh, and James R. Curran. 2006. Named entity recognition for astronomy literature. In *Proceedings of the Australasian Language Technology Workshop 2006*, pages 59–66, Sydney, Australia.

Andrii Neronov. 2019. Introduction to multi-messenger astronomy. *Journal of Physics: Conference Series*, 1263(1):012001.

Mark Neumann, Daniel King, Iz Beltagy, and Waleed Ammar. 2019. ScispaCy: Fast and robust models for biomedical natural language processing. In *Proceedings of the 18th BioNLP Workshop and Shared Task*, pages 319–327, Florence, Italy. Association for Computational Linguistics.

P. Reichherzer, F. Schüssler, V. Lefranc, A. Yusafzai, A. K. Alkan, H. Ashkar, and J. Becker Tjus. 2021. Astro-COLIBRI—the COincidence LIBrary for real-time inquiry for multimessenger astrophysics. *The Astrophysical Journal Supplement Series*, 256(1):5.

Robert E. Rutledge. 1998. The Astronomer's Telegram: A Web-based Short-Notice Publication System for the Professional Astronomical Community. *Publications of the Astronomical Society of the Pacific*, 110(748):754–756.

A Appendix

Category	Definition	Example
Person	A named person or their initials	Andrea M. Ghez, Ghez A.
Organization	A named organization that is not an observatory.	NASA, University of Toledo
Location	A named location on Earth.	Canada
Observatory	A, often similarly located, group of telescopes.	Keck Observatory, Fermi
Telescope	A "bucket" to catch light.	Hubble Space Telescope, Discovery Channel Telescope
Instrument	A device, often, but not always, placed on a telescope, to make a measurement.	Infrared Array Camera, NIRCam
Survey	An organized search of the sky often dedicated to large scale science projects.	2MASS, SDSS
Mission	A spacecraft that is not a telescope or observatory that carries multiple instruments	WIND
CelestialObject	A named object in the sky	ONC, Andromeda galaxy
CelestialRegion	A defined region projected onto the sky, or celestial coordinates.	GOODS field, l=2, b=15
CelestialObjectRegion	Named area on/in a celestial body.	Inner galaxy
Wavelength	Portion of the electromagnetic spectrum	656.46 nm, H-alpha
ObservationalTechniques	Methods/technqiues for observation	Spectroscopic, helioseismic
Model	Mathematical/Physical model	Gaussian, Keplerian
Software	Software, IT tool	NuSTAR, healpy, numpy
ComputingFacility	Server, cluster for computation	Supercomputer, GPU
Dataset	Astronomical catalogues	3FGL catalog
Database	A curated set of data	Simbad database
Archive	A curated collection of the literature or data.	NASA ADS, MAST
Identifier	A unique identifier for data, images, etc.	ALMA 123.12345
Citation	A reference to previous work in the literature.	Allen et al. 2012
Collaboration	Name of collaboration	Fermi LAT Collaboration
Event	A conference, workshop or other event that often brings scientests together.	Protostars and Planets VI
Grant	An allocation of money and/or time for a research project.	grant No. 12345, ADAP grant 12345
Fellowship	A grant focused towards students and/or early career researchers.	Hubble Fellowship
Formula	Mathematical formula or equations.	$F = Gm1m2/r^2, z = 2.3$
Tag	A HTML tag.	<bold>
TextGarbage	Incorrect text, often multiple punctuation marks with no inner text.	,,,
EntityOfFutureInterest	A general catch all for things that may be worth thinking about in the future.	Earth-like, Solar-like
URL	A link to a website.	$https://www.astropy.org/$

Table 8: Classification of the named entities in the annotation guideline. The HuggingFace repository containing the annotated data and the annotation guide is only accessible to participants of the shared task. Thus, we have reproduced the same list of named entities with their definition.

Reproducibility Signals in Science: A preliminary analysis

Akhil Pandey Akella
Dept. of Computer Science
Northern Illinois University
aakella@niu.edu

Hamed Alhoori
Dept. of Computer Science
Northern Illinois University
alhoori@niu.edu

David Koop
Dept. of Computer Science
Northern Illinois University
dakoop@niu.edu

Abstract

Reproducibility is an important feature of science; experiments are retested, and analyses are repeated. Trust in the findings increases when consistent results are achieved. Despite the importance of reproducibility, significant work is often involved in these efforts, and some published findings may not be reproducible due to oversights or errors. In this paper, we examine a myriad of features in scholarly articles published in computer science conferences and journals and test how they correlate with reproducibility. We collected data from three different sources that labeled publications as either reproducible or irreproducible and employed statistical significance tests to identify features of those publications that hold clues about reproducibility. We found the readability of the scholarly article and accessibility of the software artifacts through hyperlinks to be strong signals noticeable amongst reproducible scholarly articles.

1 Introduction

Transparency in the scientific process accelerates scientific discovery and strengthens public opinions on scientifically driven matters. Reproducibility plays a crucial role in aiding this transparency, and it is encouraging to have a consensus in the scientific community to address the problem of reproducibility in science. Policymakers, government entities, open source communities, peer-reviewed journals, conferences, and the academic community at large have a shared responsibility to promote reproducible research. Effective dissemination of science cannot happen without trust and integrity in the scientific process. Practically, reproducible science has a first-hand impact in notable places such as research labs, classrooms, industries, and academia. Lack of reproducible research could restrict attaining a deeper understanding of the original researcher's thought process and, therefore, severely impact people involved in the communities mentioned earlier.

The concept of reproducibility is intricate and stratified with different but complementary issues. Before we attempt to understand how to approach the problem of reproducibility, we must first provide some definition of what we mean by this term in this context. Studies such as (Gundersen and Kjensmo, 2018; Cohen et al., 2018; Barba, 2018) highlight how the definition of *reproducibility* varies across different studies and disciplines and how differing definitions can result in confusion. For that reason, the flexible definition presented in Gundersen and Kjensmo (2018) is appealing: "the ability of an independent research team to produce the same results using the same method based on the documentation made by the original research team." Collective efforts from various players of the research community such as publishers, conference organizers, and journals in promoting good practices for ensuring reproducibility in the experimentation process is refreshing, but there is still a lack of agreement on what exactly constitutes a "good practice" which is a concern.

In this study, we attempt to understand the relationship between the structure of science (Thelwall, 2019) and the concept of reproducibility by using statistical significance tests. In doing so, our emphasis is to examine epistemic opacity (Newman, 2015) of linguistic features and structural features concerning reproducibility. We achieve this by running numerous hypothesis tests and identifying the significant factors affecting the reproducibility of scholarly articles. Our goal is to utilize statistical tests to pick signals that could help identify articles requiring more (or less) effort to reproduce.

2 Related Work

Reproducibility is an important concept that affects large communities in general (Mede et al., 2020; Hutson, 2018). The breadth of literature on re-

Proceedings of the 1st Workshop on Information Extraction from Scientific Publications, pages 140–144
Nov 20, 2022.

producibility spanning different disciplines (Open Science Collaboration, 2012; Prinz et al., 2011; Begley and Ellis, 2012; Peers et al., 2012) has broadly focused on either performing large meta-analyses that reproduce a large set of scholarly articles or qualitative studies that encourage researchers to adopt a certain methodology.

Our study falls in line with the studies that attempts to quantify the factors important for reproducibility, e.g. (Raff, 2019). Identifying such important factors would also be helpful in building machine learning models that can estimate the degree of reproducibility in scholarly articles(Yang et al., 2020).

3 Data

While scientific publications often follow similar structures, there is significant freedom in how ideas are communicated and expressed. This lack of rigidity allows authors to weave stories around fundamental ideas, and the absorption of particular ideas can sometimes be related to how they are presented. We are interested in whether the structure of a publication reveals anything about its potential for (ir-)reproducibility. To examine this, we compiled a collection of scholarly articles that have been evaluated as either reproducible or irreproducible from three different sources. For each article, we gathered comprehensive metadata and extracted structural and linguistic features. These collections of articles include:

- **Brown University**: Collberg et al. (Collberg et al., 2015) conducted a meta-analysis that involved steps in reproducing scholarly articles published in ACM computer science conferences and journals. They found that nearly 50 percent of the examined scholarly articles required extra effort to reproduce the articles. Computer scientists at Brown University led an effort named "Examining Reproducibility in Computer Science" to crowdsource a reexamination of this study (Krishnamurthi, 2015). They performed a meta-analysis of the original study and offered new insights. The data collected provides significant detail about the effort involved in reproducing the studies in the original publications. The current repository provides results for 207 papers; 142 are classified as reproducible and 65 as non-reproducible.
- **Retraction Watch Database (RetractionDB)**: The Retraction Watch Database stores information about scholarly articles that are retracted from conferences and journals (Oransky and Marcus, 2010). It also logs information about the subject/area to which the scholarly article belongs, the country where the article is published, the name of the publisher, the journal name, and most importantly, the reason why the article was retracted. We used this database to find all the scholarly articles in the field of computer science that were retracted under reasons surrounding results not being reproducible, and 34 papers fit these criteria.
- **Badged ACM Papers**: The Association for Computing Machinery (ACM) has introduced badges as a way to signal when publications have been successfully reproduced. We began with 176 articles that were badged as having results reproduced. Of these, 90 were badged as having Reusable Artifacts, and 70 of those had a Functional Artifact badge. We were able to obtain 64 of the papers that had "Results Reproduced" badges and received both a Reusable Artifact and a Functional Artifact badge.

From each of the three sources, we used the available metadata to locate each article. In some cases, we searched by article and authors' names to obtain a DOI or, in some cases, a URL for an article. If we were unable to unambiguously determine this information, the article was dropped from the dataset. Using the DOI, we were able to obtain further metadata and the full text of the article, usually in PDF format. After filling out the metadata and obtaining the full text, we had 305 papers in total; 206 were classified as reproducible, and 99 were classified as non-reproducible. Data and code will be made available as supplementary information upon publishing.

4 Methodology

4.1 Feature Engineering

The motivation for considering the below features stems from the shared intuitions highlighted in (Gundersen et al., 2018; Gundersen, 2020; Raff, 2019) along with checklists from popular publishing venues such as NeurIPS, ICML, etc.

Table 1: List of Structural Features and respective Point Biserial Correlations against target variable

Feature	p-value
Presence of Introduction Section	0.0808
Presence of Methodology Section	0.3112
Presence of Results Section	0.7006
Number of Pages	0.1630
Number of Images	0.3571
Number of Tables	0.7187
Number of Algorithms	0.0654
Number of Hyperlinks	0.0028
Number of Equations	0.4212

1. **Structural features:** Quantitative and qualitative information pertaining to the structure of the scholarly article. This includes information about the existence of particular sections as well as counts of the tables, figures, or algorithms in a given scholarly article. We developed python modules to parse the PDF of the scholarly article in order to extract this information. The features along with respective Point Biserial correlations are mentioned in Table 1.

2. **Linguistic features:** Linguistic indicators quantifying different metrics based on the language used in the scholarly article to differentiate the writing styles of various authors. These indicators include Word count, Average word length, Average sentence length, Frequency of words greater than average word length, Syllable count, and Yule's I measure of lexical diversity (Yule, 2014). These features are general to computational linguistics and are easily understandable. Additionally, we considered metrics such as *Complex words*, which refer to the number of polysyllable words in a given text. This feature was extracted using the python *textblob* library. *Mean Readability* was measured by obtaining the mean of readability metrics such as Flesch Reading Ease Level, SMOG Index, Coleman-Liau index, Automated Readability Index, Dale-Chall Readability Score, Linsear Write Formula, and Gunning FOG. We obtained the values from *textstat*, a python package, to obtain the readability metrics. We also collected the *Sentiment* score for the full text of a given scholarly article and attached a sentiment label (positive = 1, negative = 0) for the respective articles. A similar process was used to obtain the sentiment label for the title of the article.

Table 2: List of Linguistic Features and respective Point Biserial Correlations against target variable

Feature	p-value
Word count	0.5357
Average word length	0.2379
Frequency of words greater than average word length	0.9804
Complex words	0.8394
Syllable count	0.7467
Yule's I measure of lexical diversity	0.1102
Mean Readability	0.0000
Article's sentiment	0.5659
Title's sentiment	0.7335

We gathered this information by implementing python programs that used the python libraries such as *spaCy* and *NLTK* to build the methods for calculating the metrics. All of these linguistic measures were based on the full text of the scholarly article. The features along with respective Point Biserial correlations, are mentioned in Table. 2.

4.2 Point Biserial Correlation

A preliminary statistical analysis of the dependent and independent variables could be performed using correlations. Since our target is a nominal variable, we could not use *Pearson* correlation or *Spearman* correlation as both of them presume the target variable to be continuous. The *point biserial* (Gupta, 1960) correlation matrix measures the correlation between a dichotomous target variable and continuous variables. The results in Table 1 and Table 2 are values obtained by calculating the point biserial correlation coefficient(s) and the associated p-value(s).

4.3 Significance tests

The features mentioned in Tables 1 and 2 are a combination of ordinal and nominal attributes. In order to determine the significance of the features, we had to employ different statistical significance tests such as the *Mann-Whitney U* test (Mann and Whitney, 1947) and *Chi-squared* test (Yates, 1934).

5 Results

We computed correlations and performed statistical significance tests on the combined data sources to identify features that played a significant role in indicating the reproducibility of scholarly articles. The point biserial correlations as shown in Tables 1 and 2 suggested that only **mean readability** and **number of hyperlinks** significantly correlate with reproducibility.

The results of the *Mann-Whitney U* and *Chi-squared* tests show that **mean readability, number of hyperlinks, number of algorithms, average word length, and yule's measure of lexical diversity** to be statistically significant features that align and signal scholarly work that is reproducible with reasonable certainty. More significantly, the readability of a scholarly article and accessibility of software artifacts, either as code repositories, psuedo-code, or algorithms, could be considered strong indicators for reproducibility. It is important to note that these signals do not quantify or assure the reproducibility of a scholarly article but rather help identify articles that require more (or less) effort to reproduce.

Table 3: Mann-Whitney U Significance test for the numerical features

Feature	p-value
Yule's I measure of lexical diversity	0.0131
Word count	0.6547
Average word length	0.0003
Frequency of words greater than average word length	0.9171
Syllable count	0.3910
Complex words	0.9596
Mean Readability	0.0001
Number of Images	0.2039
Number of Tables	0.9586
Number of Algorithms	0.0283
Length of the paper	0.5039
Number of Hyperlinks	0.0011
Number of Equations	0.2148

Our findings were backed by results from statistical experiments such as Point Biserial Correlations, Chi-squared test, and Mann-Whitney U test, and p-values ($p < 0.05$) served as the basis for the significance of our findings. You can obtain a copy of the datasets, experiment setup, and additional software artifacts from Github repository. [1].

Table 4: Chi-squared Significance test for the categorical features

Feature	p-value
Presence of Introduction Section	0.1070
Presence of Methodology Section	0.3728
Presence of Results Section	0.8617
Article Sentiment	0.6646
Title Sentiment	0.8495

6 Discussion

The structure of science involves a well-formed process that begins with factual and valid data, continues through detailed descriptions of experimental procedures, and follows on to clearly presented results. The scientific process has many tenets, but these represent some. They have been promulgated over the years to allow the scientific process to flourish with checks and balances in the form of peer reviews. Contextually, factors such as discipline, year, type of scientific study, etc., play a major role in identifying the effort required to reproduce articles. Therefore, the dataset we built is an essential factor to consider while interpreting our findings that the readability of the scholarly article and accessibility of the software artifacts through hyperlinks are significant features among reproducible scholarly articles. Our motivation is to discover additional latent variables that consider these contextual factors while identifying the effort required to reproduce articles.

7 Conclusions and Future Work

In this study, our pursuit of identifying features that can signal reproducible science involved correlations and significance tests. We found the readability of the scholarly article and accessibility of the software artifacts through hyperlinks to be significant features among reproducible scholarly articles. Our code repository with data and experiments will be available post-publishing.

In the future, we plan on expanding the scope of our study by 1) Gathering more Badged data from ACM; 2) Testing the validity of our findings against adversarial examples; and 3) Observing the effects

[1]https://github.com/reproducibilityproject/reproducibilitysignals

of citing a reproducible article vs non-reproducible ones.

8 Acknowledgement

This work is supported in part by NSF Grant No. 2022443.

References

Lorena A. Barba. 2018. Terminologies for reproducible research.

CG. Begley and LM. Ellis. 2012. *Drug development: Raise standards for preclinical cancer research*. Nature.

K. Bretonnel Cohen, Jingbo Xia, Pierre Zweigenbaum, Tiffany Callahan, Orin Hargraves, Foster Goss, Nancy Ide, Aurélie Névéol, Cyril Grouin, and Lawrence E. Hunter. 2018. Three dimensions of reproducibility in natural language processing. In *Proceedings of the Eleventh International Conference on Language Resources and Evaluation (LREC 2018)*, Miyazaki, Japan. European Language Resources Association (ELRA).

Christian Collberg, Todd Proebsting, and Alex M Warren. 2015. Repeatability and benefaction in computer systems research. *University of Arizona TR*, 14:4.

O. E. Gundersen. 2020. *The Fundamental Principles of Reproducibility*. ArXiv e-prints cs-LG.

O. E. Gundersen, Y. Gil, and D. W. Aha. 2018. On reproducible ai: Towards reproducible research, open science, and digital scholarship in ai publications. *AIMag*, 39(3):56–68.

Odd Erik Gundersen and Sigbjørn Kjensmo. 2018. State of the art: Reproducibility in artificial intelligence. In *Thirty-Second AAAI Conference on Artificial Intelligence*.

S.D. Gupta. 1960. Point biserial correlation coefficient and its generalization. *Psychometrika*, 25:393–408.

M. Hutson. 2018. *Artificial intelligence faces reproducibility crisis*. American Association for the Advancement of Science.

Shriram Krishnamurthi. 2015. Examining reproducibility in computer science.

H. B. Mann and D. R. Whitney. 1947. On a test of whether one of two random variables is stochastically larger than the other. *The Annals of Mathematical Statistics*, 18(1):50–60.

N. G. Mede, M. S. Sch"afer, R. Ziegler, and M. Weißkopf. 2020. The "replication crisis" in the public eye: Germans' awareness and perceptions of the (ir) reproducibility of scientific research. *Public Understanding of Science*, 9636.

Julian Newman. 2015. Epistemic opacity, confirmation holism and technical debt: Computer simulation in the light of empirical software engineering. In *HaPoC*, volume 487, pages 256–272.

Open Science Collaboration. 2012. An open, Large-Scale, collaborative effort to estimate the reproducibility of psychological science. *Perspect. Psychol. Sci.*, 7(6):657–660.

I. Oransky and A. Marcus. 2010. The retraction watch database.

I. S. Peers, P. R. Ceuppens, and C. Harbron. 2012. In search of preclinical robustness. *Nature reviews Drug discovery*, 10:733.

F. Prinz, T. Schlange, and K. Asadullah. 2011. Believe it or not: how much can we rely on published data on potential drug targets? *Nature reviews Drug discovery*, 10.

E. Raff. 2019. A step toward quantifying independently reproducible machine learning research. *Advances in Neural Information Processing Systems 32*, pages 5485–5495.

Mike Thelwall. 2019. The rhetorical structure of science? a multidisciplinary analysis of article headings. *Journal of Informetrics*, 13(2):555–563.

Y. Yang, W. Youyou, and B. Uzzi. 2020. Estimating the deep replicability of scientific findings using human and artificial intelligence. *Proceedings of the National Academy of Sciences*, 117:10762–10768.

F. Yates. 1934. Contingency tables involving small numbers and the x2 test. *Journal of the Royal Statistical Society*, 1(2):217–235.

C Udny Yule. 2014. *The statistical study of literary vocabulary*. Cambridge University Press.

A Majority Voting Strategy of a SciBERT-based Ensemble Models for Detecting Entities in the Astrophysics Literature (Shared Task)

Atilla Kaan Alkan[*,†], **Cyril Grouin**[*], **Fabian Schüssler**[†], **Pierre Zweigenbaum**[*]
[*]Université Paris-Saclay, CNRS, Laboratoire interdisciplinaire des sciences du numérique, 91405, Orsay, France
[†]IRFU, CEA, Université Paris-Saclay, F-91191 Gif-sur-Yvette, France
{atilla.alkan, cyril.grouin, pierre.zweigenbaum}@lisn.upsaclay.fr
fabian.schussler@cea.fr

Abstract

Detecting Entities in the Astrophysics Literature (DEAL) is a proposed shared task in the scope of the first Workshop on Information Extraction from Scientific Publications (WIESP) at AACL-IJCNLP 2022. It aims to propose systems identifying astrophysical named entities. This article presents our system based on a majority voting strategy of an ensemble composed of 32 SciBERT models. The system we propose is ranked second and outperforms the baseline provided by the organisers by achieving an F1 score of 0.7993 and a Matthews Correlation Coefficient (MCC) score of 0.8978 in the testing phase.

1 Introduction

Astronomy and astrophysics consist of observing and studying various cosmic phenomena such as tidal disruption events, gamma-ray bursts, and many other messengers such as neutrinos and gravitational waves (Neronov, 2019; Abbott et al., 2016). Missions and observations performed by astronomical facilities worldwide significantly increase the number of astrophysics papers. Most published papers are freely available and accessible through the Astrophysics Data System (ADS[1]), where researchers can search and access more than 15 million records covering astronomy, astrophysics, and general physics publications. However, some domain keywords can be easily confused when searching for articles in the literature. For instance, "*Planck*" can refer to the person, the mission, the constant, or several institutions. One approach for this word sense disambiguation problem would be automatically recognised entities. Named Entity Recognition (NER) consists of recognising mentions of entities from text belonging to predefined semantic types: person, location or organisation (Yadav and Bethard, 2018). It is, therefore, an essential technique to extract relevant information from unstructured human-written data.

Detecting Entities in the Astrophysics Literature (DEAL) is a shared task that tackles the challenge of developing a system that identifies named entities in the astrophysics literature (Grezes et al., 2022). The shared task was organised in two stages: validation and test. Evaluation metrics used were both the CoNLL-2000 shared task seqeval[2] F1-Score at the entity level and scikit-learn's Matthews correlation coefficient (MCC[3]) method at the token level. Organisers provided the NER system's baseline (see Table 3 in Appendix) using astroBERT (Grèzes et al., 2021), a deep contextual language model pre-trained on 395 499 publications (3 819 322 591 tokens, 16GB on disk) from the ADS database. The model astroBERT is not available yet, but preliminary results are exposed in the companion paper.

As part of this shared task, we used and explored an ensemble of contextual Pre-Trained Language Models (PLTMs) for NER purposes.

The paper is organised as follows: Section 2 briefly presents existing methods and approaches for named entity recognition in astrophysics and other scientific domain. Section 3 provides information about the corpus. Section 4 describes our system as well as the experimental setup. Section 5 presents our results.

2 Strategies for Entities Detection

2.1 State-of-the-Art Methods

The use of neural networks constitutes the current state-of-the-art in many tasks of NLP, including NER. Indeed, for a few years, word embeddings and the combination of two algorithms: bi-

[1]https://ui.adsabs.harvard.edu/

[2]https://github.com/chakki-works/seqeval

[3]https://scikit-learn.org/stable/modules/generated/sklearn.metrics.matthews_corrcoef.html

Proceedings of the 1st Workshop on Information Extraction from Scientific Publications, pages 145–150
Nov 20, 2022.

directional LSTM and Conditional Random Fields (CRF), have been widely used for sequence tagging (Huang et al., 2015). The use of PLTMs (Devlin et al., 2019), and their domain-adapted version such as SciBERT for scientific literature (Beltagy et al., 2019), or BioBERT for the biomedical field (Lee et al., 2019) give state-of-the-art results on NER tasks. Some studies in the biomedical domain have shown that combining multiple PLTMs instead of a single prediction system help to increase performances on NER (Schneider et al., 2022; Dang et al., 2020).

2.2 What About Astrophysics?

Becker et al. (2005); Hachey et al. (2005) built the Astronomy Bootstrapping Corpus (ABC) composed of 209 abstracts of astronomical papers extracted from the ADS. This study explored an active learning approach to detect relevant features and reduce annotation costs for NER using a conditional Markov model tagger (Finkel et al., 2004).

Murphy et al. (2006) built a larger corpus than the ABC for named entities. The annotated corpus consists of 7840 sentences. Similarly, the study investigates the features improving the performances of a NER system based on an adaptation of a Maximum Entropy tagger (Curran and Clark, 2003).

NER studies are limited in astrophysics, and the explored approaches are feature-based only. Since methods presented in the previous section (2.1) have been successfully applied to other specific domains, such as the biomedical one, we were confident that their application to the astrophysics domain would be successful. That is why we explored a method based on an ensemble of PLTMs for NER purposes as part of this shared task.

3 The Corpus

The shared task corpus comprises full-text fragments and acknowledgements sections extracted from ADS papers. Three sets of corpus were accessible for participants[4]: training, development and testing sets. Some statistics of the corpora are provided in Table 1.

The annotation guide comprises 31 named entities and covers the entities of interest, such as astronomical facilities, celestial objects, coordinates, formulae or observational techniques. Detailed tags list is presented in Table 5 (Appendix).

[4]Data are accessible for participants only. We do not know how organisers will make the collection publicly available.

Corpus	Docs	Tokens
Train	1753	573 132
Validation	1366	447 366
Test	2505	794 739

Table 1: Corpus statistics.

For the shared task, only labels of the training corpus were provided. Figure 1 shows entities' distribution in the training corpus. The training corpus comprises full-text fragments (blue) and acknowledgements sections (orange) of approximately equal size. Most frequent categories are `Citation`, `Organization`, `Grant` or `Person`, but classes' distribution within the type of document (acknowledgments vs. full-text fragments) is not similar.

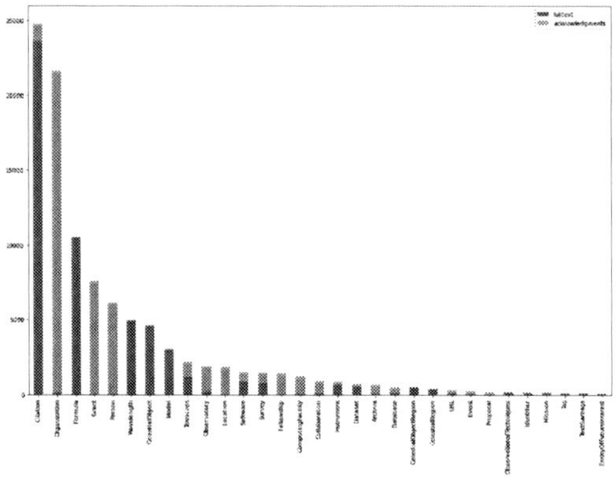

Figure 1: Entities' distribution in the training corpus. In blue are full-text fragments, and in orange are acknowledgements sections.

4 System Description

4.1 The SciBERT-cased Model

We did not apply text preprocessing to the original tokens provided by the organisers. Since some entities, such as astronomical facilities, organisations, and people's names, are proper names and therefore written in the upper-case letter, we decided to opt for the PyTorch HuggingFace's `scibert_scivocab_cased` version of SciBERT model (Beltagy et al., 2019). We assumed that preserving the type case would help the system distinguish these specific entities from standard terms. A first experiment demonstrated our assumption : the SciBERT's cased version performed better than the uncased by increasing the F1-score from 0.797 to 0.801 on the official validation set.

4.2 Setup

Internal Training and Validation Data Since we were limited to 15 daily submissions (and 100 in total) for the validation phase, we decided to create our internal validation set by splitting the original training set and conducting several experiments. Thus, our internal training set consists of 1653 annotated documents (542 550 tokens), and the internal development set comprises 100 documents (30 582 tokens).

Entities Filtering Among the defined categories, two were difficult to interpret (`TextGarbage` and `EntityOfFutureInterest`). Moreover, their low distribution in the training corpus did not make the system efficient in predicting these classes. These two reasons led us to remove them from the fine-tuning phase. Deleting these classes did not impact the overall performance since the evaluation metric was based on the micro F1-score.

Sliding Window for Long Sequences We used `BertTokenizerFast`, one of BERT's tokenizers. During the fine-tuning stage, Transformer-based models segment original tokens into subwords (or word pieces), extending thus an original sequence of N tokens into a sequence of length $N + n_{subwords}$, where $n_{subwords}$ is the number of sub-words generated by the tokenizer. This extension can exceed the size of 512, the limit sequence length that a Transformer-based model can handle. The standard way to deal with this is to apply a sliding window across the input sequence, where each window contains a passage of tokens that fit in the model's context.

4.3 Hyper-Parameters Tuning

When we started our experiments, we wanted to know the optimal combination of hyper-parameters. To do so, we proceeded to a grid search by varying two hyper-parameters: the learning rate α ($[1.10^{-5}, 2.10^{-5}, 5.10^{-5}]$) and the training batch size ($[4, 8, 16]$), representing a total of nine combinations. In order to ensure reliable results regarding the impact of hyper-parameters, each combination of hyper-parameters was used five times with five different seeds randomly chosen ($[0, 123, 762, 5000, 6822]$). We fine tuned all models on 15 epochs using our internal training corpus and evaluated them on the internal validation set at each epoch. On average, one epoch lasts approximately 170 seconds. The ranking of the nine combinations is in Table 4 (appendix).

4.4 Ensemble Strategy

In our study, we wanted to test the influence of an ensemble approach composed of several NER classifiers. Therefore, we conducted experiments comparing the performance of a single system to an ensemble of multiple systems. We used the different models fine-tuned during the grid search to design our ensemble. We wonder two main questions:

- Which different models should we use, and how many models should be included in the system?
- What method should we use to combine the predictions of the different models in our ensemble?

Regarding the first question, we first rank the combinations of the models by performances according to their hyper-parameters during the grid search stage (Table 4, appendix). Then, we proceeded by adding models progressively to the ensemble.

Regarding the second question, related studies showed that there are mainly two approaches: the first consists of a soft strategy, where each model returns its predicted probabilities, and the class label is obtained by applying the argmax function to the sum of all probabilities (Schneider et al., 2022). The second is a majority voting strategy where the system selects the majority class of the class labels predicted by each classifier (Dang et al., 2020). We opted for the majority voting strategy.

5 Results on Official Sets

The official validation and test corpora results (Table 2) show that an ensemble composed of classifiers leads to a higher F1 score.

To determine the number of models to include in our ensemble, we progressively formed an ensemble consisting of the five models of the first performant combination (C2), then added the five models of the second performant combination (C5) and so on. We notice that the performance decreases beyond a certain number of models. Our ensemble comprises the first six combinations that gave the best results during the grid search. This represents 30 models (6 combinations $*$ 5 models / combination). A last submission in the validation phase

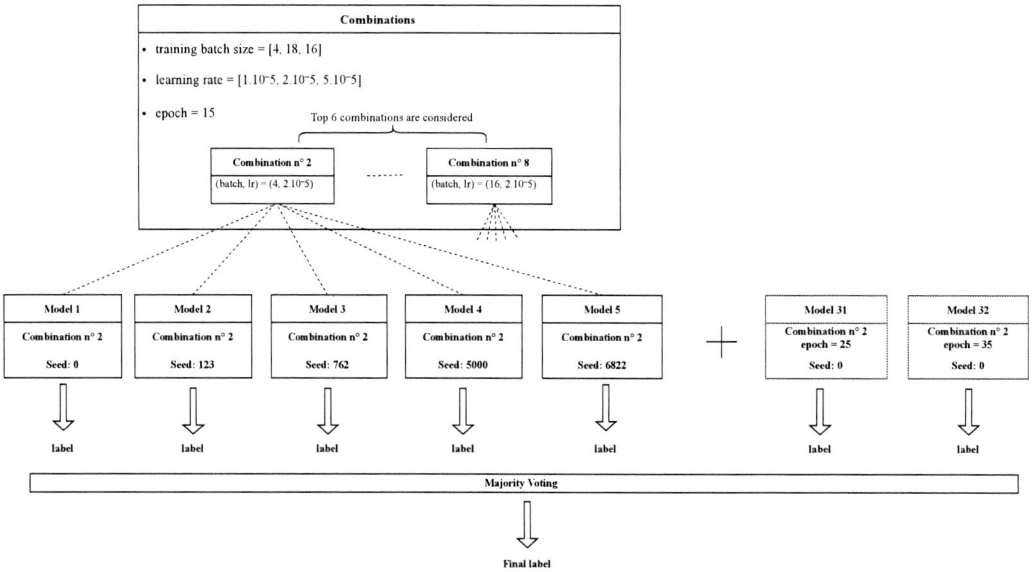

Figure 2: Final architecture of our NER ensemble based on a majority voting strategy.

Ensemble	**Validation**					**Test**				
	P	**R**	**F1**	**MCC**	s	**P**	**R**	**F1**	**MCC**	s
Single system	0.7751	0.8284	0.8009	0.9025	4	0.7990	0.7957	0.7973	0.8968	1
$\sum_{i=1}^{6} S_i$	0.8140	0.8366	0.8251	0.9132	17	0.8008	0.7966	0.7988	0.8974	2
$\sum_{i=1}^{6} S_i$ + 2 models	0.8145	0.8383	**0.8262**	0.9140	24	0.8013	0.7972	**0.7993**	0.8978	4

Table 2: Results on official validation and test sets with the corresponding submission number (s) on the Codalab platform. Metrics used are Precision (P), Recall (R), F1-score and MCC.

(s=24) showed us that adding two additional models from combination n°2 (fine-tuned on a few additional epochs) increases the F1 score. Ultimately, our ensemble consists of 32 models. Figure 2 illustrates our architecture.

6 Conclusion

This shared task aimed to tackle the challenge of detecting entities in the astrophysics literature by proposing a NER system. We exposed in this paper our approach, which first consists of identifying the different hyper-parameters combination giving the highest F1-score. To do so, we proceeded to do a grid search on our internal training and validation sets. In the second stage, we built an ensemble of classifiers based on the top 6 combinations identified during the grid search. Our submissions on the official validation and test sets show that adopting a majority voting strategy of an ensemble of SciBERT-based classifiers gives better results than a single model approach. Finally, we ranked second, achieving an F1 score of 0.7993 and an MCC coefficient of 0.8978 using an ensemble of 32 SciBERT models.

References

B. P. Abbott, R. Abbott, T. D. Abbott, M. R. Abernathy, F. Acernese, K. Ackley, C. Adams, T. Adams, P. Addesso, R. X. Adhikari, and et al. 2016. Observation of gravitational waves from a binary black hole merger. *Physical Review Letters*, 116(6).

Markus Becker, Ben Hachey, Beatrice Alex, and Claire Grover. 2005. Optimising selective sampling for bootstrapping named entity recognition. In *In Proceedings of the ICML Workshop on Learning with Multiple Views*, pages 5–11.

Iz Beltagy, Kyle Lo, and Arman Cohan. 2019. Scibert: A pretrained language model for scientific text. In *EMNLP*. Association for Computational Linguistics.

James Curran and Stephen Clark. 2003. Language independent NER using a maximum entropy tagger. In *Proceedings of the Seventh Conference on Natu-*

ral Language Learning at HLT-NAACL 2003, pages 164–167.

Huong Dang, Kahyun Lee, Sam Henry, and Özlem Uzuner. 2020. Ensemble BERT for classifying medication-mentioning tweets. In *Proceedings of the Fifth Social Media Mining for Health Applications Workshop & Shared Task*, pages 37–41, Barcelona, Spain (Online). Association for Computational Linguistics.

Jacob Devlin, Ming-Wei Chang, Kenton Lee, and Kristina Toutanova. 2019. BERT: Pre-training of deep bidirectional transformers for language understanding. In *Proceedings of the 2019 Conference of the North American Chapter of the Association for Computational Linguistics: Human Language Technologies, Volume 1 (Long and Short Papers)*, pages 4171–4186, Minneapolis, Minnesota. Association for Computational Linguistics.

Jenny Finkel, Shipra Dingare, Huy Nguyen, Malvina Nissim, Christopher Manning, and Gail Sinclair. 2004. Exploiting context for biomedical entity recognition: From syntax to the web. In *Proceedings of the International Joint Workshop on Natural Language Processing in Biomedicine and its Applications (NLPBA/BioNLP)*, pages 91–94, Geneva, Switzerland. COLING.

Felix Grezes, Thomas Allen, Tirthankar Ghosal, and Sergi Blanco-Cuaresma. 2022. Overview of the first shared task on detecting entities in the astrophysics literature (deal). In *Proceedings of the 1st Workshop on Information Extraction from Scientific Publications*, Taipei, Taiwan. Association for Computational Linguistics.

Félix Grèzes, Sergi Blanco-Cuaresma, Alberto Accomazzi, Michael J. Kurtz, Golnaz Shapurian, Edwin A. Henneken, Carolyn S. Grant, Donna M. Thompson, Roman Chyla, Stephen McDonald, Timothy W. Hostetler, Matthew R. Templeton, Kelly E. Lockhart, Nemanja Martinovic, Shinyi Chen, Chris Tanner, and Pavlos Protopapas. 2021. Building astroBERT, a language model for astronomy & astrophysics. *CoRR*, abs/2112.00590.

Ben Hachey, Beatrice Alex, and Markus Becker. 2005. Investigating the effects of selective sampling on the annotation task. In *Proceedings of the Ninth Conference on Computational Natural Language Learning (CoNLL-2005)*, pages 144–151, Ann Arbor, Michigan. Association for Computational Linguistics.

Zhiheng Huang, Wei Xu, and Kai Yu. 2015. Bidirectional lstm-crf models for sequence tagging. *ArXiv*, abs/1508.01991.

Jinhyuk Lee, Wonjin Yoon, Sungdong Kim, Donghyeon Kim, Sunkyu Kim, Chan Ho So, and Jaewoo Kang. 2019. BioBERT: a pre-trained biomedical language representation model for biomedical text mining. *Bioinformatics*.

Tara Murphy, Tara McIntosh, and James R. Curran. 2006. Named entity recognition for astronomy literature. In *Proceedings of the Australasian Language Technology Workshop 2006*, pages 59–66, Sydney, Australia.

Andrii Neronov. 2019. Introduction to multi-messenger astronomy. *Journal of Physics: Conference Series*, 1263(1):012001.

Elisa Schneider, Renzo M. Rivera-Zavala, Paloma Martinez, Claudia Moro, and Emerson Paraiso. 2022. UC3M-PUCPR at SemEval-2022 task 11: An ensemble method of transformer-based models for complex named entity recognition. In *Proceedings of the 16th International Workshop on Semantic Evaluation (SemEval-2022)*, pages 1448–1456, Seattle, United States. Association for Computational Linguistics.

Vikas Yadav and Steven Bethard. 2018. A survey on recent advances in named entity recognition from deep learning models. In *Proceedings of the 27th International Conference on Computational Linguistics*, pages 2145–2158, Santa Fe, New Mexico, USA. Association for Computational Linguistics.

A Appendix

Model	P	R	F1	MCC
random	0.119	0.0274	0.0166	0.1089
BERT	0.4779	0.4697	0.4738	0.7405
SciBERT	0.5457	0.5741	0.5595	0.8016
astroBERT	**0.5511**	**0.6080**	**0.5781**	**0.8104**

Table 3: Baseline scores for the DEAL shared task. Metrics used are Precision (P), Recall (R), F1-score and MCC.

Rank	Comb.	Designation	Hyp.-params.
1	C2	S1	$(4, 2.10^5)$
2	C5	S2	$(8, 2.10^5)$
3	C9	S3	$(16, 5.10^5)$
4	C6	S4	$(5, 5.10^5)$
5	C1	S5	$(4, 1.10^5)$
6	C8	S6	$(16, 2.10^5)$
7	C3	S7	$(4, 5.10^5)$
8	C4	S8	$(8, 1.10^5)$
9	C7	S9	$(16, 1.10^5)$

Table 4: Grid search: ranking of the combination (Comb.) giving the best results. After having ranked the different combinations, we denote by S_i the set of five models (having the same hyper-parameters) ranked in position i

Category	Definition	Example
Person	A named person or their initials	Andrea M. Ghez, Ghez A.
Organization	A named organization that is not an observatory.	NASA, University of Toledo
Location	A named location on Earth.	Canada
Observatory	A, often similarly located, group of telescopes.	Keck Observatory, Fermi
Telescope	A "bucket" to catch light.	Hubble Space Telescope, Discovery Channel Telescope
Instrument	A device, often, but not always, placed on a telescope, to make a measurement.	Infrared Array Camera, NIRCam
Survey	An organized search of the sky often dedicated to large scale science projects.	2MASS, SDSS
Mission	A spacecraft that is not a telescope or observatory that carries multiple instruments	WIND
CelestialObject	A named object in the sky	ONC, Andromeda galaxy
CelestialRegion	A defined region projected onto the sky, or celestial coordinates.	GOODS field, l=2, b=15
CelestialObjectRegion	Named area on/in a celestial body.	Inner galaxy
Wavelength	Portion of the electromagnetic spectrum	656.46 nm, H-alpha
ObservationalTechniques	Methods/technqiues for observation	Spectroscopic, helioseismic
Model	Mathematical/Physical model	Gaussian, Keplerian
Software	Software, IT tool	NuSTAR, healpy, numpy
ComputingFacility	Server, cluster for computation	Supercomputer, GPU
Dataset	Astronomical catalogues	3FGL catalog
Database	A curated set of data	Simbad database
Archive	A curated collection of the literature or data.	NASA ADS, MAST
Identifier	A unique identifier for data, images, etc.	ALMA 123.12345
Citation	A reference to previous work in the literature.	Allen et al. 2012
Collaboration	Name of collaboration	Fermi LAT Collaboration
Event	A conference, workshop or other event that often brings scientests together.	Protostars and Planets VI
Grant	An allocation of money and/or time for a research project.	grant No. 12345, ADAP grant 12345
Fellowship	A grant focused towards students and/or early career researchers.	Hubble Fellowship
Formula	Mathematical formula or equations.	$F = Gm1m2/r^2, z = 2.3$
Tag	A HTML tag.	<bold>
TextGarbage	Incorrect text, often multiple punctuation marks with no inner text.	,,,
EntityOfFutureInterest	A general catch all for things that may be worth thinking about in the future.	Earth-like, Solar-like
URL	A link to a website.	$https://www.astropy.org/$

Table 5: Classification of the named entities in the annotation guideline. The HuggingFace repository containing the annotated data and the annotation guide is only accessible to participants of the shared task. Thus, we have reproduced the same list of named entities with their definition.

Author Index

Ahuja, Aman, 121
Akella, Akhil Pandey, 140
Alhoori, Hamed, 140
Alkan, Atilla Kaan, 131, 145
Allen, Thomas, 1
ARAMAKI, Eiji, 26

Basuchowdhuri, Partha, 100
Binder, Arne, 54
Blanco-Cuaresma, Sergi, 1
Botev, Viktor, 43
Brinner, Marc, 32

Dai, Xiang, 78
Devera, Alan, 121
D'Souza, Jennifer, 105

Fox, Edward Alan, 121

Ghosal, Tirthankar, 1
Ghosh, Madhusudan, 100
Grezes, Felix, 1
Grouin, Cyril, 131, 145

Haouat, Patrick, 67
Heger, Tina, 32
Hennig, Leonhard, 54
Hoelscher-Obermaier, Jason, 43
Huang, Po-Wei, 84

Iqbal, Sk Asif, 100

Karimi, Sarvnaz, 78
Koop, David, 140

Liew, Kongmeng, 26

Martin, Anna, 105
Matsubara, Shigeki, 8
Minton, Jeremy, 43
Mutinda, Faith, 26

Pedersen, Ted, 105

Rosati, Domenic, 91

Santra, Payel, 100
Schussler, Fabian, 131, 145
Stauber, Valentin, 43
Stevinson, Edward, 43

Tahri, Chyrine, 67
Tannier, Xavier, 67
Tensmeyer, Chris, 20
Tsunokake, Masaya, 8

Verma, Bhuvanesh, 54

Wakamiya, Shoko, 26
Wigington, Curtis, 20
Wu, Ronin, 43

Yada, Shuntaro, 26
Yang, Sean, 20

Zarriess, Sina, 32
Zhelev, Ivaylo, 43
Zweigenbaum, Pierre, 131, 145

Association for Computational Linguistics
209 N. Eighth Street
Stroudsburg, Pennsylvania 18360

ISBN 978-1-7138-6756-2

CURRAN ASSOCIATES INC.
proceedings.com